HOME-KITCHEN FOOD STORAGE

P9-AET-986

Pantry-shelf Storage, Room Temperature

food item	storage time	keep in mind
baking powder, baking soda	18 months	keep dry, tightly covered
bouillon cubes & powders	1 year	
breads & rolls	3 days	in original wrapping
cake mixes	1 year	keep dry
cakes, baked	2-3 days	refrigerate if with cream or custard filling
canned foods, all kinds	1 year or more	use oldest first
coffee, vacuum can	1 year, un-opened	store in refrigerator or freezer 1 week after opening
coffee, instant	6 months, unopened	store in refrigerator or freezer 1 week after opening
coffee lightener, nondairy	6 months	keep dry
cookies, packaged	4 months, unopened	1 week after opening
crackers	3 months	keep dry, tightly closed
crumbs, cracker/bread	6 months	keep dry, tightly closed
flour, all-purpose/cake	6 months	keep dry, tightly closed
frostings, mixes & canned	6 months	
fruit, dried	6-8 months	
gelatin, unflavored/fruit	6 months	keep dry
herbs & spices, whole	1 year	keep tightly closed
herbs & spices, ground	6 months	keep tightly closed
honey	1 year	do not refrigerate
hot-roll/quick-bread mixes	1 year	keep dry
jam, jelly	1 year	refrigerate after opening
molasses	1 year	
nonfat dry milk	6 months	keep dry; refrigerate after reconstituting
oil, salad & cooking	3 months	keep tightly closed
pancake, waffle mixes	6 months	keep dry, tightly closed
pasta	6 months, unopened	keep dry
peanut butter	6 months	2 months after opening
piecrust mixes	6 months	
pies & pastries	3 days	refrigerate cream, custard
pudding mixes	1 year	
rice, brown & wild	1 year	
rice, white	2 years	
rice, flavored mixes	6 months	
salad dressings	6 months	refrigerate after opening
sauce/soup/gravy mixes	3 months	
sauces/ketchup, barbecue	2 months	keep tightly closed
shortening, hydrogenated	8 months	keep tightly closed
soft drinks	3 months	
sugar, granulated	2 years	keep dry
sugar, brown & confectioners	4 years	
syrups	1 year	close tightly after use
tea, loose or bags	6 months	
tea, instant	1 year	
vegetables: onions, potatoes, rutabagas, sweet potatoes, winter squash	1 week	keep dry; provide for air circulation, will keep 2-3 months at 55°

Refrigerator Storage, Fruits & Vegetables
(in crisper or closed plastic bags)

food item	storage time	keep in mind
apples	1 month	or store at room temperature
apricots, avocados, pears, melons, bananas, grapes, nectarines, peaches, plums	5 days	ripen before refrigerating
berries & cherries	3 days	
citrus fruits	2 weeks	or store at room temperature
pineapples	2 days	
asparagus	3 days	
beets, carrots, parsnips, radishes, turnips	5 days	remove tops before storing
cabbage, cauliflower, celery, cucumbers, green beans, eggplant, peppers	1 week	
tomatoes	1 week	ripen tomatoes before refrigerating
corn on the cob	1 day	refrigerate in husks
lettuce, spinach, all green leafy vegetables	5 days	remove damaged leaves before refrigerating
lima beans, peas	5 days	leave in pods

Refrigerator Storage, Dairy Products
(tightly covered or wrapped)

food item	storage time	keep in mind
butter	2 weeks	
buttermilk	2 weeks	
cheese, spreads	2 weeks	if mold forms on hard cheese, remove before serving — it will do no harm
cheese, cottage & ricotta	5 days	
cheese, cream & neufchatel	2 weeks	
cheese, sliced	2 weeks	
cheese, in whole cuts	2 months	
cream, sweet/sour	1 week	ultrapasteurized, 1 month in original carton
eggs, whole in shell	1 month	
whites, separated	4 days	tightly covered
yolks, separated	4 days	cover with water
margarine	1 month	
milk, whole & skim	1 week	
milk, reconstituted nonfat, opened condensed & evaporated	1 week	

Refrigerator Storage, Meat, Fish & Poultry (uncooked)

food item	storage time	keep in mind
beef, pork, lamb & veal: steaks, chops, roasts	5 days	leave in store plastic wrap or rewrap loosely
ground & stew meats	2 days	
fresh sausage	2 days	
variety meats	2 days	
bacon, frankfurters	1 week	after opening
ham, canned	6 months	unopened
ham, slices	3 days	
ham, whole	1 week	
luncheon meats, cold cuts	5 days	after opening
sausage, dry & semidry	3 weeks	
fish, shellfish (all kinds)	1 day	keep closely wrapped
poultry, fresh or thawed	2 days	

Refrigerator Storage, Leftovers & Packaged Foods (after opening)

food item	storage time	keep in mind
broth, gravy, soup	2 days	tightly covered
cakes, pies: cream or custard fillings	2-3 days	
casserole dishes, stews	3 days	
coffee	1 week	after opening
coffee lighteners, frozen	3 weeks	after thawing
flour: rye, whole wheat, wheat germ	1 year	tightly covered container — not original package
fruits	3 days	
juices, beverages	6 days	
meat, fish, poultry	2 days	remove stuffing from poultry
nutmeats	6 months	tightly covered
pickles, olives	1 month	original container
refrigerated doughs: rolls, biscuits, cookies, breads	check final-use date on package; do not open until ready to use	
salad dressings	3 months	original container
salads: potato, chicken, fish, coleslaw	2 days	tightly covered
wine, white table	3 days	after opening

Continued on back Endsheet

Freezer Storage, Commercial Frozen Foods

food item	storage time	keep in mind
breads, rolls (baked)	3 months	overwrap commercial wrappings
breads, unbaked loaves	3 months	overwrap commercial wrappings
cakes: butter, pound-type	6 months	unfrosted, overwrap
cake, angel food	2 months	overwrap
cake, frosted layer	4 months	
coffee lighteners	1 year	
doughnuts, danish pastry	3 months	overwrap
fish (fat types): trout, mackerel, salmon	3 months	overwrap if package damaged
fish, (lean types): cod, flounder, sole	6 months	if thawed, do not refreeze
shellfish, breaded, cooked	3 months	
lobster, scallops	3 months	
king / queen crab	10 months	
shrimp, uncooked, unbreaded	1 year	
fruit	1 year	
ice cream, sherbet	1 month	overwrap leftovers
main-dish pies, fish or meat	3 months	
main-dish pies, poultry	6 months	
meats, beef roasts, steaks	1 year	overwrap
ground beef	4 months	overwrap
lamb, veal roasts, & steaks	9 months	overwrap
pork chops	4 months	overwrap
pork roasts	8 months	overwrap
pancake / waffle batter	3 months	
pies, unbaked	8 months	
pies, ready to thaw & eat	4 months	
poultry: chicken, turkey parts	6 months	
whole chicken, turkey	1 year	
duck, goose	6 months	
turkey rolls, roasts	6 months	
vegetables, all	8 months	

USEFUL SUBSTITUTIONS

if the recipe calls for	use instead
2 tablespoons all-purpose or whole wheat flour (for thickening)	1 tablespoon cornstarch or arrow-root or potato starch or quick-cooking tapioca
1 cup beef or chicken broth	1 bouillon cube or 1 envelope or 1 rounded teaspoon bouillon powder + 1 cup boiling water
2 egg yolks	1 whole egg
1 cup grated coconut	1⅓ cups flaked coconut
1 pound fresh mushrooms	12 ounces canned mushrooms, drained, or 3 ounces dried mush-rooms, rehydrated
1 teaspoon lemon juice	½ teaspoon distilled white vinegar
1 teaspoon grated lemon peel	½ teaspoon lemon extract
1 cup homogenized milk	1 cup skim milk + 2 tablespoons butter or margarine; or ½ cup evaporated milk + ½ cup water, or ¼ cup powdered whole milk + 1 cup water
1 square (1 ounce) unsweetened chocolate	3 tablespoons cocoa + 1 table-spoon butter or margarine
½ cup butter or margarine	7 tablespoons vegetable shortening
1 cup sifted cake flour	⅞ cup sifted all-purpose flour
1 teaspoon baking powder	½ teaspoon cream of tartar + ¼ teaspoon baking soda
1 cup sour cream (for use in cooking)	1 tablespoon lemon juice + evapo-rated milk (undiluted) to make 1 cup, or ⅓ cup butter + ¾ cup yogurt or buttermilk

1 cup buttermilk or sour milk	1 tablespoon lemon juice or white vinegar + milk to make 1 cup (let stand 5 minutes)
1 cup honey or corn syrup	1¼ cups sugar + ¼ cup liquid
1 tablespoon snipped fresh herb	1 teaspoon dried herb, same kind
1 medium onion, chopped	1 tablespoon instant minced onion, rehydrated
1 cup light cream or half-and-half	3 tablespoons butter + ⅞ cup milk
1 cup heavy (whipping) cream	⅓ cup butter + ¾ cup milk
2 cups tomato sauce	¾ cup tomato paste + 1 cup water
1 cup tomato juice	½ cup tomato sauce + ½ cup water
1 small clove garlic	⅛ teaspoon garlic powder or ¼ tea-spoon commercial garlic juice
1 tablespoon gelatin	1 envelope
1 cake compressed yeast	1 envelope active dry yeast
1 cup yogurt (in cooking)	1 cup buttermilk

FOOD-MEASURE EQUIVALENTS

start out with	to end up with
apples, 3 medium (1 pound)	3 cups sliced
bananas, 3 medium (1 pound)	1½ cups mashed
bread, 1-pound loaf	14 to 20 slices
bread, 1 slice (including crust)	½ cup crumbs
butter or margarine, ¼ pound	½ cup (1 stick or cube)
cheese, ¼ pound	1 cup shredded
cheese, cottage, 8-ounce container	1 cup
cheese, cream, 3-ounce package	6 tablespoons
chocolate, unsweetened, 1 square	1 ounce
chocolate, semisweet pieces, 6 ounces	1 cup
coconut, flaked, 3½-ounce can	1⅓ cups
coconut, shredded, 4-ounce can	1⅓ cups
cream, heavy or whipping, 1 cup	2 cups whipped
cream, sour, 8-ounce container	1 cup
egg whites, large, 8 to 10	1 cup
egg yolks, large, 12 to 14	1 cup
flour, all-purpose, 1 pound	about 3½ cups
flour, cake, 1 pound	about 4 cups
lemon, 1 medium	3 tablespoons juice, 1 tablespoon grated peel
lime, 1 medium	2 tablespoons juice, 1 teaspoon grated peel
milk, evaporated, 5⅓ or 6-ounce can	⅔ cup
12- or 14½-ounce can	1⅔ cups
sweetened condensed, 14-ounce can	1¼ cups
nuts, 1 pound almonds in shell	1 to 1¼ cups nutmeats
almonds, 1 pound shelled	3 cups
brazil nuts, in shell, 1 pound	1½ cups nutmeats
brazil nuts, shelled, 1 pound	3¼ cups
filberts, in shell, 1 pound	1½ cups nutmeats
filberts, shelled, 1 pound	3½ cups
peanuts, in shell, 1 pound	2 to 2½ cups nutmeats
peanuts, shelled, 1 pound	3 cups
pecans, in shell, 1 pound	2¼ cups nutmeats
pecans, shelled, 1 pound	4 cups
walnuts, in shell, 1 pound	2 cups nutmeats
walnuts, shelled, 1 pound	4 cups
onion, 1 large	¾ to 1 cup chopped
orange, 1 medium	¼ to ⅓ cup juice, 2 tablespoons grated peel
potatoes, 1 pound sweet, white	2¼ cups diced
raisins, 1 pound	3 cups
rice, long grain regular, 1 cup	3 cups cooked
salad oil, 16 ounces	2 cups
sugar, 1 pound granulated	2¼ to 2½ cups
brown, 1 pound	2¼ cups (packed)
confectioners, 1 pound	4 to 4½ cups
syrup, corn, 16 ounces	2 cups
maple, 12 ounces	1½ cups

Famous Brands

CHOCOLATE CLASSICS

Brand Name Publishing Corp.

Viennese Mocha Torte (page 12); Cold Mocha Soufflé (page 118).
General Foods

Acknowledgments

The editors wish to thank the following companies for permission to use their recipes, photographs, and product names in this volume:

Almond Board of California

American Dairy Association

Amstar Corp. Domino® Sugar is a registered trademark of the Amstar Corp.

Beatrice Companies, Inc.

C & H Sugar Company

CPC International Inc.

California Dried Fig Advisory Board

California Raisin Advisory Board

Caloric Corporation

Carnation Company. Contadina® Tomato Products, Carnation® Evaporated Milk, and Carnation® Nonfat Dry Milk are products of Carnation Company.

Chicago Dietetic Supply, Inc.

Corning Glass Works

Cumberland Packing Corporation. Butter Buds®, Nu-Salt®, and Sweet 'N Low® are registered trademarks of the Cumberland Packing Corporation.

John DeKuyper & Son

Durkee Famous Foods

Eagle® Brand Sweetened Condensed Milk Division of Borden Inc.

Florida Department of Citrus

General Foods Corporation

General Mills, Inc. Bisquick® is a registered trademark of General Mills, Inc.

Hamilton Beach Scovill Inc.

Hecker's Unbleached, All-Purpose, Naturally White Flour

HERSHEY Food Corporation. All recipes developed and tested in the HERSHEY Test Kitchen.

Heublein Inc.

International Multifoods

Knox Gelatine, Inc., Englewood Cliffs, NJ 07632

Libby, McNeill & Libby, Inc., The Great Pumpkin Cookbook, A Harvest of Libby's Favorite Recipes. Libby's® is a registered trademark of Libby, McNeill & Libby, Inc.

©Mars Inc., 1984

Missouri Egg Council

Nabisco Brands, Inc.

Nestlé Foods Corporation. NESTLÉ TOLL HOUSE Semi-Sweet Chocolate Morsels, NESTLÉ Little Bits Semi-Sweet Chocolate, NESTLÉ Butterscotch Flavored Morsels, NESTLÉ Milk Chocolate Morsels, NESTLÉ Peanut Butter Morsels, NESTLÉ CHOCO-BAKE Unsweetened Baking Chocolate Flavor, TOLL HOUSE Cookies, and NESTLÉ QUIK Chocolate Flavor are registered trademarks of Nestlé Foods Corporation.

None-Such® Mincemeat Division of Borden Inc.

Ocean Spray Cranberries, Inc.

Oklahoma Peanut Commission

The Quaker Oats Company

Consumer Products Division, Reynolds Metal Company

Riceland Foods

Rich Products Corporation

Joseph E. Seagram & Sons, Inc.

Sioux Honey Association

Solo Food Products, Division of Sokol & Company

Sunbeam Appliance Co., a member company of Allegheny International, Inc. Sunbeam® is a registered trademark of the Sunbeam Corporation.

Invitation

The Famous Brands Cookbook Library invites you, the modern cook, to a new experience in your own kitchen. Have you ever wished you had a larger repertoire of company's-coming menus? Ever searched for a different and exciting way to prepare favorite products? Ever felt that if you could just have a certain technique explained simply, you could master an entire new world of cooking?

The solutions to these dilemmas and others are the cornerstone of the twelve volumes that comprise *The Famous Brands Cookbook Library*. Whether you are just getting to know your kitchen—or have a long-standing relationship with it—the recipes and hints provided here offer the very best and latest information available from the test kitchens of many of America's finest food companies. Once you have had a chance to discover the treasures inside this volume, you'll want to collect each of the other volumes in this series—and an invaluable home cooking library will be yours.

Famous Brands Desserts
Famous Brands Every Oven Microwave Cookbook
Famous Brands Great Vegetable Dishes
Famous Brands Meat Cookbook
Famous Brands Chicken & Poultry
Famous Brands Breads, Quick Breads, & Coffee Cakes
Famous Brands Soups & Salads
Famous Brands Pasta Dishes
Famous Brands Fish & Seafood Cookbook
Famous Brands Cooking with Eggs & Cheese
Famous Brands Main Dishes
Famous Brands Chocolate Classics

Published by Brand Name Publishing Corp., 1950 Craig Road, St. Louis, Missouri 63146 and Brand Name Books, Inc., 122 East 25th Street, New York, New York 10010.

Printed in Italy by Mondadori, Verona

Front cover: *Chocolate Mousse Pie au Rhum (page 83)*. General Foods

Any Flavor, As Long as It's Chocolate

There are those who would sell their souls for the wealth of princes, for the perfumes of Araby, for beauty everlasting, for the wisdom of the ages. Then again, there are those who would trade their hope of paradise for one perfect, delicate *soufflé au chocolat*.

It's difficult to find a person who doesn't like chocolate, a flavor so versatile, so adaptable, that the whole world enjoys it. It all began with Montezuma, who sipped a soothing cup of his favorite beverage while those pale-skinned outlanders were marching up from the sea to invade his kingdom, and carries on until this very moment, when hundreds of junkies are sitting in soda fountains slurping up triple-dip sundaes drowned in hot fudge. And there is no doubt that this love affair will continue, world without end. More than our favorite flavor, with some of us chocolate is an addiction, a must-have that runs far ahead of Mom, baseball, and apple pie, that threatens to sink us in our own adipose tissues if we can't get the urge under control.

Even for those who can take it or leave it—social chocolate consumers, as it were—this delicious substance is first rank among the whole spectrum of sweets. Any candy is better when chocolate-robed. Who can resist a quivering chocolate chiffon pie, a layer-on-layer devil's food cake crowned with rich frosting, a handful of crisp-yet-yielding chocolate chip cookies, an old-fashioned chocolate pudding sporting a dollop of whipped cream and a shower of chopped nuts?

Deeply dark or mild and milky, chocolate forms a beautiful partnership with many other flavors we enjoy: with spices, particulary clove and cinnamon; with fruits, especially oranges, cherries, and berries; with nuts of any kind. As for liqueurs, it's difficult to tell which enhances which: the almond delicacy of amaretto di Saronna, the cool refreshment of crème de menthe, the coffee richness of kahlua, the fresh-berry goodness of framboise, the elegant bitter orange of Curaçao. Indeed, a perfect always-on-hand, quick/easy dessert consists of a helping of chocolate ice cream sauced with one of these liqueurs.

Two relatively new variations on the chocolate theme have put in a come-lately appearance: truffles, and the chocolate fair. Truffles are big rich candies with a (surprisingly easy to make) chocolate center, more often than not flavored with liqueur or brandy or champagne, either robed in more chocolate or rolled in cocoa or finely chopped nuts. Incredibly delicious, they can take the place of dessert, or be served with coffee after the meal. As for the fairs, they are gatherings at which chocolate buffs can indulge themselves to satiety and the makers of all kinds of chocolate goodies can display their wares.

Whether you are a chocolate maven or a rank beginner, you can expand your repertoire with the recipes in *Famous Brands Chocolate Classics,* learning how to manipulate that glorious flavor into magnificent cakes and tortes, pies and tarts, cookies and brownies, breads and coffee cakes, puddings and frozen desserts that will have friends—even strangers—competing for an invitation to your house for dinner.

Contents

Crowning Glories

Majestic cakes and tortes—some extravagantly filled, some lushly frosted, all wonderfully delicious—to serve at the glorious conclusion of a meal or simply as a special treat for family and friends.

Wellesley Fudge Cake
Makes 1 cake

  4 squares Baker's Unsweetened Chocolate
  ½ cup hot water
  ½ cup sugar
  2 cups sifted cake flour
  1 teaspoon baking soda
  1 teaspoon salt
  ½ cup shortening★
  1¼ cups sugar
  3 eggs
    Milk★
  1 teaspoon vanilla extract
    Hungarian Frosting (recipe follows)

Melt chocolate with water in top of double boiler over hot water, stirring until chocolate is melted and mixture thickens. Add ½ cup sugar to mixture; cook and stir 2 minutes longer. Cool to lukewarm. Sift flour with soda and salt. Cream shortening; gradually add 1¼ cups sugar; cream until light and fluffy. Add eggs, 1 at a time, beating thoroughly after each addition. Alternately add flour mixture and milk, beating after each addition until smooth. Blend in vanilla and chocolate mixture. Pour batter into three 9-inch layer pans that have been greased and floured. Bake at 350°F. for 25 minutes, or until cake springs back when touched lightly. Cool in pans 10 minutes; remove from pans and cool thoroughly on racks. Frost with Hungarian Frosting.

★ With butter, use ¾ cup milk; with vegetable shortening, 1 cup milk.

Hungarian Frosting
Makes 2⅔ cups

  5 squares Baker's Unsweetened Chocolate
  3 cups confectioners sugar
  ⅓ cup hot water
  2 egg yolks or use 1 whole egg
  8 tablespoons (1 stick) butter or margarine, at
     room temperature

Melt chocolate in saucepan over very low heat, stirring constantly until smooth. Pour into mixer bowl. Add sugar and water, all at once; blend well. Add egg yolks, 1 at a time, beating well after each addition. Add butter, 1 tablespoon at a time, beating thoroughly after each addition. (If frosting is too soft to spread, place bowl in large bowl of cold water and stir until of spreading consistency.)

Our Favorite Devil's Food Cake
Makes 1 cake

  1 cup Domino Granulated Sugar
  ¾ cup firmly packed Domino Light Brown Sugar
  ½ cup butter or margarine, softened
  3 ounces unsweetened chocolate, melted
  3 egg yolks
  ¼ cup water
  1 teaspoon vanilla extract
  2 cups sifted cake flour
  ½ teaspoon salt
  1 teaspoon baking soda
  1 cup milk
  3 egg whites, stiffly beaten

Cream sugars and butter. Add melted chocolate. Beat yolks, add water and extract, and blend. Gradually add yolk mixture to chocolate mixture; beat until light and fluffy. Sift together flour, salt, and baking soda. Alternately add flour mixture and milk, blending well after each addition. Beat egg whites until stiff but not dry; fold into batter.

Turn into two greased and floured 9-inch round cake pans or one greased and floured 13×9×2-inch pan. Bake layers or loaf in moderate 350°F. oven about 30 to 35 minutes, or until cake springs back when touched lightly. Turn out on cooling rack.

Peanut Butter Fudge Cake

Makes 1 cake
- 1 cup butter
- ¼ cup cocoa
- 1 cup water
- ½ cup buttermilk
- 2 eggs, well beaten
- 2 cups sugar
- 2 cups all-purpose flour
- 1 teaspoon baking soda
- 1 teaspoon vanilla extract
- 1½ cups creamy peanut butter
- 1½ tablespoons peanut oil
  - Frosting (recipe follows)

In saucepan, combine butter, cocoa, water, buttermilk, and eggs. Stir constantly over low heat until mixture bubbles. In large bowl, mix sugar, flour, and baking soda. Stir hot mixture into dry ingredients. Beat until smooth; stir in vanilla. Spread mixture evenly into greased and floured 13×9×2-inch pan. Bake at 350°F. for 25 minutes. In a bowl, mix peanut butter and oil until smooth. Cool cake in pan. Spread peanut butter evenly over cooled cake. Set aside. Prepare Frosting and spread evenly over peanut topping. Cut into squares.

Frosting
- ½ cup butter
- ¼ cup cocoa
- 6 tablespoons buttermilk
- 1 package (1 pound) confectioners sugar
- 1 teaspoon vanilla extract

In saucepan, heat butter, cocoa, and buttermilk until bubbly. Place sugar in large bowl. Beat in hot mixture. Beat until smooth. Stir in vanilla.

Cocoa Chocolate Cake

Makes two 9-inch layers
- 1½ cups sugar
- ½ cup shortening
- 2 eggs
- ⅔ cup unsweetened cocoa
- 2 cups all-purpose flour
- 1¼ teaspoons baking soda
- 1 teaspoon salt
- ½ teaspoon baking powder
- 1⅓ cups milk
- 1 pint strawberries
- 2 cups heavy cream, whipped

Cream sugar and shortening. Beat in eggs until mixture is light and fluffy. Add cocoa and beat until smooth. Combine flour, baking soda, salt, and bak-

ing powder. Add flour mixture alternately with milk to creamed mixture. Pour into two 9-inch round cake pans. Preheat oven to 350°F. Bake 25 to 30 minutes until toothpick inserted in center comes out clean. Cool in pans on wire racks 10 minutes. Invert onto wire racks and cool completely.

Chop half of the strawberries; combine with 1 cup whipped cream. Spread between layers. Frost cake with remaining whipped cream. Slice remaining strawberries; arrange on cake.

Mix Fixers

You can help along the mix you use. If you remember with longing your mother's or grandmother's butter cakes, choose the mix to which butter must be added at home—it shoots the already doubtful economy, but makes a better cake. So does a teaspoonful of good (real, that is) vanilla extract, or some other add-it-yourself flavoring. Cake mixes are relatively sturdy—they can stand some monkeying with and not fail. But don't tamper with the proportions of liquid to dry mix. If you want to add orange juice, for instance, substitute it for all or part of the water; don't use it in addition to the amount of water called for.

By now, everyone has heard about the "pound" cakes made with 2-layer-size cake mix plus water, 4 eggs, ½ cup cooking oil, and instant pudding mix. A very acceptable, darkly rich mocha "pound" cake can be made with a devil's food cake mix, chocolate instant pudding, vanilla, and a rounded teaspoon of dry instant coffee—or substitute strong cold brewed coffee for the water. For a simple mix trick, bake your chocolate pound cake in a Bundt or 10-inch tube pan instead of the more traditional loaf and dust with confectioners sugar when cooled.

Another way to make a mix more your own is to use a rich homemade frosting on top: Frost a moist loaf cake with your favorite chocolate fudge frosting or devil's food with Grandma's seafoam icing. Easy, elegant, delicious.

Chocolate Layer Cake

Makes two 8- or 9-inch cake layers
- 2¼ cups all-purpose flour
- 1½ teaspoons baking soda
- 1 teaspoon salt
- ½ cup butter, softened
- 1½ cups sugar
- 1 teaspoon vanilla extract
- 2 envelopes (2 ounces) Nestlé Choco-bake Unsweetened Baking Chocolate Flavor
- 2 eggs
- 1½ cups ice water
  - Sour Cream Velvet Frosting (recipe follows) (optional)

Preheat oven to 350°F. In a small bowl, combine flour, baking soda, and salt; set aside. In a large bowl, combine butter, sugar, and vanilla; beat until creamy. Blend in Nestlé Choco-bake Unsweetened Baking Chocolate Flavor. Add eggs, 1 at a time, beating well after each addition. Blend in flour mixture alternately with ice water. Pour into two greased and floured 8- or 9-inch round cake pans. Bake 30 to 35 minutes. Cool 10 minutes; remove from pans. Cool completely on wire racks. Frost with Sour Cream Velvet Frosting or favorite frosting.

Sour Cream Velvet Frosting

Makes 2⅔ cups frosting
- 1 12-ounce package (2 cups) Nestlé Toll House Semi-Sweet Chocolate Morsels
- ⅔ cup sour cream
- 1 teaspoon vanilla extract
- ¼ teaspoon salt
- 3 cups sifted confectioners sugar

Melt Nestlé Toll House Semi-Sweet Chocolate Morsels over hot (not boiling) water; transfer to a large bowl and cool 5 minutes. Blend in sour cream, vanilla, and salt. Gradually beat in confectioners sugar; beat until smooth and creamy. Fills and frosts two 8- or 9-inch cake layers.

Chocolate Pound Cake

Makes 1 cake
- 3 cups sifted Martha White All-Purpose Flour
- ½ cup cocoa
- ½ teaspoon salt
- ½ teaspoon baking powder
- 3 cups sugar
- 1 cup butter or margarine
- ½ cup vegetable shortening
- 5 eggs
- 1 cup milk
- 1½ teaspoons vanilla extract

Preheat oven to 325°F. Grease 10-inch tube pan; set aside. Sift flour, cocoa, salt, and baking powder into large bowl; set aside. Cream sugar, butter, and shortening with electric mixer in mixing bowl until light and fluffy. Add eggs, 1 at a time, beating well after each addition. Alternately beat in flour mixture and milk, beginning and ending with flour mixture. Stir in vanilla. Pour into prepared pan. Bake 1½ hours, or until toothpick inserted in center comes out clean. Cool in pan 10 minutes. Turn out onto wire rack to cool completely.

Fudgy Almond Torte

Makes 10 servings
- **Torte Shell (recipe follows)**
- ¾ cup Hershey's® Mini Chips® Semi-Sweet Chocolate
- ⅓ cup sugar
- 1 tablespoon shortening
- 2 eggs
- 6 tablespoons butter or margarine
- 1 cup ground almonds
- ¼ teaspoon almond extract
- **Sweetened whipped cream or dessert topping**
- **Candied or maraschino cherries**

Prepare Torte Shell; set aside. Combine Mini Chips semi-sweet chocolate, sugar, and shortening in top of double boiler over hot water; stir until chocolate is smooth (or place in glass bowl and microwave on high 1 minute or until melted). Remove from heat; stir in eggs until combined. Cream butter or margarine in small mixer bowl; blend in chocolate mixture, ground almonds, and almond extract. Spoon filling into shell in cake pan. Bake at 325°F for 40 to 45 minutes, or until crust is golden brown (center does not test done). Thoroughly cool torte; remove from pan. Just before serving, garnish with dollops of whipped cream and cherries.

Torte Shell
- 1½ cups all-purpose flour
- ⅓ cup sugar
- 1 teaspoon baking powder
- ½ cup butter or margarine
- 1 egg, lightly beaten

Combine flour, sugar, and baking powder in a mixing bowl. Cut in butter or margarine until mixture is crumbly. Add egg and blend until flour is moistened. Press dough, with lightly floured fingers, evenly on bottom and sides of a greased 9-inch round cake pan—standard or removable bottom.

Grated Chocolate

Chill 1 or more squares Baker's Semi-Sweet or Unsweetened Chocolate or several 3-square strips of Baker's German's Sweet Chocolate and a hand grater; then grate chocolate quickly to prevent melting. Sprinkle grated chocolate over pudding and ice cream; fold into sweetened whipped cream or thawed Cool Whip whipped topping; or sprinkle over lace paper doily on a frosted layer cake (later removing doily carefully).

Chocolate Layer Cake (page 8) with Sour Cream Velvet Frosting (page 9). Courtesy of Nestlé Foods Corporation

Mix Fixers (page 8)

Toll House Golden Brownies (page 44); Toll House Bundt® Cake (page 11); Golden Cupcakes (page 29). Courtesy of Nestlé Foods Corporation

Spiced Rum Chocolate Cake

Makes 8 servings

½ cup butter
1 cup sugar
4 eggs, stirred
1 can (16 ounces) Hershey's® Syrup
2 tablespoons Captain Morgan Spiced Rum
1 cup all-purpose flour
   Chocolate Rum Glaze (recipe follows)

Preheat oven to 350°F. With mixer, cream butter and sugar; blend in eggs. Add syrup, Spiced Rum, and flour. Mix on low speed until batter is well blended. Pour into greased 8-inch cake pan. Bake 55 to 60 minutes. Check center for firmness. Turn cake onto wire rack. Ice when cool.

Chocolate Rum Glaze

3 ounces semisweet chocolate pieces
¼ cup confectioners sugar
2 tablespoons sweet butter
2 tablespoons water
   Pinch salt
2 tablespoons Captain Morgan Spiced Rum

In double boiler, heat chocolate, sugar, butter, water, and salt. Stir until smooth. Remove from heat and blend in Spiced Rum. Refrigerate until thickened, about 15 minutes.

Toll House Bundt® Cake

Makes one 10-inch tube or Bundt® cake

¼ cup butter, softened
2 tablespoons sugar
⅔ cup finely chopped nuts
2¾ cups all-purpose flour
2 teaspoons baking soda
1 teaspoon salt
1 tablespoon vinegar
   Whole milk
1 cup butter, softened
1 cup firmly packed brown sugar
1 tablespoon vanilla extract
4 eggs
1 12-ounce package (2 cups) Nestlé Little Bits
   Semi-Sweet Chocolate
   Chocolate Glaze (see index) (optional)

In a small bowl, combine butter, sugar, and nuts; mix until crumbly. Spoon into well-greased and floured 10-inch fluted tube pan. Chill in refrigerator while preparing cake batter.

Preheat oven to 375°F. In a small bowl, combine flour, baking soda, and salt; set aside. Place vinegar in a 1-cup liquid measure; fill with milk to 1-cup line; set aside. In a large bowl, combine butter, brown sugar, and vanilla; beat at medium speed until light and fluffy (about 3 to 5 minutes). Add eggs, 1 at a time, beating well after each addition. Turn mixer to low. Gradually add flour mixture, ⅓ at a time, alternately with milk. Remove bowl from mixer. Gently fold in Nestlé Little Bits Semi-Sweet Chocolate with a rubber spatula. Pour batter into prepared pan. Bake for 50 minutes. Check for doneness by inserting toothpick in center of cake. When it comes out clean, cake is done. Cake is a dark golden brown when baked. Loosen edges of cake with spatula; *immediately* invert on cooling rack. Cool cake completely. Drizzle top with Chocolate Glaze, if desired.

Chocolate Bundt Cake

Makes 12 servings

1¾ cups all-purpose flour
1¾ cups sugar
¾ cup Hershey's® Cocoa
1½ teaspoons baking soda
1 teaspoon salt
⅔ cup butter or margarine, softened
1½ cups sour cream
¼ cup milk
2 eggs
1 teaspoon vanilla extract
   Cocoa Glaze (recipe follows)
   Chopped nuts (optional)

Combine flour, sugar, cocoa, baking soda, and salt in large mixer bowl. Add butter, sour cream, milk, eggs, and vanilla; blend on low speed. Beat 3 minutes on medium speed. Pour batter into a well-greased and floured 10- or 12-cup Bundt pan. Bake at 350°F. for 60 to 65 minutes, or until cake tester inserted into cake comes out clean. Cool 10 minutes; remove from pan. Cool completely on wire rack. Prepare Cocoa Glaze; glaze cake and garnish with chopped nuts, if desired.

Cocoa Glaze

3 tablespoons butter
2 tablespoons Hershey's® Cocoa
3 tablespoons milk
1 cup confectioners sugar
½ teaspoon vanilla extract

Melt butter in small saucepan over low heat; add cocoa and stir until smooth. Add milk, stirring until well blended. Remove from heat; whisk or beat in confectioners sugar and vanilla until smooth. Spoon onto inverted cake, allowing some to drizzle down sides.

Mocha Bundt Cake

Makes one 10-inch cake

    1 package chocolate or devil's food cake mix
    4 eggs
    ½ cup cooking oil
    1 cup water
    1 package chocolate instant pudding mix
    1 tablespoon dry instant coffee
    1 teaspoon vanilla extract

Turn the ingredients into the large Mixmaster Mixer bowl; blend 1 minute at low; turn the dial to medium and beat 2 minutes. Bake in a greased tube pan or Bundt mold, in a preheated 350°F oven, 45 to 55 minutes, or until the cake tests done with a toothpick. Let stand in the pan about 5 minutes, then turn out to cool.

Note: This cake can be served plain, frosted, or glazed, as you like, or sprinkled with confectioners sugar.

Viennese Mocha Torte

Makes 1 cake

    1 package (2-layer size) chocolate or devil's food
        cake mix★
    1 package (4-serving size) Jell-O Chocolate or
        Chocolate Fudge Flavor Instant Pudding and
        Pie Filling
    4 eggs
    1 cup water★
    ½ cup oil
    2 cups cold milk
    1 envelope Dream Whip Whipped Topping Mix
    1 package (6-serving size) Jell-O Chocolate or
        Chocolate Fudge Flavor Instant Pudding and
        Pie Filling
    ¼ cup cooled brewed Maxwell House Coffee
    1 jar (10 ounces) apricot preserves
        Chocolate Curls (see index) (optional)

Combine cake mix, 4-serving-size pudding mix, eggs, water, and oil in large mixer bowl. Blend, then beat at medium speed of electric mixer for 4 minutes. Pour into 2 greased and floured 9-inch layer pans. Bake at 350°F for 30 to 35 minutes, or until cake tester inserted in center comes out clean and cakes begin to pull away from sides of pans. Do not underbake. Cool in pans about 15 minutes. Remove from pans and finish cooling on racks. Split cakes; makes 4 layers.

Pour milk into deep narrow-bottom mixer bowl. Add whipped topping mix and 6-serving size pudding mix. Beat at low speed of electric mixer until well blended. Gradually increase beating speed to high and whip until mixture forms soft peaks, 4 to 6 minutes.

Sprinkle each layer with 1 tablespoon of the coffee. Spread half of the jam on one layer and top with about 1 cup of the frosting. Add the second layer; spread with 1 cup of the frosting. Repeat layers. Garnish with Chocolate Curls, if desired. Chill. Store any leftover cake in the refrigerator.

★ Or use pudding-included cake mix; reduce water to ¾ cup.

Choca-Cola Cake

Makes about 12 servings

    2 cups sifted Hecker's Unbleached, All-Purpose,
        Naturally White Flour
    2 cups sugar
    1 cup butter
    3 tablespoons cocoa
    1 cup cola
 1½ cups miniature marshmallows
    ½ cup buttermilk
    2 eggs, beaten
    1 teaspoon baking soda
    1 teaspoon vanilla extract
        Icing (recipe follows)
    1 cup pecans, finely chopped

Combine flour and sugar. In a saucepan, mix together the butter and cocoa. Add the cola, and heat to boiling. Add the marshmallows, remove from heat, and mix until the marshmallows are dissolved. Pour this over the flour-sugar mixture, mixing well. Add the buttermilk, eggs, baking soda, and vanilla and mix well. Pour into a well-greased 13x9x2-inch pan. Bake in a preheated 350°F. oven 30 to 35 minutes.

Prepare Icing and frost the cake in the pan as soon as it is out of the oven. Sprinkle nuts over the top.

Icing

    ½ cup butter
    3 tablespoons cocoa
    2 tablespoons cola
    1 box (1 pound) confectioners sugar

In a saucepan, combine butter and cocoa. Add cola and heat to boiling. Pour over the sugar and mix until smooth.

A Hurry-up Hint

Frost any cupcake fast by dipping the top lightly into a fluffy (not runny) frosting. Nimble trick for little fingers, too!

Jubilee Chocolate Cake

Makes 10 to 12 servings

- ¾ teaspoon baking soda
- 1 cup buttermilk or sour milk★
- 1½ cups unsifted cake flour or 1¼ cups unsifted all-purpose flour
- 1 cup sugar
- ½ cup Hershey's® Cocoa
- ½ teaspoon salt
- ½ cup vegetable oil
- 2 egg yolks
- 2 egg whites
- ½ cup sugar
  Vanilla ice cream
  Flaming Cherry Sauce (recipe follows)

Stir baking soda into buttermilk until dissolved. Combine flour, 1 cup sugar, cocoa, and salt in large mixer bowl. Add oil, buttermilk mixture, and egg yolks; beat until smooth. Beat egg whites in small mixer bowl until foamy; gradually add ½ cup sugar, beating until very stiff peaks form. Gently fold egg whites into chocolate batter. Pour into greased and floured 13 × 9 × 2-inch pan. Bake at 350°F for 30 to 35 minutes, or until cake springs back when lightly touched in center. Cool in pan on wire rack.

To serve, cut into squares; top each square with a scoop of vanilla ice cream and a serving of Flaming Cherry Sauce.

★ To sour milk: Use 1 tablespoon vinegar plus milk to equal 1 cup.

Flaming Cherry Sauce

Makes 4 to 6 servings

- 1 can (16 or 17 ounces) dark or light sweet cherries, pitted
- 1½ tablespoons sugar
- 1 tablespoon cornstarch
  Dash salt
- ½ teaspoon grated orange peel
- ¼ cup kirsch or brandy

Drain cherries; reserve syrup. Combine ¾ cup cherry syrup with sugar, cornstarch, and salt in saucepan or chafing dish. Cook and stir until thickened; boil 1 minute. Add cherries and orange peel; heat thoroughly. Gently heat kirsch or brandy in small saucepan over low heat; pour over cherry mixture. Ignite with match. Stir gently and ladle over scoops of ice cream and chocolate cake. (Double recipe to serve entire cake.)

Quick and Easy Cherry Sauce

Combine 1 can (16 ounces) cherry pie filling with ¼ cup orange juice; heat thoroughly. Flame as above.

Father's Day Chocolate Golf-Bag Cake

Makes 8 servings

- ⅔ cup sifted cake flour
- ½ teaspoon baking powder
- ¼ teaspoon salt
- 2 squares (1 ounce each) unsweetened chocolate
- 4 eggs
- ⅔ cup sugar
- 1 teaspoon vanilla extract
- 2 tablespoons sugar
- ¼ teaspoon baking soda
- 3 tablespoons cold water
  Confectioners sugar
- ¾ cup Ocean Spray Whole Berry Cranberry Sauce
  Chocolate Fudge Frosting (recipe follows)
- 1 package (4 ounces) chocolate-covered mint wafers

Preheat oven to 375°F. Grease 15 × 10 × 1-inch jelly roll pan; line bottom with waxed paper; grease paper. Sift flour, baking powder, and salt; set aside. In top of double boiler over hot, not boiling, water, melt chocolate; set aside. In medium-size bowl, beat eggs until thick and creamy; gradually add ⅔ cup sugar, beating constantly, until very thick. Fold in flour mixture and vanilla.

Stir 2 tablespoons sugar, baking soda, and cold water into melted chocolate until thickened; fold into cake batter. Spread batter in prepared pan. Bake 15 to 20 minutes, or until top springs back when lightly touched with fingertip. Loosen cake around edges with small spatula; invert onto clean towel dusted with confectioners sugar; peel off wax paper. Starting at short end, roll up cake and towel together. Place seam side down on wire rack; cool completely.

When cake is cool, unroll carefully. Spread evenly with cranberry sauce; reroll. Place seam side down on serving plate. Spread outside of roll evenly with Chocolate Fudge Frosting. Decorate to resemble golf bag, with brown licorice for bindings and shoulder straps, golf tees on top, and chocolate mint wafers to edge bag.

Chocolate Fudge Frosting

- 2 squares (1 ounce each) unsweetened chocolate
- ¼ cup butter or margarine
- 1¾ cups confectioners sugar
- ¼ cup milk
- 1 teaspoon vanilla extract

In small heavy pan, combine chocolate and butter; melt, stirring, over low heat. Remove from heat. In medium-size bowl, combine sugar, milk, and vanilla. Add chocolate mixture and stir until smooth.

Chocolate Cream Roll
Makes 10 servings

- ¾ cup C & H Granulated Sugar
- 4 eggs
- 1 teaspoon vanilla extract
- ½ cup all-purpose flour
- ⅓ cup cocoa powder
- ¼ teaspoon *each* baking soda and salt
- 2 cups heavy cream, whipped with ⅓ cup C & H Powdered Sugar
  Chocolate Glaze (recipe follows)
  Glacéed cherries and whole blanched almonds

Preheat oven to 400°F. Grease a 15×10×1-inch jelly roll pan. Line with greased waxed paper or parchment. Gradually beat sugar into eggs and continue beating at high speed until thick and lemon colored. Beat in vanilla. Combine flour, cocoa, soda, and salt and gently fold into egg-sugar mixture. Spread batter evenly in pan. Bake 10 to 13 minutes, until edges start to pull away from sides of pan. Turn out immediately onto towel dusted with powdered

Chocolate Cream Roll. C&H Sugar Company

Mocha Bundt Cake (page 12)

sugar. Peel off paper. Trim off crisp edges. Roll cake in towel (from short side for pinwheel, from long side for log). Cool on rack. Unroll and spread with whipped cream. Reroll (without towel) and place on serving plate, seam side down. Top with Chocolate Glaze. Decorate with glacéed cherries and whole almonds.

Chocolate Glaze
- 1 tablespoon butter
- 1 ounce unsweetened chocolate
- ½ cup C & H Powdered Sugar
- ½ teaspoon vanilla extract
  Pinch salt
- 1 to 2 tablespoons heavy cream or boiling water

Melt butter and chocolate in double boiler over low heat. Remove from heat and stir in sugar, vanilla, and salt. Stir in cream. Mixture will be thick.

Peanut-Chocolate Roll

Makes 8 servings

- 4 eggs, separated, at room temperature
- 1¼ cups confectioners sugar
- 1¾ cups Planters® Dry Roasted Peanuts, finely ground
- 1 cup heavy cream
- 3 tablespoons granulated sugar
- 1 tablespoon cocoa
- 1 teaspoon vanilla extract
- 2 squares (1 ounce each) unsweetened chocolate
- 2 tablespoons Blue Bonnet® Margarine
- 1 teaspoon milk
- 2 tablespoons Planters® Dry Roasted Peanuts, coarsely chopped

Grease a 15 × 10½-inch jelly roll pan; line with waxed paper. Grease paper; set aside.

In medium bowl, with electric mixer at medium speed, beat egg yolks and 1 cup confectioners sugar until thick and lemon colored. Mix in ground Planters® Dry Roasted Peanuts. In small bowl, with electric mixer at high speed, beat egg whites until stiff but not dry. Mix one-quarter whites into yolk mixture; gently fold in remaining whites. Spread evenly in prepared pan. Bake at 400°F. for 15 minutes, or until cake is lightly browned and center springs back when touched.

Turn cake onto sheet of waxed paper; remove pan (do not remove waxed paper). Roll up cake and paper from long side. Set on rack to cool completely.

Meanwhile, in medium bowl, with electric mixer at medium speed, beat cream, granulated sugar, cocoa, and vanilla until soft peaks form. Unroll cake and carefully remove waxed paper; spread cake with chocolate-whipped cream and reroll. Place on serving platter, seam side down.

In small saucepan, over low heat, melt chocolate and Blue Bonnet® Margarine, stirring constantly. Stir in remaining ¼ cup confectioners sugar and milk until smooth. Spoon over roll. Sprinkle with chopped peanuts. Chill until ready to serve.

Chocolate Sponge Roll

Makes 16 servings

- 6 eggs, at room temperature
- ¾ cup sugar
- 1 teaspoon vanilla extract
- ⅓ cup all-purpose flour
- ⅓ cup unsweetened cocoa
- ¼ cup Argo or Kingsford's Corn Starch
- 3 tablespoons Mazola Margarine, melted and cooled
- **Chocolate Cream Filling (recipe follows)**

Line bottom of 15 × 10 × 1-inch jelly roll pan with waxed paper. In large bowl, with mixer at high speed, beat eggs, sugar, and vanilla 10 minutes, or until light and fluffy (mixture will triple). Sift together flour, cocoa, and cornstarch. Sift over beaten egg mixture, about one third at a time, gently folding in with rubber spatula after each addition. Drizzle margarine over mixture; gently fold in. Pour into prepared pan. Bake in 350°F. oven 20 to 25 minutes, or until cake springs back when lightly touched. With small metal spatula, loosen sides. Immediately turn out onto cloth dusted with cocoa. Remove waxed paper. Starting at long side, roll up cake and cloth together. Place cake seam side down on wire rack; cool. Unroll and spread with Chocolate Cream Filling (or 1 cup heavy cream, whipped). Roll up cake. Cover; refrigerate. Just before serving, sprinkle with confectioners sugar. Slice to serve.

Sponge Roll

Follow recipe for Chocolate Sponge Roll. Omit cocoa. Increase flour to ⅔ cup. After baking, immediately turn out onto cloth dusted with confectioners sugar.

Chocolate Cream Filling

Makes about 2 cups filling

- ¼ cup sugar
- 2 tablespoons Argo or Kingsford's Corn Starch
- ⅛ teaspoon salt
- 1 cup milk
- 2 squares (1 ounce each) semisweet or unsweetened chocolate, cut up
- 1 tablespoon Mazola Margarine
- ½ teaspoon vanilla extract
- ½ cup heavy cream, whipped

In 1-quart saucepan, stir together sugar, cornstarch, and salt. Gradually stir in milk until smooth. Stir in chocolate. Stirring constantly, bring to boil over medium-low heat and boil 1 minute. Stir in margarine and vanilla. Turn into medium bowl; cover surface with waxed paper or plastic wrap. Cool to room temperature. Gently fold in whipped cream. Cover; refrigerate about 1 hour, or until cool.

Is It Done?

Bake the minimum time the recipe suggests, then touch the center of the cake lightly with your finger. If the cake is done, it will spring back, leaving no indentation. If a depression remains, bake 5 minutes longer, test again; if necessary, repeat. A cake that is ready to be taken from the oven will have shrunk a little away from the sides of the pan—a backup for the finger test.

If you prefer, use a cake tester, which looks like a thin wire skewer, or a wooden toothpick. Insert in the center of the cake; if it comes out dry, with no batter or soft crumbs clinging to it, the cake is done.

Miniature Chocolate Fruitcakes

Makes 3½ dozen miniature cakes

- ½ **cup all-purpose flour**
- ½ **teaspoon baking powder**
- ½ **teaspoon salt**
- ¼ **teaspoon baking soda**
- 1 **6-ounce package (1 cup) Nestlé Toll House Semi-Sweet Chocolate Morsels**
- ⅓ **cup butter, softened**
- ¼ **cup firmly packed brown sugar**
- 1 **teaspoon orange extract**
- 3 **eggs**
- ¼ **cup water**
- 1¾ **cups mixed candied fruit, finely chopped**
- 1 **cup finely chopped nuts**
  Decorative Butter Cream Frosting (recipe follows)
  Red and green candied cherries (optional)

Preheat oven to 350°F. In a small bowl, combine flour, baking powder, salt, and baking soda; set aside. Melt Nestlé Toll House Semi-Sweet Chocolate Morsels over hot (not boiling) water; remove from heat and set aside. In a large bowl, combine butter, brown sugar, and orange extract; beat until creamy. Add eggs, 1 at a time, beating well after each addition. Stir in melted chocolate. Add flour mixture alternately with water. Fold in candied fruit and nuts. Spoon batter by measuring tablespoonfuls into 42 greased or paper-lined gem pans. Bake 15 minutes. Remove from pans; cool completely. Using a pastry bag fitted with a writing tip, decorate cupcakes with Decorative Butter Cream Frosting. Garnish with candied cherries, if desired.

Decorative Butter Cream Frosting

- 3 **cups confectioners sugar**
- ⅓ **cup butter, softened**
- 1 **teaspoon orange extract**
- 2 **tablespoons milk**
  Food coloring (optional)

In a small bowl, combine confectioners sugar, butter, and orange extract; beat until creamy. Blend in milk; beat until smooth. Frosting may be tinted.

Mocha Spice Cake

Makes 12 servings

- 1½ cups all-purpose flour
- 1 teaspoon baking soda
- 1 teaspoon ground cinnamon
- ½ teaspoon Calumet Baking Powder
- ½ teaspoon salt
- ½ cup butter or margarine
- 1½ cups sugar
- 2 eggs
- 2 squares (1 ounce each) Baker's Unsweetened Chocolate, melted and cooled
- 1 cup sour cream
- ½ cup water
- 1 tablespoon Maxwell House Instant Coffee
- ½ teaspoon vanilla extract
  Confectioners sugar (optional)

Mix flour, baking soda, cinnamon, baking powder, and salt. Cream butter. Gradually beat in sugar and continue beating until light and fluffy. Add eggs, 1 at a time, beating thoroughly after each addition. Blend in chocolate. Combine sour cream, water, instant coffee, and vanilla. Add flour mixture to batter alternately with sour cream mixture, beating after each addition until smooth. Pour into a greased and floured 13 × 9 × 2-inch pan. Bake at 350°F. for 30 to 35 minutes, or until cake tester inserted into center comes out clean. Cool cake in pan 10 minutes. Remove from pan and finish cooling on rack. Sprinkle with confectioners sugar, if desired.

Chocolate Zucchini Cake (page 19); Mini Chip Apple Snacking Cake (page 20); Harvest Pumpkin Torte (page 24). Courtesy HERSHEY Food Corporation

Chocolate Zucchini Cake

Makes 12 servings

- 3 eggs
- 1½ cups sugar
- 1 teaspoon vanilla extract
- ½ cup vegetable oil
- 2 cups all-purpose flour
- ⅓ cup Hershey's® Cocoa
- 1 teaspoon baking powder
- 1 teaspoon baking soda
- 1 teaspoon ground cinnamon
- ¼ teaspoon salt
- ¾ cup buttermilk or sour milk★
- 2 cups coarsely shredded raw zucchini
- 1 cup chopped nuts
- ½ cup raisins
   Creamy Mini Chip Glaze (recipe follows)
      (optional)

Beat eggs on high speed until light and fluffy in large mixer bowl. Gradually beat in sugar and vanilla until thick and light in color. Gradually pour in oil; beat until combined. Combine flour, cocoa, baking powder, baking soda, cinnamon, and salt. Add alternately with buttermilk in 2 additions, beginning and ending with flour mixture. Fold zucchini into batter. Stir in nuts and raisins; pour into greased and floured 12-cup Bundt pan. Bake at 350°F. for 50 to 55 minutes, or until cake tester inserted in center comes out clean. Cool 10 minutes; invert onto serving tray. Cool completely. Glaze with Creamy Mini Chip Glaze, if desired.

★ To sour milk: Use 2 teaspoons vinegar plus milk to equal ¾ cup

Creamy Mini Chip Glaze

Makes about ½ cup glaze

- 3 tablespoons sugar
- 2 tablespoons water
- ½ cup Hershey's® Mini Chips® Semi-Sweet Chocolate
- 1 tablespoon marshmallow creme
- 1 to 2 teaspoons hot water

Combine sugar and 2 tablespoons water in small saucepan; bring to boil. Remove from heat; immediately add Mini Chips semi-sweet chocolate and stir until melted. Blend in marshmallow creme; add hot water, ½ teaspoon at a time, until glaze is desired consistency.

Wheat Germ Chocolate Cake (page 24). International Multifoods

Baking Basics

To bake is to cook with dry heat at a wide range of temperatures within an enclosed space, such as an oven. However, foods cooked on a griddle—pancakes and English muffins, as examples—are also spoken of as baked.

When you are getting ready to bake, read the recipe through carefully and assemble all the ingredients and tools that you will need. Check to see whether dry ingredients are to be sifted together; if so, do that before beginning. When you are making a cake or cookies, the butter should be somewhat softened—at room temperature but not melted—unless the recipe specifies otherwise.

Always measure carefully, using standard measuring cups and spoons. When measuring solids, such as shortening, use graduated-size measuring cups meant for solid ingredients; fill the appropriate-size measuring cup to the brim and level off the top with a spatula. When measuring liquids, such as milk, water, or oil, use a measuring cup meant for liquids—usually of glass with the various fractions of a cup printed on the side—filled just to the line marking the measurement you need. Place the cup on a level surface when filling it. Use standard measuring spoons for small amounts, again leveling off ingredients with a spatula.

It is always safest to preheat the oven, even if you feel that your oven heats very rapidly; baking times given in recipes mean the time from the point at which the dish is put into a fully preheated oven until the time that the dish is done. Start preheating the oven when you begin to assemble the ingredients unless the preparation time is long, such as the time allowed for bread to rise.

In baking dishes that require exactness—cakes, pies, muffins, cookies, breads, cream puffs, soufflés, for example—the whole process of measuring, assembling and baking is critical. The success or failure of the recipe depends entirely on the chemical interaction of the ingredients both in mixing and in the baking process. Not only must you use the ingredients called for in the recipe but also the oven temperature recommended and the specified type and size of pan. The baking time, too, is critical; if your oven has a timer, set it or use a hand timer. Don't substitute ingredients. The time to make substitutions, even if you are a very good cook, is the second time that you make the dish, not the first time.

Chocolate Gingerbread

Makes 2 dozen squares

- ½ pound Meadow Gold butter or margarine, cut into pieces
- 1 cup hot coffee
- 1 cup brown sugar
- 1 cup molasses
- 2 ounces semisweet chocolate, melted
- 4 eggs
- 2⅓ cups Martha White All-Purpose Flour
- 1½ teaspoons baking soda
- 1 teaspoon salt
- 1 teaspoon ground ginger
- 1 teaspoon ground cinnamon
- ¼ teaspoon ground nutmeg
- 1 pound Beatrice English Maple Walnut Cream Cheese
- ⅓ cup confectioners sugar
- 1 tablespoon Meadow Gold milk

Blend butter with coffee. Blend in sugar and molasses. Blend in chocolate and eggs. Blend in flour, baking soda, salt, and spices. Pour into greased 13×9×2-inch pan. Bake 45 minutes in preheated 325°F oven. Cool. Blend cheese, sugar, and milk until smooth. Frost Gingerbread. Cut into 2×3-inch pieces.

Mini Chip Apple Snacking Cake

Makes 9 servings

- 2 eggs
- ½ cup vegetable oil
- ¼ cup bottled apple juice
- 1 teaspoon vanilla extract
- 1¾ cups all-purpose flour
- 1 cup sugar
- ½ teaspoon salt
- ½ teaspoon baking soda
- ½ teaspoon ground cinnamon
- 1½ cups diced, peeled tart apples
- ¾ cup Hershey's® Mini Chips® Semi-Sweet Chocolate
- ½ cup chopped nuts
- Confectioners sugar (optional)
- Whipped topping with cinnamon (optional)

Beat eggs lightly in large mixing bowl; add oil, apple juice, and vanilla. Combine flour, sugar, salt, baking soda, and cinnamon; stir into batter until combined. Add apples, Mini Chips semi-sweet chocolate, and nuts; stir until evenly mixed. Pour into greased and floured 9-inch square pan. Bake at 350°F for 40 to 45 minutes, or until cake begins to pull away from edge of pan. Cool. Just before serving, sprinkle top with confectioners sugar or serve with dollop of whipped topping sprinkled with cinnamon.

Spirited Raisin Chocolate Cake

Makes 8 servings

¾ cup Rum-Spirited Golden Raisins (recipe follows)
1 cup filberts with skin on (or almonds)
¾ cup semisweet chocolate pieces
½ cup butter, softened
⅔ cup sugar
3 eggs
Grated rind of 1 large orange
1 cup very fine bread crumbs
Honey Chocolate Glaze (recipe follows)
Slivered almonds or filberts

Grease an 8-inch round cake pan. Line bottom with waxed paper. Preheat oven to 375°F. Drain raisins. Grind filberts fine in blender. Melt chocolate over hot, not boiling, water. Cool slightly. Cream butter until very soft and light. Add sugar gradually, beating constantly. Add eggs, 1 at a time, beating hard after each addition. The batter will look curdled. Stir in chocolate, raisins, then the ground filberts, orange rind, and bread crumbs. Pour into prepared pan and bake 30 to 35 minutes. (The center of the cake will not seem quite done, hence its soft texture and exceptionally delicious flavor.)

Allow cake to cool in pan on a rack upright for about 30 minutes. Then run knife around edge and turn out onto rack. Very gently lift off paper. Cool completely before glazing with Honey Chocolate Glaze. Decorate with slivered almonds or filberts.
Note: This cake freezes well if wrapped securely. Bring to room temperature before serving.

Spirited Raisins

1 cup California dark seedless or golden raisins
½ cup warmed brandy, rum, orange liqueur, cocoa-based liquor, coffee-flavored liqueur, or sherry

Place raisins in sterilized jar. Pour warmed liquor over. Seal jar. Let stand 24 hours or more, shaking jar occasionally.

When using Spirited Raisins in a recipe, take out desired amount. Strain liquor back into jar. To replenish raisins, add more raisins and liquor to the jar, estimating proportions.

Honey Chocolate Glaze

2 squares (1 ounce each) unsweetened chocolate
½ cup semisweet chocolate pieces
¼ cup butter, softened
2 teaspoons honey

Combine the 2 chocolates, butter, and honey in the top of a double boiler and melt over hot water. Re-

move from heat and beat until thick and syrupy. Place cake on rack on a piece of waxed paper and pour glaze over all. Tip the cake so the glaze runs evenly over the top and down the sides, smoothing sides with a metal spatula, if necessary.

Storing Chocolate

A temperature beween 60° and 70°F. is best for storing chocolate. In too warm a place, or in hot summer weather, chocolate may develop a gray-white film over the outside. This is called "bloom" and is caused by part of the cocoa butter content rising to the surface. It's not particularly pretty, but it does not affect the usefulness of the chocolate. The same thing sometimes happens to chocolate candy in warm weather.

In storing cocoa, the thing to remember is to replace the top of the carton firmly. Humidity makes cocoa lumpy and hard. The 60° to 70°F. range is best for cocoa, too.

We generally bake cakes containing chocolate at a somewhat lower temperature than white cakes—usually about 25 degrees lower—because too high a temperature can change the flavor of the chocolate. Also, the crust of chocolate cake scorches more easily than that of its white counterpart.

Chocolate Almond Cake l'Orange

Makes 1 cake

6 tablespoons butter or margarine
1 cup sugar
⅛ teaspoon salt
3 eggs
4 squares (1 ounce each) Baker's Unsweetened Chocolate, melted and cooled
¾ cup ground almonds
¼ cup dry bread crumbs
3 tablespoons orange liqueur
1 teaspoon vanilla extract
Sweetened whipped cream (optional)
Orange rind (optional)

Cream butter. Gradually beat in sugar and salt and continue beating until light and fluffy. Add eggs, 1 at a time, beating thoroughly after each. Stir in chocolate, almonds, bread crumbs, 2 tablespoons of the liqueur and the vanilla.

Pour into greased and floured 8-inch layer pan. Baked at 375°F. about 25 minutes, or until cake tester inserted in center comes out clean. Cool in pan 5 minutes. Invert onto rack and drizzle with remaining 1 tablespoon liqueur. Cool. Garnish with sweetened whipped cream and thinly slivered orange rind, if desired.

Heavenly Chocolate Mousse-Filled Cake

Makes 1 cake

    1 package (14½ ounces) angel food cake mix
    3 to 4 drops red food color
       Chocolate Mousse Filling (recipe follows)
       Whipped Cream Frosting (recipe follows)
       Chocolate Hearts (recipe follows) (optional)

Prepare cake according to package directions, adding red food color to stiffly beaten egg white portion of the batter.

Place baked cake on serving plate. Slice 1-inch layer from the top and set aside. With sharp knife, cut cake 1 inch from outer edge to 1 inch from bottom. Cut around cake 1 inch from inner edge down to 1 inch from bottom, leaving walls 1 inch thick. Remove cake from center, leaving 1-inch thick base on bottom of cake. Prepare Chocolate Mousse Filling; spoon into cavity. Replace top. Prepare Whipped Cream Frosting; frost cake. Chill completely. Before serving, garnish with Chocolate Hearts, if desired.

Chocolate Mousse Filling

Makes 3 cups filling

    2 teaspoons unflavored gelatin
    2 tablespoons cold water
    ⅓ cup water
    ⅓ cup Hershey's® Cocoa
    ⅔ cup sugar
    1½ cups heavy cream
    2 teaspoons vanilla extract

Sprinkle gelatin onto 2 tablespoons water in small bowl; set aside to soften. Bring ⅓ cup water to boil in small saucepan; stir in cocoa over low heat until smooth and thickened. Add softened gelatin, stirring until dissolved. Remove from heat; mix in sugar. Cool to room temperature. Whip cream with vanilla until stiff peaks form. Gradually add chocolate while beating on low speed just until well blended. Chill 30 minutes; spoon into cake cavity.

Whipped Cream Frosting

Makes about 2 cups frosting

    1 cup heavy cream
    ¼ cup confectioners sugar
    1 teaspoon vanilla extract
    2 or 3 drops red food color

Whip cream with sugar, vanilla, and red food color until stiff. Frost cake.

Chocolate Hearts

Melt either ⅔ cup Hershey's® Mini Chips® Semi-Sweet Chocolate or a 4-ounce Hershey's® Milk Chocolate Bar or equivalent in top of double boiler over hot water. Stir until completely melted. Spread onto waxed paper-covered cookie sheet with spatula into 7-inch square about ⅛ inch thick. Chill 5 to 8 minutes, or until chocolate begins to set. Cut heart shapes in chocolate using cookie cutter, but do not remove. Chill several hours, overnight, or until very firm. Peel hearts from paper; place on tray and refrigerate until needed.

Chocolate Nut Cake

Makes 2 cakes

    2¼ cups all-purpose flour
    1 teaspoon baking soda
    1 teaspoon salt
    1 cup butter or margarine
    2 cups sugar
    5 eggs
    3 squares (1 ounce each) Baker's Unsweetened
       Chocolate, melted and cooled
    1 cup buttermilk
    2 teaspoons vanilla extract
    1 cup finely chopped nuts (optional)
       Bittersweet Glaze (recipe follows) (optional)
       Coarsely chopped nuts (optional)

Mix flour with soda and salt. Cream butter. Gradually beat in sugar and continue beating until light and fluffy. Add eggs, 1 at a time, beating thoroughly after each addition. Blend in chocolate. Add flour mixture alternately with buttermilk, beating after each addition until smooth. Mix in vanilla and nuts.

Pour into 2 greased and floured 9 × 5 × 3-inch loaf pans. Bake at 350°F about 60 minutes, or until cake tester inserted into center comes out clean. Cool cakes in pans 10 minutes. Remove from pans and finish cooling on racks. Frost or glaze with favorite frosting or Bittersweet Glaze and, top with coarsely chopped nuts, if desired.

Bittersweet Glaze

Makes 1 cup

    2 squares Baker's Unsweetened Chocolate
    2 tablespoons butter or margarine
    1¾ cups confectioners sugar
       Dash salt
    3 tablespoons hot water (approximately)

Heat chocolate and butter in saucepan until melted and smooth. Remove from heat. Add sugar and salt alternately with water until of spreading consistency.

Heavenly Chocolate Mousse-Filled Cake; Chocolate-Fluted Kiss Cups (page 95). Courtesy HERSHEY Food Corporation

Harvest Pumpkin Torte

Makes 8 to 10 servings

    4 eggs, separated
    ½ cup sugar
    ½ cup all-purpose flour
    ⅓ cup Hershey's® Cocoa
    ¼ cup sugar
    ½ teaspoon baking soda
    ¼ teaspoon salt
    ⅓ cup water
    1 teaspoon vanilla extract
    1 tablespoon sugar
       Pumpkin Filling (recipe follows)
       Harvest Chocolate Glaze (recipe follows)
       Slivered almonds (optional)

Line a 15 × 10 × 1-inch jelly roll pan with aluminum foil; generously grease foil. Beat egg yolks 2 minutes on medium speed. Gradually add ½ cup sugar; continue beating 2 minutes. Combine flour, cocoa, ¼ cup sugar, baking soda, and salt; add alternately with water on low speed just until batter is smooth. Add vanilla. Set aside. Beat egg whites until foamy; add 1 tablespoon sugar and beat until stiff peaks form. Carefully fold into chocolate mixture. Spread batter evenly into prepared pan. Bake at 375°F for 14 to 16 minutes, or until top springs back when touched lightly. Invert onto slightly dampened towel; carefully remove foil. Cool. Cut cake crosswise into 4 equal parts, each measuring approximately 3¾ × 10 inches. Place one layer on flat rectangular serving plate. Spread with about ¾ cup Pumpkin Filling. Carefully stack layers, alternating cake and filling, ending with plain cake layer on top. Glaze top of cake with Harvest Chocolate Glaze; garnish with slivered almonds, if desired. Chill.

Pumpkin Filling

Makes about 2¼ cups

    1 cup canned pumpkin
    ¼ cup all-purpose flour
    ⅓ cup butter
    3 tablespoons shortening
    1 teaspoon ground cinnamon
    ¼ teaspoon ground nutmeg
    1¾ cups confectioners sugar

Combine pumpkin and flour in small saucepan. Place over medium heat, bring to a boil, stirring constantly (mixture will be very thick). Remove from heat; cool thoroughly. Combine butter and shortening in small mixer bowl; add cinnamon and nutmeg. Gradually add confectioners sugar; beat until light and fluffy. Slowly blend pumpkin into creamed mixture. Chill until mixture begins to set before spreading between cake layers.

Harvest Chocolate Glaze

Makes about ½ cup glaze

    1 tablespoon butter or margarine
    2 tablespoons Hershey's® Cocoa
    1½ tablespoons water
    ⅔ cup confectioners sugar
    ¼ teaspoon vanilla extract

Melt butter in small saucepan over low heat; add cocoa and water, stirring constantly, until mixture thickens. Do not boil. Remove from heat. Beat in confectioners sugar and vanilla until smooth. Add additional water, ½ teaspoon at a time, until desired consistency.

Sour Milk Trick

Many chocolate cake recipes call for buttermilk or sour milk—neither of which is a household standard (soured pasteurized milk should never be used). If you hate to buy a pint or quart when you need only 1 cup, try this magical alternative: Place 1 tablespoon lemon juice or white vinegar in a measuring cup and add fresh whole milk to make 1 cup. Let the mixture stand 5 minutes and—presto!—1 cup of sour/buttermilk at your service.

Wheat Germ Chocolate Cake

Makes 12 to 16 servings

    1¼ cups unsifted Robin Hood All Purpose Flour
    ¾ cup Kretschmer Wheat Germ, Regular or
          Brown Sugar & Honey
    1 cup sugar
    ¾ teaspoon baking soda
    1⅓ cups buttermilk
    ¾ cup butter or margarine
    3 tablespoons cocoa
    1 egg, beaten
    2 teaspoons vanilla extract
       Chocolate Icing (recipe follows)
    2 tablespoons chopped walnuts
    1 tablespoon Kretschmer Wheat Germ, Regular
          or Brown Sugar & Honey

Combine flour, ¾ cup wheat germ, sugar, and baking soda in large bowl. Stir well to blend. Heat buttermilk, butter, and cocoa together until butter melts. Add buttermilk mixture to blended dry ingredients. Blend well. Stir in egg and vanilla. Line bottoms of 2 ungreased 8-inch layer pans with waxed paper. Pour batter into prepared pans. Bake at 400°F for 20 to 25 minutes, until top springs back when lightly touched in center. Cool in pans 5 minutes. Remove from pans. Cool on rack. Place first layer, top side down, on serving plate. Spread with Chocolate Icing. Place second layer, top side up, on frosted layer. Spread top with remaining icing. Sprinkle top of cake with walnuts and 1 tablespoon wheat germ.

Chocolate Icing
  ¼ cup butter or margarine
  ¼ cup boiling water
  ¼ cup cocoa
  2 to 2½ cups confectioners sugar
  2 tablespoons Kretschmer Wheat Germ, Regular or Brown Sugar & Honey
  1 teaspoon vanilla extract

Combine butter, water, cocoa, and 2 cups confectioners sugar in small bowl. Beat until creamy. Stir in wheat germ and vanilla. Add additional confectioners sugar gradually, beating until of spreading consistency.

Variation
Prepare cake as directed, but spread sweetened whipped cream between layers. Frost sides and top with icing. Garnish as directed. Refrigerate until ready to serve.

Keeping Cakes
If you're lucky, there may be cake leftovers for tomorrow or the day after. A covered cake keeper is the place for frosted cakes, either butter or foam; if you don't have one, invert a big bowl, large enough so that it doesn't touch the frosting, over the cake. If the cake has a cooked cream filling or a whipped cream filling or frosting, store it in the refrigerator. If it has an ice cream filling, store it in the freezer. Otherwise, store at room temperature.

Wrap up unfrosted cake in plastic wrap or foil; store at room temperature.

Chocolate Torte with Grand Marnier Pastry Creme and Cranberry Topping
Makes one 8-inch torte
  1⅔ cups sifted all-purpose flour
  1½ cups sugar
  1¼ teaspoons baking soda
  1 teaspoon salt
  ½ cup cocoa
  ½ cup vegetable shortening
  1 cup milk
  1 teaspoon vanilla extract
  3 eggs
    Pastry Creme (recipe follows)
    Icing (recipe follows)
  ½ cup slivered almonds
  1 can (16 ounces) Ocean Spray Whole Berry Cranberry Sauce
  2 tablespoons Grand Marnier

Preheat oven to 350°F. Into a large bowl, sift together flour, sugar, baking soda, salt, and cocoa. Add vegetable shortening, milk, and vanilla. With electric mixer beat 2 minutes on medium speed. Add eggs and beat for 2 minutes. Turn mixture into two greased and floured 8-inch layer cake pans. Bake in oven for 35 to 40 minutes or until tops spring back when touched lightly with fingertip. Cool in pans for 10 minutes. Remove from pans and let cool on wire racks.

Cut cake layers in half horizontally to make 4 layers. Place one layer on serving platter. Spread with prepared Pastry Creme; top with second cake layer. Repeat with remaining cake layers and Pastry Creme, ending with cake on top. With prepared Icing, frost sides of cake. Spread a very thin layer of Icing on top of cake. Press sliced almonds onto sides of torte into frosting. Using a pastry bag fitted with a star tip, pipe remaining frosting around outer edge of cake. In medium bowl, combine whole berry cranberry sauce and Grand Marnier until well blended; spread over top of cake. Chill torte until ready to serve.

Pastry Creme
  1 package French vanilla-flavor instant pudding
  ¾ cup milk
  ¼ cup Grand Marnier
  ½ cup heavy cream, whipped

In medium bowl, following label directions, prepare pudding mix with milk and Grand Marnier. Whip cream until stiff. Fold into pudding. Cover with plastic wrap. Chill.

Icing
  4 squares unsweetened chocolate
  ½ cup butter
  1 package (1 pound) confectioners sugar
  ½ cup milk
  2 teaspoons vanilla extract

In small heavy saucepan, combine chocolate and butter. Place over low heat, just until melted. Remove from heat. In a medium-size bowl, combine confectioners sugar, milk, and vanilla and stir until smooth; add melted chocolate mixture. In pan of ice and water, set bowl; beat with wooden spoon until frosting is thick enough to spread and hold its shape.

Chocolate Swirl Cake

Makes one 10-inch cake
   1 12-ounce package (2 cups) Nestlé Toll House
      Semi-Sweet Chocolate Morsels, divided
   3 tablespoons water
2½ cups all-purpose flour
   1 tablespoon baking powder
   1 teaspoon salt
1½ cups sugar
   1 cup butter, softened
   1 teaspoon vanilla extract
   4 eggs
   1 cup milk
   ¼ cup water
   1 to 1½ cups sifted confectioners sugar
      Pecan halves

Preheat oven to 350°F. Combine over hot (not boiling) water, 1½ cups Nestlé Toll House Semi-Sweet Chocolate Morsels and water; stir until smooth. Combine flour, baking powder, and salt. Beat sugar, butter, and vanilla. Beat in eggs, 1 at a time. Add flour mixture alternately with milk; mix well. Pour one-third the batter into well-greased and floured 10-inch tube pan (not fluted pan). Spread with half the morsel mixture. Repeat layers. Swirl batter. Bake 60 to 70 minutes. Cool 15 to 20 minutes; remove from pan; cool.

Combine over hot (not boiling) water, ½ cup Nestlé Toll House Semi-Sweet Chocolate Morsels and ¼ cup water; stir until smooth. Stir in confectioners sugar. Spoon mixture over cake. Top with pecan halves. Let stand 15 minutes before serving.

Q. *I love the look of "marbled" cakes and pies. But when I try to achieve it, my chocolate batter sinks right to the bottom of the white. Or, as soon as I begin to mix the chocolate blends completely with the white. How do I get the right pattern?*
A. First, you shouldn't pour the chocolate batter; spoon it gently on top of the white batter. Be sure both batters are at room temperature when you start. And you shouldn't be mixing at all; use a swirling motion to keep control of the colors. Swirl through the batters with a knife or spatula; it's better if the knife is cold.

Mocha Lace Cake

Makes 9 servings
1½ cups all-purpose flour
   ¾ cup sugar
   1 teaspoon baking soda
   ¼ teaspoon salt
   ⅔ cup strong coffee or water
   ½ cup Hellmann's or Best Foods Real Mayonnaise
   ⅓ cup chocolate-flavored syrup
   ½ tablespoon vinegar
   1 teaspoon vanilla extract
      Confectioners sugar (optional)

In 8 × 8 × 2-inch baking pan, stir together flour, sugar, baking soda, and salt. Add coffee, mayonnaise, chocolate-flavored syrup, vinegar, and vanilla. Stir with fork, scraping corners and sides of pan until mixture is uniform in color. Bake in 350°F oven 30 to 35 minutes, or until cake tester inserted in center comes out clean. Cool completely in pan on wire rack. If desired, place a paper doily on top of cake; sprinkle with confectioners sugar. Remove carefully. Cut into squares.
Note: Cake may also be made in a 9-inch round cake pan.

Mocha Lace Cake. Hellmann's / Best Foods Real Mayonnaise

Mississippi Mud Cake

Makes 1 cake

- 2 cups sugar
- 1 cup vegetable shortening
- 2 eggs
- 1½ cups sifted Martha White All-Purpose Flour
- ⅓ cup cocoa
- ½ teaspoon salt
- 2 teaspoons vanilla extract
- 1 cup chopped nuts
- 2 cups miniature marshmallows
  Mississippi Mud Icing (recipe follows)

Preheat oven to 325°F. Grease and flour 13x9x2-inch baking pan; set aside. Cream sugar and shortening with electric mixer in mixing bowl until light and fluffy. Add eggs; beat at low speed until well blended. Combine flour, cocoa, and salt in a separate bowl. Add to creamed mixture; blend well. Stir in vanilla and nuts. Pour into prepared pan. Bake 35 to 40 minutes, or until toothpick inserted in center comes out clean. Remove from oven. Sprinkle marshmallows evenly over top. Return to oven 10 minutes, or until marshmallows are melted. Cool in pan on wire rack. Frost with Mississippi Mud Icing. Chill before cutting.

Mississippi Mud Icing

- 4½ cups (16 ounces) sifted confectioners sugar
- ⅓ cup cocoa
- 1 cup butter or margarine, melted
- ½ cup evaporated milk, undiluted, or half and half
- 1 teaspoon vanilla extract
- ½ cup chopped nuts

Combine confectioners sugar and cocoa in small mixing bowl. Add butter; blend well. Add milk and vanilla; beat with electric mixer until smooth. Stir in nuts.

Crunchy Topped Cocoa Cake

Makes 9 servings

- 1½ cups all-purpose flour
- 1 cup sugar
- ¼ cup Hershey's® Cocoa
- 1 teaspoon baking soda
- ½ teaspoon salt
- 1 cup water
- ¼ cup plus 2 tablespoons vegetable oil
- 1 tablespoon vinegar
- 1 teaspoon vanilla extract
  Broiled Topping (recipe follows)

Combine flour, sugar, cocoa, baking soda, and salt in large mixing bowl. Add water, oil, vinegar, and vanilla; beat with spoon or wire whisk just until batter is smooth and ingredients are well blended. Pour into greased and floured 8-inch square pan.

Peanut Butter Cheesecake (page 28). Courtesy of Nabisco Brands, Inc.

Cocoa Chocolate Cake (page 8). Caloric Corporation

Bake at 350°F for 35 to 40 minutes, or until tester inserted in center comes out clean. Meanwhile, prepare Broiled Topping; spread on warm cake. Set oven control at broil. Place cake about 4 inches from heat; broil 3 minutes or until top is bubbly and golden brown. Remove from oven; cool on wire rack.

Broiled Topping

- ¼ cup butter or margarine, softened
- ½ cup packed light brown sugar
- ½ cup coarsely chopped nuts
- ½ cup flaked coconut
- 3 tablespoons light cream or evaporated milk

Combine all ingredients in small bowl, blending well.

Chocolate Chip Cheesecake

Makes one 9-inch cheesecake

1½ cups finely crushed creme-filled chocolate
    sandwich cookies (about 18 cookies)
2 to 3 tablespoons margarine or butter, melted
3 packages (8 ounces each) cream cheese, softened
1 can (14 ounces) Eagle® Brand Sweetened
    Condensed Milk (not evaporated milk)
3 eggs
2 teaspoons vanilla extract
1 cup mini chocolate chips
1 teaspoon all-purpose flour

Preheat oven to 300°F. Combine cookie crumbs and
margarine; press firmly on bottom of 9-inch springform pan. In large mixer bowl, beat cheese until
fluffy. Gradually beat in sweetened condensed milk
until smooth. Add eggs and vanilla; mix well. In
small bowl, toss ½ cup chips with flour to coat; stir
into cheese mixture. Pour into prepared pan. Sprinkle
remaining ½ cup chips evenly over top. Bake 1 hour,
or until cake springs back when lightly touched.
Cool to room temperature. Chill thoroughly. Garnish as desired. Refrigerate leftovers.

Peanut Butter Cheesecake

Makes 12 servings

⅓ cup Blue Bonnet® Margarine, melted
24 Nutter Butter® Peanut Butter Sandwich
    Cookies, finely rolled
2 packages (8 ounces each) cream cheese, softened
1½ cups sugar
⅔ cup Nut Butter (recipe follows)
5 eggs
½ cup sour cream
2 teaspoons lemon juice
1 cup mini semisweet chocolate morsels
1 cup sour cream
¼ cup sugar
1 teaspoon vanilla extract
1 tablespoon Planters® Dry Roasted Unsalted
    Peanuts, chopped
    Strawberry slices

In medium bowl, combine melted Blue Bonnet®
Margarine and Nutter Butter® Peanut Butter Sandwich Cookie crumbs. Press evenly onto bottom and
up sides of 9-inch springform pan; set aside.

In medium bowl, with electric mixer at medium
speed, combine cream cheese and sugar until smooth;
beat in Nut Butter, eggs, sour cream, and lemon
juice. Mix in chocolate morsels. Spread in prepared
crust. Bake at 350°F for 70 to 80 minutes, until center
is firm. Let stand at room temperature 15 minutes.

Meanwhile, in small bowl, blend sour cream,
sugar, and vanilla; spread over cheesecake. Bake for
10 minutes. Cool, then refrigerate at least 3 hours
before serving. Garnish with chopped peanuts and
strawberry slices.

Nut Butter

Makes 1 cup

1 jar (8¼ ounces) Planters® Dry Roasted Unsalted
    Peanuts
2 tablespoons Planters® Peanut Oil
1 tablespoon honey

Place peanuts in a blender or food processor and blend
on high speed until finely ground. While continuing to
blend, add oil and honey until smooth and creamy. Store
refrigerated in covered container.

Cheesecake Chic

Traditional dishes in British and Irish homes in the
17th and 18th centuries, cheesecakes today enjoy great
popularity in America. The addition of chocolate to
cheesecake is a fairly recent innovation, but to those
who succumb to the voluptuous flavors and texture, a
chocolate or chocolate-laced cheesecake is perhaps the
ultimate dessert, to be savored in small, prolonged
bites. Cheesecakes are easy to make, but benefit from
some special care: Ingredients, unless otherwise indi-
cated, should be at room temperature. If overbaked
even a little, the cakes will have a dry, shriveled appearance; some normal shrinkage may occur during
cooling, however. For deliciously different flavors,
vary the crumb crusts.

Chocolate Cheesecake

Makes about 6 servings

Crust

2 cups chocolate wafer crumbs
6 tablespoons butter or margarine, melted
3 tablespoons Domino Granulated Sugar

Combine ingredients and mix well. Press firmly
into an 8- or 9-inch springform pan. Bake at 325°F
for 10 minutes. Cool.

Filling

3 packages (8 ounces each) cream cheese
1 cup plus 2 tablespoons Domino Light Brown
    Sugar, firmly packed
1½ tablespoons vanilla extract
1½ packages (9 ounces) semisweet chocolate bits,
    melted
3 eggs
    Whipped cream (optional)

Combine cheese, sugar, and vanilla. Mix until well
blended. Add melted chocolate. Add eggs, 1 at a

time, beating well after each addition. Pour mixture over crumb crust. Bake at 325°F. for 35 to 40 minutes. Cool. Chill. Serve with whipped cream, if desired.

Raisin Fudge Cups

Makes 1 dozen
  2 cups chocolate sandwich cookie crumbs
  ¼ cup butter or margarine, melted
  1 package (6 ounces) semisweet chocolate pieces
  ¼ cup butter or margarine
  1 egg, beaten
  ½ teaspoon vanilla extract
  ⅔ cup all-purpose flour
  ⅓ cup firmly packed brown sugar
  1 teaspoon baking powder
  ¼ teaspoon salt
  1 cup miniature marshmallows
  1 cup raisins

Combine cookie crumbs and melted butter; mix well. Press mixture onto bottoms and sides of twelve 2½-inch muffin cups, dividing equally; set aside. In saucepan melt chocolate and butter over low heat. Stir in egg, vanilla, flour, brown sugar, baking powder, and salt to blend well. Stir in marshmallows and raisins. Spoon mixture into crumb-lined cups, dividing equally. Bake in preheated 350°F. oven 15 to 20 minutes (centers should still be soft). Remove to rack; loosen edges and remove from muffin cups while still warm.

Golden Cupcakes

Makes 16 cupcakes
  1 cup plus 2 tablespoons all-purpose flour
  ½ teaspoon baking soda
  ½ teaspoon salt
  ½ cup butter, softened
  6 tablespoons sugar
  6 tablespoons firmly packed brown sugar
  ½ teaspoon vanilla extract
  1 egg
    Topping (recipe follows)

Preheat oven to 375°F. In a small bowl, combine flour, baking soda, and salt; set aside. In a large bowl, combine butter, sugar, brown sugar, and vanilla; beat until creamy. Beat in egg. Blend in flour mixture. Spoon mixture into 16 paper-lined muffin cups, using 1 rounded tablespoon batter for each. Bake 15 minutes. Remove from oven. Increase oven temperature to 425°F. Spoon 1 tablespoon topping over each cupcake. Return to oven. Bake 8 to 10 minutes longer. Cool completely before removing from muffin cups.

Topping

  ½ cup firmly packed brown sugar
  1 egg
  ⅛ teaspoon salt
  1 6-ounce package (1 cup) Nestlé Toll House Semi-Sweet Chocolate Morsels
  ½ cup chopped nuts
  ½ teaspoon vanilla extract

In a small bowl, combine brown sugar, egg, and salt; beat at high speed until thick, about 5 minutes. Stir in Nestlé Toll House Semi-Sweet Chocolate Morsels, nuts, and vanilla.

Sacher Bites

Makes 3 dozen bars
  1½ cups sugar
  ¾ cup butter, melted
  3 envelopes (1 ounce each) Nestlé Choco-bake Unsweetened Baking Chocolate Flavor
  1½ teaspoons vanilla extract
  3 eggs
  1¼ cups all-purpose flour
  ¾ cup apricot preserves
  1 6-ounce package (1 cup) Nestlé Toll House Semi-Sweet Chocolate Morsels
  1 tablespoon vegetable shortening

Preheat oven to 325°F. Combine sugar, butter, Nestlé Choco-bake Unsweetened Baking Chocolate Flavor, and vanilla; mix well. Beat in eggs, 1 at a time. Gradually stir in flour. Turn into a greased 15 × 10 × 1-inch baking pan. Bake 20 to 25 minutes; cool. Place preserves in blender container; blend until smooth. Spread over cake; cut in half lengthwise, then in quarters crosswise; remove from pan. Make 4 stacks, 2 layers each, preserves side up; trim edges. Cut each stack into 1 × 1½-inch bars. Place on wire racks over waxed paper. Combine over hot (not boiling) water, the morsels and shortening; stir until smooth. Drizzle over bars. Chill.

Decorate with Chocolate

The Chocolate Mint Way: As soon as a cake is out of the oven, place chocolate-covered mint patties on the hot surface. Give them a few moments to melt and then swirl them over the cake in a marblelike pattern of chocolate and creamy filling.

The Chocolate Bits Way: As soon as the cake is done, sprinkle the hot surface generously with semisweet chocolate bits. Return the cake to the oven briefly—the bits will soften but not melt entirely. Then remove the cake from the oven and sprinkle the chocolate surface with chopped pecans, walnuts, or pistachios. Stop there, or add a few miniature marshmallows for a rocky road topping to delight children—and adults.

Magic Morsels

The cookie jar can't hide the marvelous goodness of just-baked cookies, brownies, squares, and bars. Try these recipes and you'll find you've never been more popular.

Original Toll House® Cookies

Makes 100 cookies

2¼ cups all-purpose flour
1 teaspoon baking soda
1 teaspoon salt
1 cup butter, softened
¾ cup sugar
¾ cup firmly packed brown sugar
1 teaspoon vanilla extract
2 eggs
1 12-ounce package (2 cups) Nestlé Toll House Semi-Sweet Chocolate Morsels
1 cup chopped nuts

Preheat oven to 375°F. In a small bowl, combine flour, baking soda, and salt; set aside. In a large bowl, combine butter, sugar, brown sugar, and vanilla; beat until creamy. Beat in eggs. Gradually add flour mixture; mix well. Stir in Nestlé Toll House Semi-Sweet Chocolate Morsels and nuts. Drop by rounded teaspoonfuls onto ungreased cookie sheets. Bake 8 to 10 minutes.

Pan Cookie Variation

Prepare Toll House Cookie dough as directed. Spread into greased 15 × 10 × 1-inch baking pan. Bake at 375°F for 20 minutes. Cool; cut into thirty-five 2-inch squares.
Note: Recipe may be divided in half (use a 6-ounce package of Nestlé Toll House Semi-Sweet Chocolate Morsels; halve the amounts of all other ingredients). Spread dough into greased 9-inch square baking pan. Bake at 375°F for 20 to 25 minutes. Cool; cut into about sixteen 2-inch squares. For a crisper pan cookie, spread dough into greased 13 × 9 × 2-inch baking pan. Bake at 375°F for 12 to 15 minutes. Cool; cut into twenty-four 2-inch squares.

Original Toll House® Cookies. Courtesy of Nestlé Foods Corporation

Whole Wheat Toll House Cookies

Substitute unsifted whole wheat flour for either the total amount of flour (2¼ cups) or substitute unsifted whole wheat flour for half the amount of flour (use 1 cup plus 2 tablespoons each whole wheat and all-purpose flour).
Note: Cookies made with whole wheat flour are darker than traditional Toll House Cookies.

Chocolate Chip Cookies

Makes 7½ dozen cookies

2 cups all-purpose flour
½ teaspoon baking soda
¼ teaspoon salt
2 eggs
1 cup firmly packed dark brown sugar
¾ cup Hellmann's or Best Foods Real Mayonnaise
2 teaspoons vanilla extract
1 package (12 ounces) semisweet chocolate pieces
1 cup chopped nuts or raisins

In small bowl, stir together flour, baking soda, and salt. In large bowl with mixer at high speed, beat together eggs, sugar, mayonnaise, and vanilla for 2 minutes. Reduce speed to low; beat in flour mixture. With wooden spoon, stir in chocolate pieces and nuts. Drop by rounded teaspoonfuls 2 inches apart on greased cookie sheets. Bake in 375°F oven 8 to 10 minutes, or until browned. Immediately remove from cookie sheets. Cool on wire rack. Store in tightly covered container.

Mini Chip Pumpkin Cookies

Makes about 4 dozen cookies
- ¼ **cup butter or margarine**
- 1 **cup sugar**
- 1 **cup canned pumpkin**
- 2 **eggs**
- 2¼ **cups all-purpose flour**
- 2 **teaspoons baking powder**
- ¾ **teaspoon pumpkin pie spice**
- ½ **teaspoon baking soda**
- ½ **teaspoon salt**
- 1 **cup Hershey's® Mini Chips® Semi-Sweet Chocolate**
- ½ **cup chopped pecans (optional)**
  Decorative Glaze (recipe follows) (optional)

Cream butter and sugar in large mixer bowl until light and fluffy. Add pumpkin and eggs; blend well. Combine flour, baking powder, pumpkin pie spice, baking soda, and salt; add to pumpkin mixture. Beat well. Stir in Mini Chips semi-sweet chocolate and pecans, if desired. Drop by heaping teaspoonfuls onto a lightly greased cookie sheet. Bake at 350°F. for 12 to 14 minutes, or until lightly browned. Remove from cookie sheet; cool completely on wire rack. Meanwhile, prepare Decorative Glaze, if desired. Place cooled chocolate mixture in pastry bag. With writing tip, pipe decorative design on top of each cookie.

Decorative Glaze
- ⅔ **cup Hershey's® Mini Chips® Semi-Sweet Chocolate**
- 2 **teaspoons butter**

Combine Mini Chips semi-sweet chocolate and butter in top of double boiler over hot, not boiling, water. Stir until melted. Remove from heat; cool, stirring occasionally, for 20 minutes, or until desired consistency.

Chocolate Butterscotch Cookies

Makes 3½ dozen cookies
- ¾ **cup pecans**
- ½ **cup semisweet chocolate pieces**
- ½ **cup butterscotch pieces**
- ½ **cup butter or margarine, softened**
- ½ **cup sugar**
- ¼ **cup firmly packed brown sugar**
- 1 **egg**
- 1 **teaspoon vanilla extract**
- 1 **cup sifted all-purpose flour**
- ½ **teaspoon baking soda**
- ½ **teaspoon salt**

Heat oven to 375°F. Put pecans into blender container. Cover; blend at medium speed until chopped. Empty into mixing bowl; add chocolate and butterscotch pieces. Put remaining ingredients into blender container in order listed. Cover; blend at high speed until smooth. If necessary, stop blender during processing and push ingredients toward blades with rubber spatula. Empty into bowl with nut mixture; mix well. Drop by teaspoonfuls, 2 inches apart, onto greased cookie sheets. Bake 10 to 12 minutes, or until lightly browned. Cool on cookie sheets 1 minute. Transfer to wire racks with spatula; cool.

Chocolate Nut Cookies

Makes 3½ dozen cookies
- 2 **cups all-purpose flour**
- ½ **teaspoon baking soda**
- ½ **teaspoon salt**
- ½ **cup butter or margarine, softened**
- 1 **cup Domino Granulated Sugar**
- 1 **teaspoon vanilla extract**
- 1 **egg**
- 2 **ounces unsweetened chocolate, melted**
- ½ **cup milk**
- 1 **cup chopped walnuts**

Sift together flour, baking soda, and salt. Cream butter and sugar; beat well. Add vanilla. Beat in egg. Stir in chocolate. Alternately add flour mixture and milk, mixing until blended after each addition. Stir in nuts. Drop by teaspoonfuls onto ungreased baking sheets. Bake in moderate 350°F. oven for 10 to 12 minutes.

Double Chocolate Cookies
Add 1 cup semisweet chocolate chips with nuts.

Two-Tone Peanut Butter Cookies

Makes 5 dozen cookies
- 1½ **cups sifted all-purpose flour**
- 2 **teaspoons baking soda**
- ½ **teaspoon salt**
- 1 **cup smooth peanut butter**
- 1 **cup shortening**
- 2 **cups firmly packed brown sugar**
- 4 **eggs**
- 2 **teaspoons vanilla extract**
- 2 **squares (2 ounces) unsweetened chocolate, melted**

Sift together flour, baking soda, and salt. In large-size bowl, beat peanut butter and shortening until light; gradually add sugar; cream until light and fluffy. Beat in eggs and vanilla. At low speed on mixer, fold in dry ingredients. Combine ½ the batter with melted chocolate well. Gently swirl chocolate batter into white batter for marbled effect. Drop batter by teaspoonfuls on ungreased cookie sheets. Bake at 375°F. for 10 to 12 minutes.

Oatmeal Kiss Cookies

Makes about 6 dozen cookies
- ½ cup butter or margarine
- ½ cup shortening
- 1 cup sugar
- 1 cup firmly packed brown sugar
- 2 eggs
- 2 cups all-purpose flour
- 1 teaspoon baking soda
- 1 teaspoon salt
- 2¼ cups quick-cooking rolled oats
- 1 cup chopped nuts
- 1 package (14 ounces) Hershey's₀ Kisses₀ Chocolates

Cream butter and shortening in large mixer bowl. Gradually add sugar; beat until light and fluffy. Add eggs; beat well. Combine flour, baking soda, and salt; add to creamed mixture, blending thoroughly. Stir in rolled oats and nuts. Shape dough into 1-inch balls, using a rounded teaspoonful for each. Place on ungreased cookie sheet; bake at 375°F. for 10 to 12 minutes, until light brown. Remove from oven; immediately place unwrapped chocolate Kiss on top of each cookie, pressing down slightly. Remove from cookie sheet; cool.

Krunchy Kiss Kookies

Makes about 3 dozen cookies
- ½ cup light corn syrup
- ¼ cup firmly packed light brown sugar
- 1 cup creamy peanut butter
- 1 teaspoon vanilla extract
- 2 cups crisp rice cereal
- 1 cup cornflakes, slightly crushed
- 36 Hershey's₀ Kisses₀ Chocolates, unwrapped

Combine corn syrup and brown sugar in saucepan; bring to full boil, stirring constantly. Remove from heat; blend in peanut butter and vanilla. Add rice cereal and cornflakes; stir until well coated. Drop by teaspoonfuls onto cookie sheet. Loosely shape into balls; gently press chocolate Kiss in center, forming mixture into cookie shape. Store at room temperature in covered container.

Peanut Butter Cup Cookies

Makes 37 cookies
- ½ cup butter or margarine
- ½ cup peanut butter
- ½ cup firmly packed light brown sugar
- ¼ cup sugar
- 1 egg
- 1⅔ cups all-purpose flour
- 1 teaspoon baking soda
- 1 egg white
- 1 tablespoon water
- 1 cup finely chopped unsalted peanuts or crushed cornflake cereal
- 1 package (9 ounces) Reese's® Peanut Butter Cups (37 cups)

Cream butter, peanut butter, brown sugar, sugar, and egg until light and fluffy. Combine flour and baking soda; add to creamed mixture and blend well. Roll dough into 1-inch balls. Combine egg white and water; beat with fork until foamy. Roll balls in egg white mixture, then in chopped peanuts. Place on ungreased cookie sheet and press with thumb or fingertip in center to make a depression about 1 inch wide. Bake at 375°F. for 8 to 10 minutes, or until set. Remove from oven; cool on cookie sheet 1 minute. Unwrap peanut butter cups; place a cup in center of each warm cookie, pressing down slightly. Carefully remove from cookie sheet onto wire rack. Cool completely until peanut butter cups are firm.

Chou(x) Paste

You may find it in your cookbooks under its full French name, pâte à chou. Whatever you call it, it's the pastry from which the shells for cream puffs and eclairs are made, as well as some other elegant concoctions, such as Paris Brest. The familiar pastry we use for pies is made by cutting fat into flour, adding ice water. The totally different method for chou paste consists of melting butter in water, vigorously stirring in the flour, then beating in eggs one by one.

Cookbooks often call for shaping chou paste with a pastry tube, but you can manage very creditable cream puff and eclair shells by shaping them with 2 spoons. Tiny puffs of chou paste, filled with a savory mixture after baking, serve as handsome and delectable appetizers, not at all difficult to achieve, but looking and tasting as if you'd labored long and lovingly.

Baked chou paste freezes well. Keep a stock of appetizers on hand. Eclair or cream puff shells filled with ice cream and stashed in the freezer equal instant—and impressive—dessert. Serve with hot fudge or butterscotch sauce for total bliss.

Clockwise from top: *Butterscotch People; Chocolate-Dipped Shortbread Cookies (page 37); Chocolate Shortbread (page 36); Milk Chocolate Pecan Bars (page 41).* Courtesy of Nestlé Foods Corporation

Butterscotch Thins

Makes 8 dozen cookies

  1 6-ounce package (1 cup) Nestlé Butterscotch
      Flavored Morsels
  ½ cup butter
  ⅔ cup firmly packed brown sugar
  1 egg
  1⅓ cups all-purpose flour
  ¾ teaspoon baking soda
  ⅓ cup chopped nuts
  ¾ teaspoon vanilla extract

Over hot (not boiling) water, combine Nestlé Butterscotch Flavored Morsels and butter; stir until morsels melt and mixture is smooth. Transfer to a large bowl. Add brown sugar and egg; beat until light and fluffy. Add flour and baking soda. Stir in nuts and vanilla. Wrap in waxed paper; chill in refrigerator until firm enough to handle (about 1 hour). Shape into a log about 12 × 1½ inches; wrap and return to refrigerator.

To bake, preheat oven to 375°F. Cut log into slices ⅛ inch thick. Place on ungreased cookie sheets. Bake 5 to 6 minutes.

Butterscotch People

Omit nuts. Prepare dough as directed and chill until firm enough to handle (about 1 hour). On a floured board or pastry cloth, roll out dough to ⅛-inch thickness. Cut out cookies, using an 8-inch gingerbread cookie cutter (or, if desired, a 2- to 2½-inch cookie cutter). Bake 8-inch cookies for 7 to 9 min-utes; bake 2- to 2½-inch cookies 4 to 5 minutes. If desired, glaze cookies with Butterscotch Orange Glaze (recipe follows) and outline each cookie with Chocolate Outline (recipe follows). *Makes nine 8-inch cookies or about 6 dozen 2- to 2½-inch cookies.*

Butterscotch Orange Glaze

Makes ⅔ cup glaze

  1 6-ounce package (1 cup) Nestlé Butterscotch
      Flavored Morsels
  1 teaspoon vegetable oil
  1 teaspoon grated orange rind
  2 teaspoons orange juice

Over hot (not boiling) water, combine Nestlé Butterscotch Flavored Morsels and vegetable oil; stir until morsels melt. Remove from heat. Stir in orange rind and juice. Use as a glaze for cakes, cupcakes, or cookies.

Chocolate Outline

Makes ½ cup

  1 6-ounce package (1 cup) Nestlé Toll House
      Semi-Sweet Chocolate Morsels
  1 tablespoon vegetable shortening

Over hot (not boiling) water, combine Nestlé Toll House Semi-Sweet Chocolate Morsels and vegetable shortening; stir until morsels melt and mixture is smooth. Remove from heat; transfer mixture to a pastry bag fitted with a writing tip. Outline cookies or cakes as desired.

Caramel-Chocolate-Pecan Bars (page 42). Land O'Lakes, Inc.

Chocolate Melting Moments

Makes about 3 dozen cookies

1 cup all-purpose flour
½ cup Argo or Kingsford's Corn Starch
½ cup confectioners sugar
¼ cup unsweetened cocoa
¼ teaspoon salt
¾ cup Mazola Margarine
1 teaspoon vanilla extract

In medium bowl, stir together flour, cornstarch, confectioners sugar, cocoa, and salt. In large bowl, with mixer at medium speed, beat margarine until smooth. Add flour mixture and vanilla; beat until well blended. If necessary, refrigerate 1 hour, or until easy to handle. Shape into 1-inch balls. Place about 1½ inches apart on ungreased cookie sheets; flatten with lightly floured fork. Bake in 375°F oven 10 to 12 minutes, or until edges are lightly browned. Remove and cool completely on wire rack. Store in tightly covered container.

Minted Chocolate Wafers

Makes about 2 dozen cookies

½ cup butter or margarine
1 cup sugar
1 egg
1 teaspoon vanilla extract
1¾ cups all-purpose flour
⅓ cup Hershey's® Cocoa
½ teaspoon baking soda
¼ teaspoon salt
   Creamy Mint Filling (recipe follows)

Cream butter and sugar in large mixer bowl until light and fluffy. Add egg and vanilla; blend well. Combine flour, cocoa, baking soda, and salt; blend into creamed mixture until mixture leaves sides of bowl and forms a ball. Cover; chill about 2 hours. Divide dough in half; roll each half into a 12 × 8-inch rectangle. Cut each rectangle into six strips, each measuring 2 × 8 inches. Carefully place strips on ungreased cookie sheets about 2 inches apart. Bake at 375°F for 4 to 5 minutes, or until set. Cool on cookie sheet for 1 minute; cool thoroughly on wire rack. Prepare Creamy Mint Filling. Alternate filling and cookie strips to form 5 layers using about ¼ cup filling for each layer, beginning and ending with cookie strips. Wrap in foil and chill until serving. Cut into 1-inch pieces with sharp, serrated knife.

Creamy Mint Filling

1 package (3 ounces) cream cheese, softened
2 tablespoons butter, softened
3⅔ cups (1 pound) confectioners sugar
2 tablespoons milk
1 teaspoon vanilla extract
¼ teaspoon peppermint extract
4 to 5 drops green food color

Combine cream cheese and butter in small mixing bowl until smooth. Add confectioners sugar alternately with milk; blend in flavorings and food color. (If too thick add additional milk, a teaspoonful at a time, until desired consistency.) Any remaining filling can be made into mints by shaping in candy molds lightly sprinkled with granulated sugar or by forming into ¾-inch balls, dipping each ball in granulated sugar. Flatten each ball with tines of fork; let dry overnight.

Chocolate Shortbread

Makes 3 dozen cookies

1 6-ounce package (1 cup) Nestlé Toll House Semi-Sweet Chocolate Morsels
1¼ cups sifted confectioners sugar
¾ cup butter, softened
1 teaspoon vanilla extract
1 cup all-purpose flour
¼ teaspoon salt
1 cup ground nuts
   Chocolate Glaze (recipe follows)

Preheat oven to 350°F. Melt Nestlé Toll House Semi-Sweet Chocolate Morsels over hot (not boiling) water; remove from heat. In a large bowl, combine confectioners sugar, butter, and vanilla; beat until creamy. Gradually blend in flour and salt. Add melted chocolate and nuts; mix well. Shape into crescents, using 1 level tablespoon of dough for each. Place on ungreased cookie sheets. Bake 30 minutes. Remove from cookie sheets; cool completely. Dip half of each crescent cookie into Chocolate Glaze. Place on waxed paper-lined cookie sheets. Chill in refrigerator until chocolate sets (about 30 minutes).

Chocolate Glaze

1 6-ounce package (1 cup) Nestlé Toll House Semi-Sweet Chocolate Morsels
2 tablespoons vegetable shortening

Over hot (not boiling) water, combine Nestlé Toll House Semi-Sweet Chocolate Morsels and vegetable shortening; stir until morsels melt and mixture is smooth.

Pressed Chocolate Shortbread

After adding nuts, place dough in cookie press; force through desired disc onto ungreased cookie sheets. Proceed as directed.

Chocolate-Dipped Shortbread Cookies

Makes 4½ dozen cookies

- 2 cups all-purpose flour
- 1 cup butter, softened
- ½ cup sifted confectioners sugar
- 1 teaspoon vanilla extract
- 1 12-ounce package (2 cups) Nestlé Little Bits Semi-Sweet Chocolate, divided
- 1 tablespoon vegetable shortening
- ¾ cup finely chopped nuts

Preheat oven to 350°F. In a large bowl, combine flour, butter, confectioners sugar, and vanilla; mix until well blended. Stir in 1 cup Nestlé Little Bits Semi-Sweet Chocolate; mix well. Drop dough by rounded teaspoonfuls onto ungreased cookie sheets; shape into 2-inch logs or press into circles using bottom of glass dipped in flour. Bake 10 to 12 minutes. Cool completely. Over hot (not boiling) water, melt remaining 1 cup Nestlé Little Bits Semi-Sweet Chocolate and shortening; remove from heat. Dip one end of each cookie into melted chocolate. Roll in nuts. Chill in refrigerator until firm (about 1 hour).

Chocolate Mounds

Makes about 4 dozen

- 2 cups all-purpose flour
- 2 teaspoons baking powder
- 2 eggs
- 1½ cups sugar
- ½ cup Hellmann's or Best Foods Real Mayonnaise
- 4 squares (1 ounce each) unsweetened chocolate, melted
- 2 teaspoons vanilla extract
- ¼ cup confectioners or granulated sugar

In small bowl, stir together flour and baking powder. In large bowl with mixer at high speed, beat together eggs, sugar, mayonnaise, chocolate, and vanilla 2 minutes. With wooden spoon, stir in flour mixture until well mixed. Shape dough, 1 tablespoonful at a time, into balls. Roll in sugar. Place 2 inches apart on ungreased cookie sheets. Bake in 350°F oven 12 minutes. Immediately remove from cookie sheets. Cool on wire rack. Store in tightly covered container.

Super Fudgy Chocolate Cookies

Makes about 5 dozen cookies

- 2½ cups semisweet chocolate morsels
- 1 can (14 ounces) Eagle® Brand Sweetened Condensed Milk (not evaporated milk)
- 3 tablespoons margarine or butter
- 2 cups all-purpose flour
- ½ teaspoon baking soda
- 1 teaspoon vanilla extract
- ½ cup coarsely chopped nuts

In heavy saucepan, over low heat, melt morsels, Eagle Brand, and margarine. Remove from heat and add remaining ingredients. Mix well. Divide dough into thirds; shape each into 8-inch roll. Wrap in waxed paper. Chill until firm (about 2 hours). Preheat oven to 350°F. Cut dough into ¼-inch slices; place on ungreased baking sheets. Bake 7 to 9 minutes, or until tops are slightly crusted. Cool 2 to 3 minutes before removing from baking sheets. Store in tightly covered container.

Quick Chips

Are you all set to make chocolate chip cookies and you have no chips? Cut up some semisweet chocolate instead. Remember that 1 package (6 ounces) chocolate chips equals 1 cup. If your recipe calls for ½ cup chips, cut up 3 squares of chocolate.

Nutty Chocolate Stars

Makes about 3½ dozen cookies

- 3 cups Quaker Oats (quick or old fashioned, uncooked)
- 1 cup all-purpose flour
- ½ teaspoon baking soda
- ¾ cup butter or margarine, softened
- ¾ cup firmly packed brown sugar
- 1 egg
- 1 teaspoon vanilla extract
- ⅔ cup finely chopped nuts
- 1 package (6 to 7 ounces) milk chocolate candy stars or kisses

Heat oven to 350°F. Grease cookie sheet. In medium bowl, combine oats, flour and soda. In large bowl, beat together butter and sugar until light and fluffy. Blend in egg and vanilla. Add dry ingredients; mix well★. Shape into 1-inch balls; roll in nuts. Place on prepared cookie sheet. Bake 10 to 12 minutes. Remove from oven; gently press chocolate candy into center of each cookie. Cool 1 minute on cookie sheets; remove to wire cooling rack.

★ Dough may be chilled at this point. Use within 2 days.

Chocolate Finger Cookies

Makes 2½ dozen cookies
- ⅔ cup butter or margarine
- 1 cup sugar
- 2 eggs
- 2 teaspoons vanilla extract
- 2½ cups all-purpose flour
- ½ cup Hershey's® Cocoa
- ½ teaspoon baking soda
- ¼ teaspoon salt
  Chocolate Glaze (recipe follows)
  Chopped nuts (optional)
  Candied cherries

Cream butter and sugar in large mixer bowl until light and fluffy. Add eggs and vanilla; blend well. Combine dry ingredients; gradually add to creamed mixture, blending thoroughly. Shape heaping teaspoonfuls of dough into 3×1-inch fingers; place on ungreased cookie sheet. Bake at 350°F. for 8 to 10 minutes, or until set but not hard. Cool slightly; remove from cookie sheet to wire rack. Prepare Chocolate Glaze; glaze and sprinkle with chopped nuts, if desired. Garnish with cherry half.

Chocolate Glaze
- 2 tablespoons butter
- 2 tablespoons water
- 3 tablespoons Hershey's® Cocoa
- 1 cup confectioners sugar
- ½ teaspoon vanilla extract

Combine butter and water in small saucepan; bring to boil. Remove from heat; immediately stir in cocoa until well blended. Add confectioners sugar and vanilla. Beat until smooth. (If too thick, add 1 to 2 teaspoons water.)

Viennese Sandwich Cookies

Makes 3 dozen cookies
- 1 cup unsalted butter, at room temperature
- 1 cup sugar
- 1 egg yolk
- 1 teaspoon vanilla extract
- 2 cups all-purpose flour
- 2 cups confectioners sugar
- ½ cup unsalted butter, at room temperature
- 2 to 4 tablespoons fresh lemon juice
- 2 squares (1 ounce each) semisweet chocolate
- 1 tablespoon butter
  Chopped nuts, varicolored nonpareils, or shredded coconut

Fudgy Almond Torte (page 9); Mini Chip Fruit and Nut Bars (page 45); Oatmeal Kiss Cookies (page 33). Courtesy HERSHEY Food Corporation

Cream together butter and sugar. Add egg yolk, vanilla, and flour, mixing thoroughly. Chill at least 2 hours.

Make 72 balls of dough the size of small walnuts. Place 2 inches apart on ungreased cookie sheets. Preheat oven to 325°F. Dip bottom of small glass into sugar and use it to flatten each ball to a thickness of ⅛ inch. Bake 10 to 12 minutes, until cookies are lightly colored with slightly brown edges. Do not overbake. Place on cooling rack.

Cream confectioners sugar and butter. Add lemon juice to taste (it should be tart). Spread a teaspoonful on half the baked cookies. Cover each with another cookie, making a sandwich.

In a double boiler heat chocolate and butter until just melted. Dip an edge of each cookie sandwich into chocolate, then into nuts, nonpareils, or coconut. Place on cooling rack to set. Store in tightly covered container, layered with sheets of waxed paper, or freeze.

> **Q.** My kids love chocolate, but they're always getting it all over themselves. What's the best way to remove chocolate stains?
> **A.** Of course it's best to rinse with cold water the minute the spill occurs. If that is not possible, sprinkle the stain with boric acid and soak in cold water for 20 minutes. Then pour boiling water through the fabric from a great height. It doesn't always work, but in most cases your garment will become perfectly clean.

Rocky Road Brownie Bars (page 44); "Gorp" Bars (page 45). "M&M's" Chocolate Candies

Chocolate Teddy Bears

Makes 14 cookies

- ⅔ **cup butter or margarine**
- 1 **cup sugar**
- 2 **teaspoons vanilla extract**
- 2 **eggs**
- 2½ **cups all-purpose flour**
- ½ **cup Hershey's® Cocoa**
- ½ **teaspoon baking soda**
- ¼ **teaspoon salt**

Cream butter, sugar, and vanilla in large mixer bowl until light and fluffy. Add eggs; blend well. Combine flour, cocoa, baking soda, and salt; gradually add to creamed mixture, blending thoroughly. Chill until dough is firm enough to handle.

To shape teddy bears: For each cookie, form a portion of dough into 1 large ball for body (1 to 1½ inches), 1 medium-size ball for head (¾ to 1 inch), 4 small balls for arms and legs (½ inch), 2 smaller balls for ears, 1 tiny ball for nose, and 4 tiny balls for paws (optional). On an ungreased cookie sheet flatten the large ball slightly for body. Attach medium-size ball for head by overlapping slightly onto body. Place balls for arms, legs, and ears, and a tiny ball on head for nose. Arrange other tiny balls atop ends of legs and arms for paws, if desired. With a wooden pick, draw eyes and mouth; you can pierce a small hole at top of cookies for use as tree ornaments. Bake at 350°F for 6 to 8 minutes, or until set. Cool 1 minute on cookie sheet; remove to wire rack. Cool completely. Store in covered container for a gift or allow cookies to dry overnight before hanging. Pull ribbon through hole to hang as a tree ornament.

Christmas Cottages

Makes 10 cookies

- ¾ **cup butter or margarine**
- ⅔ **cup sugar**
- ⅔ **cup light corn syrup**
- 1½ **teaspoons vanilla extract**
- 1 **egg, beaten**
- 4 **cups all-purpose flour**
- 6 **tablespoons Hershey's® Cocoa**
- ¾ **teaspoon baking soda**
  Ornamental Icing (recipe follows)
  Colored sugar crystals, marshmallows, or candies for garnish

Combine butter, sugar, and corn syrup in small saucepan. Cook, stirring constantly, over medium heat until butter or margarine is melted and sugar is dissolved. Pour into mixing bowl; stir in vanilla. Cool 5 minutes, or until lukewarm. Add egg; mix well. Combine flour, cocoa, and baking soda; gradually add to egg mixture, blending well. Cover; chill 2

hours or overnight. Meanwhile, cut patterns and prepare Ornamental Icing. Roll dough onto a lightly floured surface to ⅛-inch thickness. Cut shapes using cardboard patterns; place on ungreased cookie sheet. Pierce hole in roof pieces with a wooden pick for use as tree ornaments. Bake at 350°F for 3 to 4 minutes, or until set. Remove from cookie sheet; cool on wire rack.

To assemble cottage: Pipe with decorating tube or spread a line of Ornamental Icing along edge of one end, one side wall, and 2 edges of base; attach end and side pieces to base. Prop while air drying (about 20 minutes, or until set). Join other end and side wall to base and at corners, as above; prop while drying. Fill in any space with more icing to make edges even. Attach one roof piece in place with icing; hold a few minutes to dry. Repeat with other half of roof. Decorate cottage with remaining icing, colored sugar crystals, marshmallows, or candies. Dry completely. Pull ribbon through hole in roof (tapestry needle may be used if available) to hang as a tree ornament.

Ornamental Icing

Makes 2 cups

- 3 **egg whites, at room temperature**
- 1 **box (16 ounces) confectioners sugar**
- ½ **teaspoon cream of tartar**
- ½ **teaspoon vanilla extract**

Combine all ingredients in large mixer bowl. Blend until smooth; beat at high speed until very stiff and knife drawn through mixture leaves a clean-cut path.

Note: Icing dries quickly; cover with damp cloth or paper towel. To store several days or overnight, cover tightly and place in refrigerator with a damp paper towel directly on surface.

Patterns

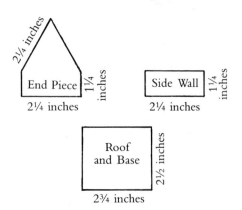

Chewy Brownies

Makes about 2 dozen brownies

½ cup butter or margarine
3 squares (1 ounce each) unsweetened chocolate
1 cup all-purpose flour
¾ teaspoon baking powder
½ teaspoon salt
3 eggs
1½ cups Domino Granulated Sugar
1½ teaspoons vanilla extract
¾ cup chopped pecans or walnuts

Melt butter and chocolate together; cool. Sift together flour, baking powder, and salt. Beat eggs until light and fluffy. Gradually add sugar, beating until thick. Add chocolate mixture and vanilla. Add flour mixture, beating just until blended. Stir in nuts. Bake in well-greased 9-inch square pan at 350°F. 28 to 30 minutes. Cool on a rack. Cut into squares.

Split-Level Brownies

Makes 32 brownies

2 cups Quaker Oats (quick or old fashioned, uncooked)
¾ cup firmly packed brown sugar
¾ cup all-purpose flour
¾ cup butter or margarine, melted
¼ teaspoon baking soda
1⅓ cups all-purpose flour
½ teaspoon baking powder
1¼ cups sugar
2 squares (1 ounce each) unsweetened chocolate, melted
2 eggs
½ cup milk
½ teaspoon vanillia extract
Frosting (recipe follows) (optional)

Heat oven to 350°F. In medium bowl, combine all oats, brown sugar, ¾ cup flour, and soda; mix well. Press firmly onto bottom of ungreased 13×9×2-inch baking pan. Bake 10 minutes.

In medium bowl, combine 1⅓ cups flour and baking powder. In large bowl, combine remaining ingredients except Frosting; mix well. Add dry ingredients; mix well. Pour over partially baked base. Bake 24 to 28 minutes, or until wooden pick inserted in center comes out clean. Cool completely on wire rack. Frost, if desired, and cut into 2×1½-inch bars.

Frosting

1½ squares (1½ ounces) unsweetened chocolate
3 tablespoons butter or margarine
2¼ cups confectioners sugar
3 tablespoons hot water
1½ teaspoons vanilla extract

In heavy medium saucepan over low heat, melt together chocolate and butter, stirring occasionally. Remove from heat. Add remaining ingredients; mix well.

Milk Chocolate Pecan Bars

Makes 4½ dozen bars

1 cup all-purpose flour
½ cup firmly packed brown sugar
½ teaspoon baking soda
¼ teaspoon salt
¼ cup butter, softened
Topping (recipe follows)

Preheat oven to 350°F. In a large bowl, combine flour, brown sugar, baking soda, and salt; mix well. Cut in butter with pastry blender or two knives until mixture resembles fine crumbs. Press evenly into greased 13×9×2-inch baking pan. Bake 10 minutes. Pour topping over cookie base; sprinkle with ½ cup pecans. Return to oven; bake 20 minutes. Cool completely; cut into 2×1-inch bars.

Topping

1 11½-ounce package (2 cups) Nestlé Milk Chocolate Morsels
2 eggs
¼ cup firmly packed brown sugar
1 teaspoon vanilla extract
¼ teaspoon salt
1 cup chopped pecans, divided

Melt Nestlé Milk Chocolate Morsels over hot (not boiling) water; remove from heat. In a small bowl, combine eggs, brown sugar, vanilla, and salt; beat 2 minutes at high speed with electric mixer. Add melted chocolate; mix well. Stir in remaining ½ cup pecans.

Cookies as Gifts

Cookies make fine gifts, at Christmas or any other occasion, for faraway friends; all year around, cookies are a great homesickness remedy for youngsters away at school or camp. To ensure that cookies will travel well, wrap individually or pack lightly into a plastic bag, and surround them with popcorn, filling all the spaces above, below, and on the sides.

Caramel-Chocolate-Pecan Bars

Makes 3 dozen bars

- 2 cups all-purpose flour
- 1 cup firmly packed brown sugar
- ½ cup Land O Lakes Sweet Cream Butter, softened
- 1 cup pecan halves (whole)
- ⅔ cup Land O Lakes Sweet Cream Butter
- ½ cup firmly packed brown sugar
- ½ cup butterscotch pieces
- ½ cup semisweet chocolate pieces

Preheat oven to 350°F. In 3-quart mixer bowl, combine flour, brown sugar, and butter. Beat at low speed, scraping sides of bowl often, until particles are fine (1 to 2 minutes). Press into ungreased 13 × 9 × 2-inch baking pan. Sprinkle pecans evenly over unbaked crumb mixture. In heavy 1-quart saucepan, combine butter and brown sugar. Cook over medium heat, stirring constantly, until mixture boils all over the top (4 to 5 minutes). Boil ½ to 1 minute, stirring constantly. Pour evenly over pecans and crumb mixture. Bake near center of 350°F. oven 18 to 20 minutes, or until filling is bubbly. Immediately sprinkle with butterscotch and chocolate pieces. Allow pieces to melt slightly (2 to 5 minutes). Slightly swirl pieces as they melt; leave some whole for a marbled effect. Do not spread pieces. Cool completely; cut into bars.

Super Oatmeal Brownies

Makes 36 brownies

- 2½ cups rolled oats
- 1 cup Durkee Flaked Coconut
- ¾ cup firmly packed light brown sugar
- ¾ cup all-purpose flour
- ½ teaspoon baking soda
- ¼ teaspoon salt
- ¾ cup butter or margarine, melted
- 1 package (22 ounces) brownie mix

Mix oats, coconut, sugar, flour, soda, and salt in bowl; stir in butter. Reserve ¾ cup mixture. Pat oatmeal mixture in bottom of greased 13x9x2-inch baking pan. Bake at 350°F. for 10 minutes. Cool 5 minutes. Prepare brownie mix according to package directions for fudgy brownies. Spread batter evenly over baked crust. Sprinkle with reserved oatmeal mixture. Bake according to brownie mix package directions; cool. Cut into squares.

Chocolate Teddy Bears (page 40); Christmas Cottages (page 40). Courtesy HERSHEY Food Corporation

Triple-Layer Brownies

Makes 4 dozen brownies

- 1 12-ounce package (2 cups) Nestlé Toll House Semi-Sweet Chocolate Morsels, divided
- 1 6-ounce package (1 cup) Nestlé Butterscotch Flavored Morsels
- 2 cups all-purpose flour
- 1½ teaspoons baking powder
- ½ teaspoon salt
- 1 cup butter, softened
- 1 cup firmly packed brown sugar
- 2 teaspoons vanilla extract
- 3 eggs
- 1 cup chopped nuts

Preheat oven to 350°F. Melt 1 cup Nestlé Toll House Semi-Sweet Chocolate Morsels over hot (not boiling) water; set aside. In another pan, melt Nestlé Butterscotch Flavored Morsels over hot (not boiling) water; set aside. In a small bowl, combine flour, baking powder, and salt; set aside. In a large bowl, combine butter, brown sugar, and vanilla; beat until creamy. Add eggs, 1 at a time, beating well after each addition. Blend in flour mixture. Stir in nuts. Divide batter in half; blend melted butterscotch into one half. Spread into well-greased 13x9x2-inch baking pan. Blend melted chocolate into remaining batter. Spread evenly over butterscotch layer. Bake 35 minutes. Remove from oven. Sprinkle remaining 1 cup

Nestlé Toll House Semi-Sweet Chocolate Morsels evenly over top. Let set for about 5 minutes to soften morsels, then spread evenly over top. Cool completely. Cut in 2x1-inch bars.

Q. *Melting chocolate takes so long. Is there any way to speed it up?*
A. Break chocolate into smaller pieces and stir frequently. Don't try to turn up the heat. That will only cause chocolate to thicken and curdle. If that happens, don't despair: add a tablespoon of vegetable oil and stir until the chocolate becomes smooth again. But you won't have saved any time.

Chocolate-Swirled Peanut Butter Brownies

Makes 30 brownies

¾ cup peanut butter
½ cup butter or margarine
1½ cups sugar
1½ cups firmly packed light brown sugar
4 eggs
2 teaspoons vanilla extract
3 cups sifted all-purpose flour
1 tablespoon baking powder
1 teaspoon salt
2 squares (2 ounces) semisweet chocolate, melted over hot water

Cream peanut butter and butter until soft and creamy. Gradually blend in sugar and brown sugar. Beat in eggs, 1 at a time. Add vanilla. Sift flour, baking powder, and salt. Add all at once and beat until smooth and well blended. Spread mixture into a greased and floured 13x9x2-inch pan. Drizzle melted chocolate over top of batter. With the tip of a knife swirl chocolate into batter. Bake at 350°F. for 35 to 40 minutes, or until brownies feel firm to the touch. Cool in pan; cut into squares.

Double Chocolate Brownies

Makes 16 brownies

¾ cup all-purpose flour
¼ teaspoon baking soda
¼ teaspoon salt
⅓ cup butter
¾ cup sugar
2 tablespoons water
1 12-ounce package (2 cups) Nestlé Toll House Semi-Sweet Chocolate Morsels, divided
1 teaspoon vanilla extract
2 eggs
½ cup chopped nuts

Preheat oven to 325°F. In a small bowl, combine flour, baking soda, and salt; set aside. In a small saucepan, combine butter, sugar, and water. Bring just to a boil, then remove from heat. Add 6 ounces (1 cup) Nestlé Toll House Semi-Sweet Chocolate Morsels and vanilla. Stir until morsels melt and mixture is smooth. Transfer to a large bowl. Add eggs, 1 at a time, beating well after each addition. Gradually blend in flour mixture. Stir in remaining 1 cup Nestlé Toll House Semi-Sweet Chocolate Morsels and the nuts. Spread into greased 9-inch square baking pan. Bake 30 to 35 minutes. Cool completely. Cut into 2¼-inch squares.

Rocky Road Brownie Bars

Makes 2½ dozen bars

¾ cup margarine
¾ cup sugar
2 eggs
1 teaspoon vanilla extract
1½ cups all-purpose flour
¼ cup cocoa powder
¾ teaspoon baking soda
¼ teaspoon salt
1 cup "M&M's" Plain Chocolate Candies
¾ cup coarsely chopped nuts
⅔ cup miniature marshmallows

Beat together margarine and sugar until light and fluffy; blend in eggs and vanilla. Add combined flour, cocoa, soda, and salt; mix well. Stir in ½ cup candies, ½ cup nuts, and raisins. Spread batter into greased 13×9×2-inch baking pan. Sprinkle with remaining ½ cup candies and ¼ cup nuts. Bake at 350°F. for 15 minutes. Sprinkle marshmallows over partially baked bars, pressing in lightly. Continue baking about 15 minutes, or until edges are set. (Do not overbake.) Cool thoroughly; cut into bars.

Toll House Golden Brownies

Makes about 3 dozen brownies

2 cups all-purpose flour
2 teaspoons baking powder
1 teaspoon salt
¾ cup butter, softened
¾ cup sugar
¾ cup firmly packed dark brown sugar
1 teaspoon vanilla extract
3 eggs
1 12-ounce package (2 cups) Nestlé Toll House Semi-Sweet Chocolate Morsels

Preheat oven to 350°F. In a small bowl, combine flour, baking powder, and salt; set aside. In a large bowl, combine butter, sugar, dark brown sugar, and vanilla; beat until creamy. Add eggs, 1 at a time, beating well after each addition. Gradually add flour mixture; mix well. Stir in Nestlé Toll House Semi-Sweet Chocolate Morsels. Spread evenly into well-greased 15×10×1-inch baking pan. Bake 30 to 35 minutes. Cool completely. Cut into 2-inch squares.

"Gorp" Bars

Makes 2½ dozen bars

    2 cups bite-size crispy cereal squares
 2½ cups thin pretzel sticks, broken in half
 1½ cups "M&M's" Plain or Peanut Chocolate
        Candies
    1 cup banana chips
    ¾ cup raisins
    ½ cup butter or margarine
    ⅓ cup creamy peanut butter
    5 cups miniature marshmallows

Combine cereal, pretzels, candies, banana chips, and raisins in a large bowl; set aside. Melt together butter and peanut butter in 3-quart saucepan over low heat. Add marshmallows; stir occasionally until marshmallows are melted and smooth. Immediately pour marshmallow mixture over cereal mixture, mixing until thoroughly coated. Press lightly into a greased 13×9×2-inch baking pan. Let stand until firm. Cut into bars to serve.

Halloween Squares

Makes 2 dozen squares

    1 6-ounce package (1 cup) Nestlé Toll House
        Semi-Sweet Chocolate Morsels
 1⅔ cups all-purpose flour
    3 tablespoons yellow cornmeal
    1 tablespoon baking powder
    1 teaspoon ground cinnamon
    ¼ teaspoon salt
    ¾ cup butter, softened
    ½ cup firmly packed brown sugar
    2 eggs
    1 can (17 ounces) sweet potatoes, drained and
        mashed
    ¼ cup frozen orange juice concentrate, thawed
    ¼ cup honey
    ½ cup chopped walnuts
    ½ cup raisins
        Butterscotch Cream Frosting (recipe follows)
        Walnut halves

Preheat oven to 350°F. Melt Nestlé Toll House Semi-Sweet Chocolate Morsels over hot (not boiling) water; set aside. In a small bowl, combine flour, cornmeal, baking powder, cinnamon, and salt; set aside. In a large bowl, combine butter and brown sugar; beat until creamy. Add eggs, 1 at a time, beating well after each addition. Blend in sweet potatoes, orange juice concentrate, and honey. Gradually blend in flour mixture. Add melted chocolate, walnuts, and raisins; mix well. Pour into greased 13x9x2-inch baking pan. Bake 30 to 35 minutes. Cool completely. Spread with Butterscotch Cream Frosting. Cut into 2-inch squares. Garnish each square with a walnut half.

Butterscotch Cream Frosting

    1 6-ounce package (1 cup) Nestlé Butterscotch
        Flavored Morsels
    2 tablespoons water
    1 package (8 ounces) cream cheese, softened
    ¼ teaspoon salt
    3 cups sifted confectioners sugar

Melt Nestlé Butterscotch Flavored Morsels over hot (not boiling) water. Add water; stir until morsels melt and mixture is smooth. Remove from heat. In a small bowl, combine cream cheese and salt; beat until creamy. Blend in melted butterscotch. Gradually beat in confectioners sugar.

Mini Chip Fruit and Nut Bars

Makes about 2 dozen bars

    ½ cup butter or margarine
    1 cup firmly packed light brown sugar
    1 egg
    1 teaspoon vanilla extract
 1½ cups all-purpose flour
    ½ teaspoon baking powder
    ½ teaspoon salt
    ¼ teaspoon ground cinnamon (optional)
    ½ cup golden raisins
    ½ cup snipped dried apricots
    ½ cup snipped pitted prunes
    ½ cup coarsely chopped pecans
    1 cup Hershey's® Mini Chips® Semi-Sweet
        Chocolate
        Mini Chip Glaze (recipe follows)(optional)

Cream butter and brown sugar in large mixer bowl until light and fluffy. Add egg and vanilla; blend well. Combine flour, baking powder, salt, and cinnamon; add to creamed mixture, mixing until well blended. Stir in dried fruits, nuts, and Mini Chips semi-sweet chocolate. Spread batter evenly in greased 13×9×2-inch baking pan. Bake at 375°F for 25 to 30 minutes, or until lightly browned. Cool on wire rack; glaze if desired. Cut into bars.

Mini Chip Glaze

Makes about 1 cup

    ⅓ cup sugar
    3 tablespoons water
    1 cup Hershey's® Mini Chips® Semi-Sweet Chocolate
    3 tablespoons marshmallow creme
    1 or 2 tablespoons water

Combine sugar and water in small saucepan; bring to boil. Remove from heat; immediately add Mini Chips semi-sweet chocolate and stir until melted. Blend in marshmallow creme and water, beating until glazing consistency.

Chocoholic's Creations

Chocolately chiffon, cream, and meringue pies; nutty chocolate crusts and fillings; delicate tarts and delicious pie toppings—for the chocoholic in you.

Chocolate Chiffon Pie

Makes 8 to 10 servings

- 1 package (8½ ounces) chocolate wafer cookies
- ½ cup butter, melted
- 2 tablespoons Domino Superfine Sugar
- 1 tablespoon unflavored gelatin
- 1 cup water
- ¾ cup Domino Superfine Sugar
- 3 eggs, separated
- 2 squares (1 ounce each) unsweetened chocolate, melted
- Topping (recipe follows)
- Grated chocolate or Chocolate Curls (see index) (optional)

Preheat oven to 350°F. Crush cookies into fine crumbs or crumb in blender or processor (you will have about 2⅓ cups cookie crumbs). Combine crumbs with melted butter and Superfine sugar. Press into 10-inch pie plate. Bake 8 minutes. Cool.

In small saucepan, sprinkle gelatin over water; let stand one minute. Heat, stirring until gelatin dissolves; remove from heat. In top of double boiler over boiling water, combine ½ cup of the Superfine sugar with egg yolks. Beat with rotary beater or whisk, until light yellow. Remove from heat. Beat in melted chocolate. Gradually add gelatin mixture, beating until foamy. Chill until almost set. Beat egg whites until foamy. Gradually beat in remaining ¼ cup Superfine sugar. Beat until stiff but not dry. Fold egg whites into chocolate mixture. Pour into prepared crumb crust. Chill. Spread Topping attractively over top of chilled pie. If desired, garnish with grated chocolate or Chocolate Curls. Refrigerate until serving time.

Topping

- 1½ cups heavy cream
- 3 tablespoons Domino Superfine Sugar

In medium bowl, combine heavy cream with Superfine sugar. Beat until cream holds peak.

Fudge Chiffon Pie

Makes 8 to 10 servings

- 1 9-inch baked pastry shell or crumb crust
- 1 envelope unflavored gelatin
- ¼ cup cold water
- 3 eggs, separated
- 1 teaspoon vanilla extract
- 1 cup sugar, divided
- ½ cup Hershey's® Cocoa
- ½ teaspoon salt
- 1¼ cups milk
- 1 cup heavy cream or 1¾ cups non-dairy whipped topping, thawed

Prepare pie shell; cool. Mix gelatin and water in small bowl; allow to soften. Beat egg yolks lightly with vanilla in mixing bowl; set aside. Combine ¾ cup sugar, cocoa, and salt in saucepan; stir in milk. Cook and stir until mixture comes to a full boil; add gelatin and return to boil. Remove from heat; immediately whisk into beaten egg yolks (mixture will thicken slightly). Cool; chill until mixture mounds from a spoon, stirring occasionally. Whip cream until stiff; fold into chocolate or fold whipped topping into chocolate. Beat egg whites with remaining ¼ cup sugar until stiff peaks form; fold in. Pour into pie shell; chill until set.

Fudge Chiffon Pie; Chocolate Pecan Pie (page 48); Fruited Chocolate Tarts (page 61). Courtesy HERSHEY Food Corporation

Chocolate Substitute

Carob enjoys (or suffers from) a number of different names—caroub, algarroba, locust bean, St. John's bread. Whatever you choose to call it, it is the long brown pod of the carob tree, which grows in Israel and in various other places along the Mediterranean. Sweet and quite chocolatelike in flavor, except for a few small hard seeds, the entire pod is edible. It is sold fresh—sometimes by street peddlers, to be eaten out of hand—in the places where it grows, and is available dried elsewhere. Look for carob in natural-food stores if you have difficulty finding it.

The dried fruit is powdered, resulting in a meal that resembles a pale cocoa powder. This powder, as well as a carob syrup, is used to flavor such foods as puddings and candies, delicious in their own right and particularly useful to those who are allergic to chocolate. Carob is a favorite of natural-food nuts (as opposed to those who approach the subject sensibly) as a chocolate substitute; actually it is in no way more "natural" than chocolate—both are derived from plants, both are cultivated, both are processed. As a substitute for chocolate or cocoa, carob must be used in recipes tailored for its use.

Carob is rich in sugar and fairly high in protein.

Chocolate Pecan Pie

Makes 8 to 10 servings
- 1 9-inch unbaked pastry shell
- ¼ cup butter or margarine
- ½ cup Hershey's® Mini Chips® Semi-Sweet Chocolate
- 1 cup light corn syrup
- ⅓ cup sugar
- 1 teaspoon vanilla extract
- 3 eggs
- 1½ cups pecan halves or broken pecans
  Chocolate Whipped Cream or Mocha Whipped Cream (see index) (optional)

Prepare pastry shell; set aside. Melt butter in small saucepan; remove from heat and immediately add Mini Chips semi-sweet chocolate, stirring until melted and smooth. With fork, beat in corn syrup, sugar, vanilla, salt, and eggs until well blended. Arrange pecans on bottom of pie crust; carefully pour chocolate mixture over them. Bake at 350°F for 50 to 55 minutes, or until knife inserted 1 inch from edge comes out clean; cool on rack. Wrap tightly and refrigerate or freeze. If desired, serve with Chocolate or Mocha Whipped Cream.

Mocha Pecan Pie

Makes 1 pie
- 1 package (4 ounces) Baker's German's Sweet Chocolate
- 3 tablespoons butter or margarine
- 1 teaspoon Maxwell House Instant Coffee
- ⅓ cup sugar
- 1 cup light corn syrup
- 3 eggs, lightly beaten
- 1 teaspoon vanilla extract
- 1 cup coarsely chopped pecans
- 1 unbaked 9-inch pie shell
  Coffee Whipped Cream Topping (recipe follows)
  Pecan halves (optional)

Melt chocolate and butter in saucepan over very low heat. Stir in instant coffee. Combine sugar and syrup in saucepan. Bring to a boil over high heat, stirring until sugar is dissolved. Reduce heat and boil gently for 2 minutes, stirring occasionally. Remove from heat; add chocolate mixture. Pour slowly over eggs, stirring constantly. Stir in vanilla and nuts. Pour into pie shell. Bake at 375°F for 45 to 50 minutes, or until filling is completely puffed across top. Cool. Garnish with Coffee Whipped Cream Topping and pecan halves, if desired.

Coffee Whipped Cream Topping

Makes 1 cup
- 1 teaspoon Maxwell House Instant Coffee
- ½ cup heavy cream
- 1 teaspoon confectioners or granulated sugar
- ¼ teaspoon vanilla extract

Combine instant coffee, cream, sugar, and vanilla in a chilled bowl. Whip just until soft peaks form. (Do not overbeat.)

Chocolate-Almond Pie

Makes one 9-inch pie
- 1 6-ounce package (1 cup) Nestlé Toll House Semi-Sweet Chocolate Morsels
- 1 cup light corn syrup
- 3 eggs
- ⅓ cup sugar
- ¼ cup butter, melted
- ½ teaspoon salt
- 1 cup coarsely chopped almonds, toasted
- 1 9-inch unbaked pie shell
  Whipped cream and whole almonds (optional)

Preheat oven to 375°F. Melt Nestlé Toll House Semi-Sweet Chocolate Morsels over hot (not boiling) water; remove from heat and cool at room temperature 5 minutes. In a large bowl, combine corn syrup, eggs, sugar, butter, and salt; beat well. Gradually blend in melted chocolate; beat until smooth. Stir in chopped almonds. Pour into unbaked pie shell. Bake 45 to 50 minutes. Cool. Garnish with dollops of whipped cream and whole almonds, if desired.

Fudgy Chocolate Pie

Makes one 9-inch pie

- 1 **9-inch unbaked pastry shell**
- 1 **package (4 ounces) sweet cooking chocolate**
- ¼ **cup margarine or butter**
- 1 **can (14 ounces) Eagle® Brand Sweetened Condensed Milk (not evaporated milk)**
- 2 **eggs, lightly beaten**
- ½ **cup hot water**
- 1 **teaspoon vanilla extract**
- ⅛ **teaspoon salt**
- ½ **cup chopped pecans**
- 1 **cup flaked coconut**

Preheat oven to 350°F. In heavy saucepan, over low heat, melt chocolate and margarine; remove from heat. In large mixer bowl, combine Eagle Brand and warm chocolate mixture; mix well. Stir in eggs, hot water, vanilla, and salt; mix well. Pour into crust. Top with pecans and coconut. Bake 35 to 40 minutes, or until coconut is lightly browned. Serve warm or chilled. Refrigerate leftovers.

Amaretto Chocolate Pie

Makes 8 servings

- 1 **cup Arrow Amaretto Cream Originale**
- 2 **ounces sweet cooking chocolate**
- ¾ **cup sugar**
- ½ **cup butter or margarine**
- 2 **teaspoons vanilla extract**
- 1 **cup all-purpose flour**
- 1 **teaspoon baking powder**
- ¼ **teaspoon salt**
- 1 **egg**
- 1 **9-inch unbaked pie shell**
- ½ **cup sliced almonds**
    Amaretto Originale Whipped Cream (recipe follows)

In medium saucepan, combine ½ cup Amaretto Cream, chocolate, ¼ cup sugar, and ¼ cup butter. Cook over low heat, stirring, until chocolate is melted. Stir in 1½ teaspoons vanilla. Set aside. In medium bowl, combine remaining ½ cup Amaretto Cream, ½ cup sugar, ½ teaspoon vanilla, flour, baking powder, salt, and egg. Beat 2 minutes. Pour into pie shell. Pour chocolate mixture over batter. Sprinkle with almonds. Bake in preheated 350°F. oven 50 minutes, or until wooden pick inserted in center comes out clean. Serve with Amaretto Originale Whipped Cream.

Amaretto Originale Whipped Cream

- 1 **cup heavy cream**
- ¼ **cup chilled Arrow Amaretto Cream Originale**

Beat cream and Amaretto Cream until stiff.

Celebration Chocolate Chip Pie

Makes 8 to 10 servings

- 1 **9-inch unbaked pastry shell**
- 2 **eggs**
- 1 **cup sugar**
- ½ **cup butter or margarine, melted**
- 3 **to 4 tablespoons bourbon or 1 teaspoon vanilla extract**
- ¼ **cup cornstarch**
- 1 **cup finely chopped pecans**
- 1 **cup (6-ounce package) Hershey's® Mini Chips® Semi-Sweet Chocolate**
    Festive Whipped Cream (recipe follows)

Prepare pastry shell; set aside. Beat eggs lightly in small mixer bowl; gradually add sugar. Add melted butter and bourbon; mix well. Blend in cornstarch. Stir in pecans and Mini Chips semi-sweet chocolate; pour into unbaked pastry shell. Bake at 350°F for 45 to 50 minutes. Cool 1 hour and serve warm with a dollop of Festive Whipped Cream.
Note: This pie freezes well. To serve, remove from freezer and warm at 300°F. for 35 to 40 minutes.

Festive Whipped Cream

- ½ **cup whipping cream or 1 cup non-dairy whipped topping★**
- 2 **tablespoons confectioners sugar**
- 1 **to 2 teaspoons bourbon or ½ teaspoon vanilla extract**

Whip cream with confectioners sugar. Add bourbon; beat until stiff peaks form.
★ When using non-dairy whipped topping, omit confectioners sugar and vanilla; blend in bourbon, if desired.

you are invited

Autumn Bavarian Pie

Makes 1 pie

    1 9-inch baked pastry shell or crumb crust
    1 envelope unflavored gelatin
    1 cup milk
    ⅔ cup sugar
    ⅓ cup Hershey's® Cocoa
    2 tablespoons butter or margarine
    ⅔ cup milk
    ¾ teaspoon vanilla extract
    ½ cup heavy cream
       Spice Whipped Cream (recipe follows)
       Chocolate Leaves (recipe follows) (optional)

Prepare pie shell; cool. Sprinkle gelatin onto 1 cup milk in medium-size saucepan; allow to stand for 2 minutes. Combine sugar and cocoa; add to mixture in saucepan. Cook over medium heat, stirring constantly, until mixture boils. Remove from heat; add butter and stir until melted. Blend in ⅔ cup milk and vanilla. Cool; chill until mixture begins to set, stirring occasionally. Whip cream until stiff peaks form; carefully fold into chocolate mixture, blending well. Pour into pie shell; chill until set. Prepare Spice Whipped Cream. Garnish in a decorative design and top with Chocolate Leaves, if desired.

Spice Whipped Cream

    ½ cup heavy cream
    1 tablespoon sugar
    ¼ teaspoon vanilla extract
    ¼ teaspoon ground cinnamon
       Dash ground nutmeg

Combine heavy cream, sugar, vanilla, cinnamon, and nutmeg in small mixer bowl; beat until stiff.

Chocolate Leaves

Wash and dry thoroughly 6 to 8 leaves with stems (rose, lemon, or grape ivy). Melt ½ cup Hershey's® Semi-Sweet or Milk Chocolate Chips in top of double boiler over hot, not boiling, water. Remove from heat; keep pan over warm water. With a small pastry brush, spread melted chocolate in a thin layer (about ⅛ inch thick) on underside of leaf. (Avoid getting chocolate on front of leaf.) Place on waxed paper-covered tray until firm; chill if necessary. Carefully peel leaf away from chocolate leaf; store covered in cool place.

Christmas Poinsettia Pie (page 57); Chocolate Finger Cookies (page 39). Courtesy HERSHEY Food Corporation

Chocolate Coconut Pie

Makes 8 servings
   Chocolate Coconut Crust (recipe follows)
 4 **ounces unsweetened chocolate**
 1 **cup C & H Powdered Sugar**
 ½ **cup butter or margarine, softened**
   Pinch salt
 1 **teaspoon vanilla extract**
 3 **eggs**
 1 **cup heavy cream, whipped**
   Slivered orange rind

Prepare Chocolate Coconut Crust. Melt chocolate in double boiler over simmering water; cool. Cream sugar, butter, and salt together until light and fluffy. Beat in vanilla and melted chocolate. Add eggs, 1 at a time, beating at high speed after each addition. Spoon into crust; chill. Top with whipped cream. Garnish with orange rind.

Chocolate Coconut Crust
 2 **ounces unsweetened chocolate**
 2 **tablespoons butter**
 2 **tablespoons hot milk**
 ⅔ **cup C & H Powdered Sugar**
 1⅓ **cups coconut flakes**

Grease 9-inch pie pan. Melt chocolate with butter in heavy saucepan. Remove from heat; stir in remaining ingredients. Mix well. Press firmly on bottom and sides of pie pan. Chill 1 hour before filling with chiffon filling, ice cream, or cream filling such as the rich chocolate recipe above.

Extra-Chocolate Almond Pie

Makes one 9-inch pie
 2 **squares (1 ounce each) unsweetened chocolate**
 ¼ **cup margarine or butter**
 1 **can (14 ounces) Eagle® Brand Sweetened Condensed Milk (not evaporated milk)**
 ⅓ **cup hot water**
 2 **eggs, well beaten**
 ¼ **to ⅓ cup amaretto or other almond-flavored liqueur**
 ⅛ **teaspoon salt**
 1 **cup slivered almonds, toasted and chopped**
 1 **9-inch unbaked pastry shell**

Preheat oven to 350°F. In medium saucepan, over low heat, melt chocolate and margarine. Stir in sweetened condensed milk, hot water, and eggs; mix well. Remove from heat; stir in remaining ingredients. Pour into prepared pastry shell. Bake 40 to 45 minutes, or until center is set. Cool. Chill 3 hours. Garnish as desired. Refrigerate leftovers.

Chocolate Dream Pie

Makes one 9-inch pie
 2 **envelopes Dream Whip® Whipped Topping Mix**
 2¾ **cups cold milk**
 2 **packages (4-serving size) Jell-O Chocolate or Chocolate Fudge Instant Pudding and Pie Filling★**
 1 **baked 9-inch pie shell, cooled**

Prepare whipped topping mix with 1 cup of the milk as directed on package, using large mixer bowl. Add remaining 1¾ cups milk and the pie filling mix. Blend; then beat at high speed for 2 minutes, scraping bowl occasionally. Spoon into 9-inch pie shell. Chill at least 4 hours.
★ Any flavor Jell-O Brand Instant Pudding and Pie Filling may be substituted for the chocolate pudding.

Chocolate Mousse Pie

Makes one 9-inch pie
 2 **cups flaked coconut**
 ¼ **cup butter or margarine, melted**
 1 **cup semisweet real chocolate morsels**
 1 **cup Libby's Solid Pack Pumpkin**
 ¼ **pound (16 large) marshmallows**
   Dash salt
 1½ **cups whipping cream, whipped**

Preheat oven to 250°F. Combine coconut and butter; press into 9-inch pie plate. Bake 30 to 35 minutes, or until evenly browned. Cool. In medium saucepan, combine chocolate morsels, pumpkin, marshmallows, and salt. Cook over low heat, stirring constantly, until morsels and marshmallows melt and mixture is smooth. Cool. Beat with wire whisk; fold in whipped cream. Spoon into crust. Chill.

Chocolate-Coconut Mousse Pie

Makes one 9-inch pie
 ¼ **cup butter**
 2 **3⅓-ounce cans (2⅔ cups) shredded coconut**
 1 **11½-ounce package (2 cups) Nestlé Milk Chocolate Morsels**
 ¼ **pound (16 large) marshmallows**
 ½ **cup milk**
 ⅛ **teaspoon salt**
 1 **cup heavy cream**

Melt butter in a large skillet. Add coconut; stir occasionally until lightly toasted. Press evenly on bottom and sides (not over rim) of buttered 9-inch pie pan. Chill in refrigerator 30 minutes.
   Over hot (not boiling) water, combine Nestlé Milk Chocolate Morsels, marshmallows, milk, and salt;

heat until morsels and marshmallows melt and mixture is smooth. Cool mixture thoroughly in refrigerator (1 to 1½ hours).

In a small bowl, beat heavy cream until stiff peaks form. Fold into cooled chocolate mixture. Pour into prepared crust. Chill

Chocolate Bar Pie

Makes one 9-inch pie

    Chocolate Crumb Crust (recipe follows)
  1 8-ounce Hershey's® Milk Chocolate or Special
    Dark® Sweet Chocolate Bar
  ⅓ cup milk
  1½ cups miniature marshmallows
  1 cup heavy cream
    Sweetened whipped cream or dessert topping
  1 1.45-ounce Hershey's® Milk Chocolate Bar
    (optional)

Prepare Chocolate Crumb Crust; set aside. Break bar into sections; melt with milk and marshmallows in top of double boiler over hot water, stirring constantly until smooth. Cool to room temperature. Whip 1 cup cream until stiff; fold into chocolate mixture. Pour into crust; chill several hours until firm. Garnish with dollops of sweetened whipped cream or dessert topping and squares of chocolate bar.

Chocolate Crumb Crust

  1½ cups vanilla wafer or graham cracker crumbs
  ⅓ cup Hershey's® Cocoa
  ⅓ cup confectioners sugar
  6 tablespoons butter or margarine, melted

Combine ingredients in mixing bowl. Press onto bottom and up sides of 9-inch pie pan; bake at 350°F. for 8 to 10 minutes. Cool.

Heavenly Cream Cheese Pie

Makes one 9-inch pie

  1 6-ounce package (1 cup) Nestlé Toll House
    Semi-Sweet Chocolate Morsels
  1 tablespoon vegetable shortening
  1½ cups finely chopped nuts
  1 6-ounce package (1 cup) Nestlé Toll House
    Semi-Sweet Chocolate Morsels
  1 package (8 ounces) cream cheese, softened
  ¾ cup sugar, divided
  ⅛ teaspoon salt
  2 eggs, separated
  1 cup heavy cream
  3 tablespoons brandy
    Whipped cream (optional)

Line a 9-inch pie pan with foil. Over hot (not boiling) water, melt 1 package Nestlé Toll House Semi-Sweet Chocolate Morsels and shortening; stir in nuts. Spread evenly on bottom and sides (not over rim) of prepared pie pan. Chill in refrigerator until firm (about 1 hour). Lift out of pan; peel off foil. Replace crust in pan; chill until ready to fill.

Melt 1 package Nestlé Toll House Semi-Sweet Chocolate Morsels over hot (not boiling) water; cool 10 minutes. In a large bowl, combine cream cheese, ½ cup sugar, and the salt; beat until creamy. Beat in egg yolks, 1 at a time. Stir in cooled chocolate; set aside. In a small bowl, beat egg whites until foamy. Gradually add ¼ cup sugar and beat until stiff, glossy peaks form. Set aside. In a small bowl, beat heavy cream and brandy until stiff peaks form. Fold whipped cream and beaten egg whites into chocolate mixture. Pour into chocolate nut crust. Chill in refrigerator until firm (about 3 hours). Garnish with whipped cream, if desired.

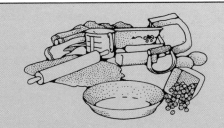

Secrets to Making Pies and Pastry

Measure ingredients for pastry and fillings accurately to ensure perfect results.

Handle pastry delicately—too much handling will toughen it.

To help prevent soggy bottom crusts in custard pies, reserve 1 teaspoonful of beaten egg and brush over pastry crust; chill, then add filling.

Pastry and crumb crusts may be made ahead and frozen if desired.

Cook fillings for cream pies in a heavy saucepan and stir constantly to prevent scorching.

Avoid overcooking filling that has a cornstarch base to prevent thinning the filling.

Refrigerate chiffon, custard, and cream pies and those with whipped cream toppings.

To chill chiffon pies quickly, place saucepan containing filling in a large pan or bowl filled with ice cubes and water. Stir filling until mixture begins to thicken and mounds when spooned. Remove from chilled water immediately and quickly fold in any remaining ingredients.

Chocolate Cream Pie

Makes 1 pie
- 1 **cup sugar, divided**
- 2 **tablespoons cornstarch**
- 1 **tablespoon Martha White All-Purpose Flour**
- ¼ **teaspoon salt**
- 2¼ **cups milk, divided**
- 3 **egg yolks, lightly beaten**
- 2 **squares (1 ounce each) unsweetened chocolate**
- 1 **tablespoon butter or margarine**
- 1 **teaspoon vanilla extract**
- 1 **baked 9-inch pie shell**
  Sweetened whipped cream

Combine ⅓ cup sugar, cornstarch, flour, and salt in small bowl. Stir in ¼ cup milk and egg yolks; set aside. Combine remaining ⅔ cup sugar and 2 cups milk in saucepan. Add unsweetened chocolate and stir mixture until chocolate is melted. Bring to a boil over high heat, stirring constantly. When mixture reaches full boil, remove from heat. Slowly stir 1 cup milk mixture into egg yolk mixture. Return all to saucepan. Bring to a boil over moderate heat, stirring constantly. Boil 5 minutes, stirring constantly. Remove from heat. Stir in butter and vanilla. Let stand until cool. Pour into pie shell. Refrigerate at least 2 hours. Top with sweetened whipped cream.

> **Q.** *I don't keep a whole array of chocolate products in my pantry. Can one chocolate product be substituted for another?*
> **A.** Use this chart:
> - 3 **tablespoons cocoa plus 1 tablespoon shortening equals 1 square (1 ounce) baking chocolate**
> - 3 **tablespoons cocoa plus 1 tablespoon oil or melted shortening equals 1 envelope (1 ounce) pre-melted unsweetened chocolate**
> - 6 **tablespoons cocoa plus ¼ cup shortening equals one 6-ounce package semisweet chocolate morsels**

Creamy Layered Chocolate Pie

Makes 1 pie
- 1 **baked 9-inch pie shell or graham cracker crumb crust**
- 2 **envelopes Featherweight Chocolate Pudding**
- 3 **cups skim milk**
- 1 **envelope Featherweight Whipped Topping**

Place bottom of double boiler containing water on high heat. Place 3 cups of skim milk in top of double boiler. Add contents of chocolate pudding envelopes. Mix well and stir until simmer point (185°–195°F) is reached. Continue stirring for 3 minutes. Pour pudding mixture into baked pie crust, reserving ½ cup, and chill until partially set. Prepare whipped topping as directed on package. Blend 1 cup of whipped topping into remaining ½ cup of pudding. Pour onto partially set pie. Chill until set (about 4 hours), then garnish with remaining whipped topping.

Chocolate Meringue Pie

Makes one 9-inch pie
- ⅔ **cup sugar**
- ⅓ **cup all-purpose flour**
- ½ **teaspoon salt**
- 2¾ **cups milk**
- 2 **squares Baker's Unsweetened Chocolate**
- 3 **egg yolks, lightly beaten**
- 2 **teaspoons butter or margarine**
- 2 **teaspoons vanilla extract**
- 1 **baked 9-inch pie shell, cooled**
- 3 **egg whites**
- 6 **tablespoons sugar**

Combine ⅔ cup sugar, flour, and salt in saucepan, mixing well. Gradually stir in milk. Add chocolate. Cook and stir over medium heat until chocolate is melted and mixture is thickened and smooth. Then cook and stir 5 minutes longer. Stir a small amount of the hot mixture into the egg yolks, mixing well. Return to remaining hot mixture in saucepan. Continue cooking 2 minutes longer. Blend in butter and vanilla. Cool 30 minutes without stirring. Pour into pie shell.

Beat egg whites until foamy throughout. Gradually beat in 6 tablespoons sugar and continue beating until mixture forms stiff shiny peaks. Pile lightly on filling, sealing well at edge of shell. Bake at 425°F for 8 minutes, or until meringue is lightly browned. Cool to room temperature.

Chocolate Coconut Pie (page 52). C&H Sugar Company

Chocolate Bar Pie (page 53); Peanut Butter Cup Cookies (page 33).
Courtesy HERSHEY Foods Corporation

*Chocolate Coconut Meringue Pie (page 56); Chocolate Sponge Roll
(page 16); Chocolate Melting Moments (page 36).* Argo/Kingsford's
Corn Starch

Chocolate Coconut Meringue Pie

Makes 8 servings

    1 cup sugar, divided
    ¼ cup Argo or Kingsford's Corn Starch
    ⅛ teaspoon salt
    2½ cups milk
    3 egg yolks, lightly beaten
    2 squares (1 ounce each) unsweetened chocolate,
        cut up
    1⅓ cups flaked coconut, divided
    1 teaspoon vanilla extract
    3 egg whites
    1 baked 9-inch pastry shell

In 2-quart saucepan, stir together ⅔ cup of the sugar, cornstarch, and salt. Gradually stir in milk until smooth. Stir in egg yolks until well blended. Stir in chocolate. Stirring constantly, bring to boil over medium-low heat and boil 1 minute. Remove from heat. Stir in 1 cup of the coconut and vanilla. Turn into large bowl; cover surface with waxed paper or plastic wrap; cool completely. Spoon into pastry shell. In small bowl, with mixer at high speed, beat egg whites until foamy. Gradually beat in remaining ⅓ cup sugar until stiff peaks form. Spread some meringue around edge of filling first, touching crust all around; then fill in center. Sprinkle remaining ⅓ cup coconut over meringue. Bake in 350°F. oven 15 to 20 minutes, or until lightly browned. Cool at room temperature away from drafts.

Chocolate Black Bottom Pie

Makes one 9-inch pie

    3 egg yolks, lightly beaten
    ⅔ cup sugar
    ¼ teaspoon salt
    1¾ cups milk
    4 squares Baker's Unsweetened Chocolate
    2 teaspoons vanilla extract
    1 baked 9-inch pie shell, cooled
    1 envelope unflavored gelatin
    ¼ cup water
    3 egg whites
    ½ cup sugar
    ½ cup thawed Birds Eye Cool Whip Non-Dairy
        Whipped Topping

Combine egg yolks, ⅔ cup sugar, and the salt in saucepan; stir in milk. Cook and stir over medium heat until mixture coats a metal spoon, 12 to 15 minutes. Remove from heat. Add chocolate and vanilla; stir until chocolate is melted and mixture is smooth. Measure 1¼ cups into pie shell.

Add gelatin to water and let stand about 5 minutes. Add to remaining chocolate mixture and stir until

gelatin is dissolved. Cool. Beat egg whites until foamy throughout. Gradually beat in ½ cup sugar and continue beating until mixture forms stiff, shiny peaks. Blend in cooled chocolate mixture and whipped topping. Pour carefully over chocolate layer in shell. Chill until set, about 3 hours. Garnish with additional whipped topping, if desired.

From Tree to Kitchen

The cacao grows only in tropical areas not far north and south of the equator. At maturity the trees are 20 to 25 feet tall, bearing long shiny leaves and clusters of pink and white scentless flowers that turn, in their season, into pods 6 to 8 inches long, each bearing from 20 to 50 cacao beans. Each tree produces between 20 and 40 pods a year, and the growth cycle is continuous—leaves, blossoms, and pods appear at one time on the tree.

The mature pods are harvested and the beans removed. Fermentation separates the beans from the pulp; then the beans are dried in the sun. They are shipped from their tropical home to processing plants, where they are cleaned, roasted, and husked. Milled, the beans release a large amount of their "butter," the natural fat of the cocoa bean, so that a liquor is formed. From this liquor all the various forms of chocolate are processed.

In making baking chocolate, the cocoa butter content is maintained; in making cocoa—chocolate in a powdered, less rich form—more than half the butter is removed. That cocoa butter is added, along with milk and sugar, to chocolate liquor to produce milk chocolate. Omission of the milk results in the semisweet chocolate used for some kinds of baking—chocolate bits, for example—and for eating as candy.

Black Bottom Pecan Pie

Makes one 9-inch pie

    4 eggs
    ¾ cup dark corn syrup
    ½ cup sugar
    ¼ cup butter, melted
    4 tablespoons rum, divided (optional)
    1 teaspoon vanilla extract
    ½ teaspoon salt
    1½ cups pecan halves
    1 6-ounce package (1 cup) Nestlé Toll House
        Semi-Sweet Chocolate Morsels, divided
    1 9-inch unbaked pie shell
    1 cup heavy cream

Preheat oven to 350°F. Lightly beat together eggs, corn syrup, sugar, butter, 3 tablespoons of rum, vanilla, and salt. Do not overbeat. Stir in pecan halves and ½ cup morsels; pour into pie shell. Cover edges with foil. Bake at 350°F. for 25 minutes. Remove foil.

Bake 20 to 25 minutes more, or until knife inserted in center comes out clean. Cool, then chill. Melt remaining ½ cup morsels over hot (not boiling) water; stir until smooth. Cool. Whip cream and remaining 1 tablespoon rum until soft peaks form; gently fold in melted morsels. Serve with pie. Store pie and whipped cream in refrigerator.

Black Beauty Pie

Makes 1 pie
 16 stewed California dried figs
  3 cups milk
  1 envelope unflavored gelatin
 ½ cup sugar
  2 teaspoons instant coffee
  1 teaspoon ground cinnamon
  1 package chocolate pudding mix
  1 teaspoon vanilla extract
 ½ cup slivered, toasted almonds
 ½ cup toasted whole almonds
  1 9-inch baked pie shell
  1 cup heavy cream, whipped, sweetened, and
     vanilla-flavored

Drain stewed figs thoroughly. Set aside several figs to garnish pie top. Cut up remaining figs into small bits, discarding stems. In ½ cup of the milk, dissolve the gelatin. Place remaining milk in saucepan with coffee, sugar, cinnamon, and package of chocolate pudding. Stir over low heat until pudding thickens and bubbles up. Stir in the gelatin. Cool. Then add vanilla and slivered almonds. Pour into pie shell and chill. Top with sweetened, vanilla-flavored whipped cream. Dry the whole figs carefully and use with toasted whole almonds to garnish pie top.

Chocolate Linzer Torte

Makes one 9-inch pie
 ¾ cup butter, softened
  1 cup sifted confectioners sugar
  3 tablespoons mayonnaise
  1 teaspoon ground cinnamon
 ¼ teaspoon ground cloves
 1½ cups all-purpose flour
  1 cup coarsely chopped almonds
  1 6-ounce package (1 cup) Nestlé Toll House
     Semi-Sweet Chocolate Morsels
  1 cup raspberry preserves

Preheat oven to 300°F. In a large bowl, combine butter and confectioners sugar; beat until creamy. Blend in mayonnaise, cinnamon, and cloves. Gradually add flour; mix well. Stir in almonds and Nestlé Toll House Semi-Sweet Chocolate Morsels. Divide

dough into two balls; cover and refrigerate 30 minutes. Place one ball of dough in 9-inch pie pan. Flatten dough to fit in bottom of pan. Spread raspberry preserves on top of dough. Roll out remaining dough between 2 sheets of waxed paper. Remove waxed paper; place dough on top of pie. Crimp edges, if desired. With sharp knife, score top crust into 16 wedges. Bake 45 minutes. Remove from oven; cool completely.

Christmas Poinsettia Pie

Makes 1 pie
  1 8- or 9-inch baked pastry shell or crumb crust
  1 teaspoon unflavored gelatin
  1 tablespoon cold water
  2 tablespoons boiling water
 ½ cup sugar
 ¼ cup Hershey's® Cocoa
  1 cup heavy cream (very cold)
  1 teaspoon vanilla extract
     Rum Cream Topping (recipe follows)
 ¼ cup flaked coconut
     Maraschino or candied red and green cherries

Prepare pie shell; cool. Sprinkle gelatin over cold water in small bowl; stir gently and let stand 1 minute to soften. Add boiling water; stir until gelatin is completely dissolved (mixture must be clear). Stir together sugar and cocoa in small cold mixer bowl; add heavy cream and vanilla. Beat on low speed about 30 seconds, or until smooth; beat on medium speed about 1 minute, or until stiff peaks form. Gradually add gelatin mixture; beat until blended. Pour into crust. Spread Rum Cream Topping over chocolate filling; sprinkle with coconut. Chill at least 2 hours. Cut cherries into eighths for petals; arrange decoratively on top of pie.

Rum Cream Topping

Makes about 2 cups
 ½ teaspoon unflavored gelatin
  1 tablespoon cold water
  1 tablespoon boiling water
  1 cup heavy cream
  2 tablespoons confectioners sugar
  2 teaspoons white rum or ¼ teaspoon rum extract
     or 1 teaspoon vanilla extract

Sprinkle gelatin over cold water in cup; stir gently and let stand 1 minute to soften. Add boiling water; stir until gelatin is completely dissolved. Combine heavy cream, sugar, and rum or vanilla in small mixer bowl. Beat to blend; slowly add gelatin mixture. Beat until stiff peaks form.

Creme de Cacao Silk Pie

Makes 8 servings

   1 baked 9-inch Chocolate Crumb Crust (recipe
       follows)
   1 cup unsalted butter or margarine
   ⅓ cup sugar
   2 squares (1 ounce each) semisweet chocolate,
       melted
   2 eggs
   ½ cup DeKuyper Creme de Cacao (brown)
   ½ cup heavy cream, whipped
       Chocolate Curls (see index)

Prepare Chocolate Crumb Crust. In large bowl of electric mixer, cream butter and sugar until light and fluffy; beat in chocolate. Add 1 egg; beat at high speed until well blended. Continue beating, adding ¼ cup Creme de Cacao in a thin stream. Add second egg; beat until well blended. Add remaining Creme de Cacao in thin stream, beating continuously. Spoon mixture into prepared pie crust. Chill several hours or until firm. Garnish with whipped cream and Chocolate Curls.

Chocolate Crumb Crust

   1¼ cups chocolate cookie crumbs
    2 tablespoons sugar
   ⅓ cup butter or margarine, melted

In small bowl blend crumbs, sugar and butter. Press firmly against bottom and sides of a 9-inch pie plate. Bake in a 375°F. oven 8 minutes. Cool thoroughly.

Chocolate Boston Cream Pie

Makes 6 to 8 servings

   ⅓ cup butter
   ⅔ cup sugar
    2 eggs
   ½ teaspoon vanilla extract
    1 square (1 ounce) unsweetened chocolate
   ¾ cup all-purpose flour
   ½ teaspoon baking soda
   ¼ teaspoon salt
   ⅓ cup milk
    1 package (3¾ ounces) instant vanilla pudding
       and pie filling
    1 cup sour cream
   ½ cup milk
    1 tablespoon butter
   ¾ cup confectioners sugar
    2 tablespoons sour cream
   ¼ teaspoon vanilla extract
   ½ square (½ ounce) unsweetened chocolate

For cake, cream butter and sugar in a small mixing bowl until light and fluffy. Beat in eggs and vanilla. Melt chocolate over hot, not boiling, water in small saucepan. Add melted chocolate to creamed mixture; mix well. Combine dry ingredients. Add alternately to creamed mixture with milk. Begin and end with dry ingredients; beat well after each addition. Line bottom of 9-inch round cake dish with double layers of waxed paper. Pour batter into prepared dish. Bake at 350°F. for 30 to 35 minutes, or until center springs back when lightly touched. Cool in dish 10 minutes; remove from dish and cool completely on a wire rack. Cut cake horizontally into 2 layers. For filling, combine pudding, sour cream, and milk in a small mixing bowl. Beat on high speed until thick and fluffy. Place one layer of cake on a serving plate. Spread with filling. Place second layer on top. For frosting, melt butter in small saucepan. Pour in mixer bowl. Add sugar, sour cream, and vanilla. Beat until smooth and of spreading consistency. Spread over top of cake. Melt chocolate over hot, not boiling, water. Drizzle chocolate over icing; swirl with knife edge. Refrigerate until ready to serve.

Say It with Chocolate

Here's a novel way to send a greeting—solid chunk chocolate, personalized with any message you choose.

On a piece of paper or waxed paper, draw any desired shape to desired size. Don't try to get too fancy on your first try, but a simple heart, diamond, or crescent shape is not difficult. Cut out the shape.

Melt 2 squares semisweet chocolate or 2 ounces (¼ cup) semisweet chocolate morsels in top of double boiler over hot (not boiling) water, stirring constantly. Remove from heat and allow to cool slightly, stirring occasionally.

Spread chocolate on waxed paper or aluminum foil, so that it is ¼ inch thick. Do not allow chocolate to harden completely.

Place your cut-out shape over the chocolate, and, with a sharp knife, cut the chocolate into that shape. Then, using a toothpick, write your message directly in the chocolate. Don't let the toothpick go all the way to the bottom of the chocolate; try to keep the letters no more than ⅛ inch deep.

If you like, you can decorate your "card" with candied mints, icing, raisins, or nuts.

Cover your card with waxed paper and place it in the refrigerator until it hardens completely. Remove it from the waxed paper or foil; wrap in new paper. If you decide to mail your chocolate greeting card, pack it in a sturdy box, with packing material around it.

Chocolate Meringue Pie (page 54); Chocolate Black Bottom Pie (page 56). General Foods

Shopping for Chocolate Products

Whatever chocolate delicacies—and their names are legion—you have in mind to make, there's a chocolate product to serve your purpose.

Unsweetened chocolate: This is often called baking chocolate. It's pure chocolate liquor, with nothing added, that has been poured into molds, where it hardens into cakes. When a recipe calls for "2 squares chocolate," this is what is required; a square weighs 1 ounce, in case the recipe calls for measurement in ounces. Buy it in packages of 8 individually wrapped squares, shelved near other products for baking, such as flour, baking powder, and so on.

Cocoa: Part of the cocoa butter is removed from chocolate liquor, the liquor is pressed into cakes, and the cakes are pulverized to result in the fine chocolate powder that is cocoa. Use this plain cocoa in recipes calling for the product, and to make—with milk and sugar—the cups of cocoa in which children delight (particularly with a marshmallow afloat). Usually shelved in the markets with other products for baking, or with beverages, most often in cardboard cartons with pry-off metal lids.

Breakfast cocoa: This has somewhat more cocoa butter left in. Use interchangeably with regular cocoa.

Dutch cocoa: Treated with an alkali, this cocoa is darker and has a slightly different taste and aroma. It, too, can be used interchangeably with regular cocoa.

Instant cocoa: Sugar is added to cocoa for convenience in making a hot beverage at home; don't use in cooking unless the recipe specifically calls for it. Shelved with beverages.

Hot cocoa mix: Cocoa plus sugar plus dry milk—again for making beverages, but not for cooking. It is also shelved with beverages.

Semisweet: A blend of unsweetened chocolate plus sugar and extra cocoa butter. Comes in 8-ounce bars, marked in segments for ready measuring. Can be eaten out of hand or used in recipes that specifically call for it. Do not substitute for regular baking chocolate in cooking. Shelved with baking products.

Chocolate chips: Also called, depending on the manufacturer, pieces or bits. For eating out of hand, or use in cooking. Packed in 6- and 12-ounce bags, the chips are generally made of semisweet chocolate, although at least two manufacturers also make milk chocolate chips. These milk chocolate chips can be used interchangeably with the semisweet ones in cookies and for toppings, but where the recipe calls for melting the chips, stick to the semisweet kind for best results. Some manufacturers also make miniature semisweet chocolate chips, each about half the size of the usual kind.

Sweet cooking chocolate: Also a blend of unsweetened chocolate, sugar, and cocoa butter, this is lighter and milder than semisweet. Comes in individually wrapped squares, in packages. Shelved with baking products. Do not substitute for regular baking chocolate in cooking unless recipe specifically calls for it.

Liquid chocolate: Unsweetened, for cooking; made with cocoa and vegetable shortening. Comes in packages of individual envelopes, each the equivalent of a 1-ounce square of regular unsweetened baking chocolate, for which it may be substituted. In effect, this is premelted baking chocolate. However, the flavor is not exactly the same—you may be delighted to skip the melting, or prefer to melt chocolate yourself for the familiar flavor. Shelved with baking products.

Chocolate syrup: Ready-to-use, made of cocoa sweetened with sugar. Comes in cans, jars, or bottles, shelved near baking products or sometimes near ice cream. Add it to milk for a chocolate beverage, or use as a sauce over ice cream or cake. Can be used in cooking, but not unless recipe specifically calls for it.

Milk chocolate: Sweetened chocolate with milk added—the familiar chocolate bar, plain or with nuts; also used to coat chocolate creams and various kinds of candy bars. Find it at the candy counter. Do not cook with it unless recipe specifies.

Meringue Shells with Chocolate Peanut Filling

Makes 12 shells

- 3 egg whites, at room temperature
- ¾ cup sugar
- 24 chocolate-covered peanut butter cups (small size)
- 1 cup heavy cream
- 1 teaspoon orange flavor
- Grated rind of 1 small orange
- ½ cup chopped salted peanuts

Beat egg whites until stiff. Gradually beat in sugar, 1 tablespoon at a time, until stiff and glossy. Spoon mixture in ¼-cup mounds on a foil-lined cookie sheet. Hollow out each mound with the back of a spoon until meringue is shaped like a cup. Bake at 275°F for 20 minutes. Remove from oven and top each meringue with a peanut butter cup. Replace in oven; bake another 20 minutes. Cool on cookie sheet. When ready to serve, place meringues on serving plates. In a bowl beat remaining ingredients until thick and fluffy. Spoon mixture over meringues. Top with chopped peanuts.

Petite Derby Tarts

Makes 4 dozen tarts

 2 packages (3 ounces each) cream cheese
 ½ cup shortening
 ½ cup butter or margarine
 2 cups all-purpose flour
 2 eggs
 1 cup sugar
 3 tablespoons cornstarch
 ½ cup butter or margarine, melted
 ¼ cup bourbon or apple juice
 ½ cup finely chopped pecans
 ¾ cup Hershey's₍₎ Mini Chips₍₎ Semi-Sweet
    Chocolate
    Derby Topping (recipe follows)

Combine cream cheese, shortening, and butter in large mixer bowl; blend in flour. Chill dough for 1 hour; shape into 4 dozen 1-inch balls. Press balls of dough on bottom and up sides of ungreased 1¾-inch muffin cups (tea cake pans).

Beat eggs in small mixer bowl; gradually add sugar and cornstarch. Add melted butter or margarine and bourbon; mix well. Stir in pecans and Mini Chips semi-sweet chocolate. Spoon heaping teaspoon of filling into each cup; bake at 350°F. for 20 to 25 minutes. Cool 30 minutes; remove from pan. Cool completely; garnish with a dollop of Derby Topping.

Derby Topping

 ⅔ cup heavy cream
 ¼ cup confectioners sugar
 1 to 2 teaspoons bourbon

Whip cream with confectioners sugar. Add bourbon; beat until stiff peaks form.

Fiesta Raisin Tarts

Makes 1½ dozen tarts

 1 package (11 ounces) pie crust mix
 1 package (6 ounces) semisweet chocolate morsels
 ½ cup sour cream
 1 cup California raisins
 1 cup miniature marshmallows
 ¼ cup chopped walnuts

Prepare pie crust according to package directions. Press tablespoonful into small tart pans or muffin pan cups (2½ inches in diameter) to cover bottom and sides evenly. Prick shells with fork. Bake at 450°F. for 8 to 10 minutes, or just until top edge is golden. Remove from oven and cool on racks. Meanwhile, melt chocolate over hot water. Add sour cream and blend well. Add remaining ingredients. Drop mixture by spoonful into tart shells. Store in cool place.

Chocolate-Cherry No-Bake Mini-Tarts

Makes 30 mini-tarts

    Cocoa Tart Shells (recipe follows)
 1 package (3 ounces) cream cheese
 2 cups confectioners sugar
 1 teaspoon vanilla extract
 ¼ teaspoon almond extract
 ½ cup coarsely chopped blanched almonds
 ¼ cup candied cherries, quartered
    Candied cherries, halved

Prepare Cocoa Tart Shells. Beat cream cheese in small mixer bowl; gradually blend in confectioners sugar, vanilla, and almond extract until smooth. Stir in almonds and ¼ cup candied cherries. Spoon filling into tart shells; garnish with halved candied cherries. Chill until firm.

Cocoa Tart Shells

 2 cups confectioners sugar
 1 cup vanilla wafer crumbs
 1 cup ground almonds
 ½ cup Hershey's₍₎ Cocoa
 ½ cup milk

Combine confectioners sugar, vanilla wafer crumbs, ground almonds, and cocoa in a mixing bowl. Sprinkle in milk, mixing until ingredients are moistened and cling together. Shape into walnut-size pieces; place in 30 paper-lined muffin cups (1¾ inches in diameter). Press dough against bottom and side of each cup to form shell. Chill.

Fruited Chocolate Tarts

Makes 4 to 6 tarts

 4 4-inch pastry tart shells or 6 packaged tart-size
    crumb crusts
 ⅔ cup sugar
 ¼ cup Hershey's₍₎ Cocoa
 3 tablespoons cornstarch
 ¼ teaspoon salt
 2 cups milk
 2 tablespoons butter
 1 teaspoon vanilla extract
    Assorted fresh or canned fruit

Bake pastry tart shells; cool. Combine sugar, cocoa, cornstarch, and salt in medium saucepan; blend in milk. Cook and stir constantly over medium heat to boiling; boil and stir 1 minute. Remove from heat; blend in butter and vanilla. Pour into tart shells. Press plastic wrap onto surface. Chill. Before serving, garnish with fruit as desired.

Creamy Confections

The accent is on chocolate richness in these luscious puddings—from hot and steamed to chilled pots de crème, parfaits, cakes, and mousses.

Holiday Steamed Pudding
Makes 8 servings

    1 6-ounce package (1 cup) Nestlé Toll House
        Semi-Sweet Chocolate Morsels
1½ cups chopped pecans
    1 cup currants
    1 cup uncooked quick oats
    ¾ cup chopped candied cherries
    ¾ cup all-purpose flour
    ¾ cup sugar
    2 teaspoons ground cinnamon
1¼ teaspoons baking soda
    ¾ teaspoon salt
    1 cup buttermilk or sour milk
    2 teaspoons vanilla extract
        Brandied Hard Sauce (recipe follows),
            sweetened whipped cream, or ice cream

Melt Nestlé Toll House Semi-Sweet Chocolate Morsels over hot (not boiling) water; remove from heat and set aside. In a large bowl, combine pecans, currants, oats, candied cherries, flour, sugar, cinnamon, baking soda, and salt; toss together. Add melted chocolate, buttermilk, and vanilla; mix well. Press into greased 5- to 6-cup heatproof mold. Cover tightly with foil. Place covered mold on rack or trivet in a deep kettle or roasting pan. Pour boiling water into kettle halfway up side of mold (water should not touch foil cover). Cover kettle; simmer over low heat 2 hours, or until toothpick inserted in center comes out clean. Cool 10 minutes; remove from mold and cool completely. If using as a gift, return pudding to cleaned mold.

To reheat, cover mold with foil and bake at 350°F. for 30 to 45 minutes. Serve warm with Brandied Hard Sauce or sweetened whipped cream or ice cream.

Brandied Hard Sauce
    1 jar (5½ ounces) hard sauce
    2 eggs
    1 tablespoon milk
    1 tablespoon brandy

In a small bowl, combine hard sauce, eggs, milk, and brandy; beat until creamy. Refrigerate.

Steamed Chocolate Pudding
Makes 6 to 8 servings

    ¾ cup C & H Golden Brown Sugar, packed
    ¼ cup butter or margarine, softened
    1 egg
    1 teaspoon vanilla extract
    3 ounces unsweetened chocolate
1¾ cups all-purpose flour
    1 tablespoon baking powder
    1 teaspoon *each* salt and ground cinnamon
    1 cup milk
    ½ cup chopped walnuts
        Steamed Pudding Sauce (recipe follows)

Grease 2-quart mold. Cream sugar and butter. Add egg and vanilla; beat until smooth. Melt chocolate; cool. Stir into creamed mixture. Combine flour, baking powder, salt, and cinnamon and add alternately with milk to chocolate mixture, beginning and ending with dry ingredients. Stir in walnuts. Spoon into mold and cover tightly with lid or heavy foil. Place on rack in large kettle. Add boiling water to come halfway up sides of mold. Steam 2 hours. Keep water boiling continuously. Add more boiling water as necessary. Let rest 10 minutes before unmolding. Serve warm with Steamed Pudding Sauce.

Steamed Pudding Sauce
    1 cup C & H Granulated Sugar
    ½ cup light cream
    ½ cup butter or margarine
    1 teaspoon vanilla extract

Combine all ingredients in saucepan. Heat until butter melts and sauce is hot. Pour over steamed pudding.

Steamed Chocolate Pudding. C&H Sugar Company

Chocolate Almond Pudding

Makes 6 to 8 servings
  ½ cup butter or margarine, softened
  ¾ cup sugar, divided
  3 squares (3 ounces) unsweetened chocolate,
     melted and cooled
  5 eggs, separated
  2 tablespoons almond-flavored liqueur
  1 cup ground almonds
  ½ cup all-purpose flour
    Chocolate sauce
  1 cup heavy cream, whipped
    Slivered almonds

Cream butter and ½ cup sugar until light and fluffy. Beat in chocolate. Add egg yolks, 1 at a time, beating well after each addition. Beat in liqueur, almonds, and flour; set aside. Beat egg whites until soft peaks form. Beat in remaining ¼ cup sugar and continue to beat until stiff peaks form. Stir large spoonful of whites into chocolate mixture, then fold in remaining whites just until combined.

Pour chocolate mixture into greased 1½-quart heatproof bowl. Preheat oven to 350°F. Cover bowl with aluminum foil and place in larger bowl. Add boiling water to come about halfway up side of bowl. Bake 40 minutes, or until toothpick inserted in center comes out clean. Let stand 2 to 3 minutes before inverting onto serving plate. Serve warm, topped with chocolate sauce, whipped cream, and slivered almonds.

Chocolate Nugget Pudding

Makes 6 to 8 servings
  4 slices day-old bread, crusts trimmed, quartered
  ¾ cup semisweet chocolate chips
  3 eggs, lightly beaten
  ⅓ cup sugar
  2¼ cups milk

You will need: Corning Ware 8x8x2-inch square utility dish or Pyrex 1½-quart utility casserole, buttered

Arrange 8 bread quarters in bottom of dish or casserole. Sprinkle with half the chocolate chips. Top with remaining bread; sprinkle with remaining chocolate chips. Set aside.

Combine eggs and sugar in a medium bowl; beat until pale. Add milk; beat to blend. Pour over bread. Let stand at room temperature 1 hour. Place dish or casserole in a large shallow pan; pour hot water into pan to a depth of 1 inch. Bake in preheated 350°F oven 50 to 70 minutes, or until a table knife inserted halfway between center and edge comes out clean. Cool slightly before serving.

Cho-Co Rice Pudding

Makes 6 servings
  3 cups warm, cooked Riceland Rice
  ½ cup sugar
  3 egg yolks
  ⅔ cup sugar
  ⅓ cup all-purpose flour
  3 tablespoons cocoa
  ⅛ teaspoon salt
  2 cups milk
  2 tablespoons margarine
  1 teaspoon vanilla extract
    Meringue or whipped topping (optional)

Combine warm rice and ½ cup sugar; set aside. In heavy saucepan beat egg yolks until lemon colored. Cream in ⅔ cup sugar. Slowly stir in flour, cocoa, and salt. Stir in hot milk, a small amount at a time, mixing well after each addition. Cook until thick, stirring continuously. Add margarine and vanilla. Cool. In serving dish layer rice and filling, starting with rice and ending with filling. Top with a meringue or whipped topping, if desired.

Party Parfaits

Makes 5 servings
  1 6-ounce package (1 cup) Nestlé Toll House
    Semi-Sweet Chocolate Morsels
  1 6-ounce package (1 cup) Nestlé Butterscotch
    Flavored Morsels
  2 packages (3¾ ounces each) vanilla instant
    pudding and pie filling
  2 cups milk
  2 cups sour cream

Melt Nestlé Toll House Semi-Sweet Chocolate Morsels over hot (not boiling) water; remove from heat and set aside. Repeat with Nestlé Butterscotch Flavored Morsels. In a large bowl, combine instant pudding powder, milk, and sour cream. Mix pudding according to package directions. Transfer half the pudding to a small bowl; using a wire whisk or electric beater, blend in melted chocolate. Repeat with remaining pudding, using melted butterscotch. Spoon about 2 rounded tablespoonfuls chocolate mixture alternately with equal amount butterscotch mixture into each of five 7-ounce parfait glasses. Chill in refrigerator until ready to serve.

Quick Pots de Crème

Makes 6 servings

    1 package (6 ounces) semisweet chocolate pieces
1¼ cups light cream, scalded
    1 teaspoon instant coffee (optional)
    2 egg yolks
       Dash salt
    1 teaspoon vanilla extract

Put chocolate pieces, cream, and instant coffee, if desired, into blender container. Cover; blend at high speed until smooth. Add remaining ingredients in order listed. Cover; blend until smooth. Pour into six pots de crème, demitasse or custard cups, or small sherbet glasses. Chill several hours.

Pots de Crème au Chocolat

Makes 4 to 6 servings

    1 package (4 ounces) Baker's German's Sweet
       Chocolate, broken in pieces
1¼ cups light cream or half and half
¼ cup sugar
    6 egg yolks, lightly beaten
    1 teaspoon vanilla extract
       Chocolate Curls (see index)(optional)

Heat chocolate, cream, and sugar in saucepan over very low heat, stirring constantly until chocolate is melted and mixture is smooth. Stir a small amount of the hot mixture into egg yolks, mixing well. Return to remaining hot mixture; continue cooking, stirring constantly, until slightly thickened, about 5 minutes. Add vanilla and pour into pot de crème or demitasse cups. Chill until set. Garnish with Chocolate Curls, if desired.

Spirited Pots de Crème

Makes 6 servings

    1 package (6 ounces) semisweet chocolate pieces
½ cup hot brewed coffee
    4 eggs
    3 tablespoons sugar
⅔ to 1 teaspoon brandy or rum extract
       Whipped cream (optional)

Place chocolate pieces in blender container. Blend at medium speed 10 seconds. Scrape down sides of blender container with rubber spatula, if necessary. Add coffee. Blend at medium speed 5 seconds. Add eggs, sugar, and extract. Blend at medium speed until smooth, about 30 to 45 seconds. Pour into 6 pot de crème cups. Refrigerate overnight. Garnish with whipped cream, if desired.

Surprise Chocolate Pudding

Makes 4 servings

    1 package (3⅝ ounces) chocolate pudding and pie
       filling
    3 cups milk
⅔ cup crushed peppermint candy
       Whipped cream (optional)
       Crushed peppermint candy (optional)

Make pudding according to package directions, adding ⅓ cup peppermint candy with dry mix. Stir in remaining ⅓ cup candy. Chill, covered, 2 to 3 hours. Serve topped with whipped cream and peppermint candy, if desired.

Dessert Toppings Tidbit

Dessert toppings may be found in your market freezer case, ready to thaw and use, or as a powder on the grocery shelves to be whipped with liquid before using. These are nondairy products, but may be used in place of whipped cream in a variety of delicious—and considerably lower-calorie—dishes, such as chiffon pies, soufflés, and Bavarians.

Or you may (less expensively) make a good whipped topping at home, to use in place of whipped cream on or in many desserts. Start by putting the large electric mixer bowl and the beaters in the refrigerator to be thoroughly chilled. When they are ready, put 4 teaspoons cold water in a cup and sprinkle over it 1 envelope unflavored gelatin; let stand until softened. Add ⅓ cup boiling water and stir until the gelatin is dissolved; cool to room temperature. In the chilled bowl, combine 1 cup ice water with 1⅓ cups nonfat dry milk. Beat at high speed until soft peaks form, about 5 minutes. As you continue to beat, gradually add 6 tablespoons sugar. Scrape down the sides of the bowl and, continuing to beat, gradually add ⅓ cup salad oil, 1 teaspoon vanilla, 2 teaspoons lemon juice, and the gelatin mixture. Scrape down the sides of the bowl again and continue to beat 1 minute longer. Makes about 6 cups.

To use as a topping, place in a rigid container, cover, and refrigerate or freeze. Or use as an ingredient in desserts.

Chocolate Fudge Pudding

Makes 6 to 8 servings

- ½ cup C & H Granulated Sugar
- 1 cup all-purpose flour
- 2 teaspoons baking powder
- ½ teaspoon salt
- 2 tablespoons cocoa powder
- ¾ cup chopped nuts
- ½ cup milk
- 1 teaspoon vanilla extract
- 2 tablespoons vegetable oil
- ¾ cup firmly packed C & H Dark Brown Sugar
- ¼ cup cocoa powder
- ⅛ teaspoon salt
- 1¾ cups hot water
  Sweetened whipped cream

Autumn Bavarian Pie (page 51); Autumn Chocolate Mousse (page 68); Mini Chip Pumpkin Cookies (page 32). Courtesy HERSHEY Food Corporation

Pots de Crème au Chocolat (page 65); Chocolate Sponge Mold (page 72). General Foods

Preheat oven to 350°F. Grease 8-inch square baking pan. Combine sugar, flour, baking powder, salt, and 2 tablespoons cocoa in bowl. Stir in nuts, milk, vanilla, and oil. Spread in pan. Mix brown sugar, ¼ cup cocoa, and salt; stir into hot water and pour over unbaked batter. Bake 40 to 45 minutes. As pudding bakes, batter rises through rich chocolate sauce. Serve warm or cold with whipped cream.

Q. *I tried substituting milk chocolate morsels for semisweet in a pudding; the morsels got so hard we nearly broke our teeth. What did I do wrong?*
A. You shouldn't use milk chocolate morsels in baked desserts that do not call for melting the morsels before blending them in. The milk causes them to become hard when they are baked. You may substitute milk chocolate morsels for semisweet in recipes that call for melting the morsels, such as frostings and glazes.

Autumn Chocolate Mousse

Makes 6 servings
  3 cups miniature or 30 large marshmallows
  ½ cup milk
  4 to 6 teaspoons orange-flavored liqueur or ½
      teaspoon orange extract
    Yellow and red food color
  1 cup Hershey's® Mini Chips® Semi-Sweet
      Chocolate
  1 teaspoon vanilla extract
1½ cups heavy cream
    Mandarin orange segments (optional)

Combine marshmallows and milk in medium saucepan. Stir constantly over low heat until marshmallows are melted and mixture is smooth. Pour ¾ cup marshmallow mixture into medium bowl; blend in liqueur and food color (10 drops yellow and 6 drops red). Set aside. Add Mini Chips semi-sweet chocolate to the remaining marshmallow mixture; return to low heat and stir until chips are melted. Remove from heat; add vanilla. Cool thoroughly. Whip cream until stiff; fold 1½ cups into chocolate mixture. Gradually fold remaining whipped cream into orange mixture. Alternately spoon chocolate and orange mixtures into parfait glasses or dessert dishes. Chill for 3 to 4 hours, or until set. Garnish with orange segments, if desired.

Gelatin Know-how

You'll follow the basic package or recipe directions, of course, but these extra tips will help, as well.

• To make a mixture that is clear and uniformly set, be sure the gelatin is completely dissolved in the boiling water or other liquid before adding the cold liquid.

• To make soft-set gelatin, increase the liquid about ½ cup for each 3 ounces of gelatin. The resulting dessert is softer, tastes delicious, but will be too soft to unmold.

• To double a recipe, just double the amounts of gelatin, liquid, and other ingredients used, with the exception of salt, vinegar, and lemon juice. For these, use just 1½ times the amount called for.

• To make gelatin in a microwave oven, measure 1 cup water into a glass bowl. Place in oven and heat about 2 minutes, or until water comes to a boil. Remove from oven, add gelatin (3-ounce package), and stir until dissolved. Add 1 cup cold water and chill until set.

• To store prepared gelatin overnight or longer, cover it to prevent drying. Always store gelatin cakes or pies in the refrigerator.

Fudge Mousse with Caramelized Almonds

Makes 6 to 9 servings
  4 eggs, separated
  1 cup semisweet chocolate pieces
  ⅓ cup boiling water
  3 tablespoons rum or 2 tablespoons water and 1
      teaspoon rum extract
  ½ cup whole blanched almonds
  ½ cup sugar
    Whipped cream

Whip egg whites until stiff. In electric blender, combine chocolate pieces and boiling water; process at medium speed until smooth. Continue processing; add egg yolks, 1 at a time, and rum. Fold in egg whites until well blended. Turn into individual dessert dishes and chill until set (overnight if possible).

Meanwhile, coarsely chop almonds and combine with sugar in skillet. Stir over medium-low heat until sugar melts and turns golden. Remove from heat and pour at once onto foil or a greased cookie sheet. Cool, then break up.

To serve, pipe or spoon a rosette of whipped cream on top of each mousse. Sprinkle with caramelized almonds.

Note: Keep the caramelized almonds in mind to top ice cream, frozen cheesecake, or custard.

Frozen Chocolate Spiced Rum Mousse

Makes 8 servings
  ¾ cup sugar
  ⅓ cup water
  4 egg whites
  4 squares (1 ounce each) unsweetened chocolate,
      melted
  1 cup heavy cream
  ¼ cup Captain Morgan Spiced Rum
  ½ cup heavy cream, whipped
    Chocolate shavings

Make a waxed paper collar for 4-cup soufflé dish (or use 1½-quart bowl). In small saucepan, bring sugar and water to a boil for 3 to 4 minutes. In large bowl, beat egg whites on high speed until soft peaks form. Add sugar syrup in thin stream; beat 5 minutes. Fold in melted chocolate. In separate bowl, whip cream; beat in Spiced Rum until well mixed. Fold into chocolate. Transfer into soufflé dish; cover and freeze at least 4 hours. Garnish with whipped cream and chocolate shavings just before serving.

Chocolate Mousse

Makes 4 servings

  4 squares (1 ounce each) semisweet chocolate
  ½ cup Domino Superfine Sugar
  2 teaspoons vanilla extract
  2 cups heavy cream

In top of double boiler over hot water place sugar, chocolate, and ¼ cup of cream. Stir constantly until smooth and melted. Remove from heat. Stir in vanilla. Cool to room temperature. Whip remaining cream until stiff. Fold gently into chocolate mixture. Spoon into serving dishes. Chill until serving time (at least 2 hours). Serve topped with additional sweetened whipped cream, if desired.

Chocolate Mini-Mousses

Makes about 30 servings

  2 envelopes Knox® Unflavored Gelatine
  ½ cup sugar
  3 cups milk
  1 package (12 ounces) semisweet chocolate pieces
  1 tablespoon vanilla extract
  2 cups heavy cream, whipped

In a medium saucepan, mix Knox Unflavored Gelatine with sugar; add milk and chocolate pieces. Stir over low heat until gelatine is completely dissolved and chocolate is melted, about 10 minutes. Turn into a large bowl; add vanilla. Beat with wire whip or rotary beater until chocolate is blended. Chill, stirring occasionally, until mixture mounds slightly when dropped from a spoon.

Fold in whipped cream. Set cupcake liners in muffin pan cups; spoon gelatine mixture into liners. Chill until set. Garnish with whipped cream, if desired.

Variation

Pile this filling into 16 baked 3-inch tart shells or into 2 deep 9-inch baked pie shells. Whip 1 cup heavy cream with 1 teaspoon instant coffee powder, 2 tablespoons confectioners sugar, and ½ teaspoon ground cinnamon. Garnish tarts or pies with this mixture; sprinkle with grated semisweet chocolate.

Grasshopper Dessert

Makes 10 to 12 servings

  2 envelopes unflavored gelatin
  1 cup water
  2 cups undiluted Carnation® Evaporated Milk
  1 package (8 ounces) cream cheese
  ⅔ cup sugar
  ¼ cup green crème de menthe
  ¼ cup crème de cacao
  1 teaspoon vanilla extract
  2 tablespoons butter, melted
  2 cups (about 20) icing-filled chocolate sandwich cookie crumbs
  3 egg whites
  Chocolate Curls (see index)
  Mint leaves

Soften gelatin in water; heat to dissolve. Pour into blender container. Add evaporated milk, cream cheese, ⅓ cup sugar, crème de menthe, crème de cacao, and vanilla. Cover. Blend on medium speed until smooth. Pour into large bowl. Chill until mixture mounds on spoon; beat smooth with wire whip if necessary. Stir butter into cookie crumbs. Press onto bottom and 1 inch up sides of 9-inch springform pan. Beat egg whites until foamy. Gradually add remaining ⅓ cup sugar; beat until stiff and sugar is dissolved. Fold into gelatin mixture. Spoon into prepared crust. Chill until firm. Garnish with Chocolate Curls and mint leaves before serving.

Superb Chocolate Mousse

Makes 4 servings

  1 package (6 ounces) semisweet chocolate bits
  2 eggs
  3 tablespoons strong, hot coffee
  1 to 2 tablespoons rum, brandy, or Arrow Curaçao
  ¾ cup milk, scalded

Combine all ingredients in blender. Cover and process at high speed for 2 minutes. Pour into 4 dessert dishes and refrigerate at least 4 hours before serving.

Wonderful Whipped Creams

Plain sweetened whipped cream has its place; but when you add chocolate and other flavorings, you get an even better, more flavorful finishing touch to your favorite dessert.

Chocolate Whipped Cream: Combine 2 tablespoons confectioners sugar with 1 tablespoon cocoa in a small bowl. Add ½ cup heavy cream and ½ teaspoon vanilla extract. Beat on low speed to blend, then beat on high speed until stiff peaks form.

Mocha Whipped Cream: Decrease cocoa to 2 teaspoons and combine with 2 tablespoons confectioners sugar; add ½ teaspoon instant coffee granules. Proceed as above.

Almond-Chocolate Whipped Cream: Substitute 1 teaspoon almond extract for vanilla extract. Proceed as above.

Raspberry-Chocolate Whipped Cream: Purée ¼ cup frozen raspberries. Fold in to Chocolate Whipped Cream.

Frosty Fantasies

These make-ahead marvels cool regally in the refrigerator or freezer until you're ready to serve them. When you do, listen to the raves as dessert fantasies come true.

Chocolate Delight

Makes 6 servings

- 3 tablespoons unsweetened cocoa
- 1 teaspoon instant coffee powder
- 1 envelope unflavored gelatin
- 4 packets (1¼ teaspoons) Sweet 'N Low® granulated sugar substitute
- ⅓ cup sugar
- 2 egg yolks
- 1½ cups skim milk
- 2 tablespoons rum
- 2 tablespoons margarine
- 4 egg whites
- Orange sections

In saucepan, mix cocoa, coffee, gelatin, Sweet 'N Low, and sugar. In bowl, beat egg yolks, milk, and rum; stir into dry mixture. Cook and stir until slightly thickened; remove from heat. Stir in margarine; cool about 20 minutes. In another bowl, beat egg whites until stiff. Fold into chocolate mixture. Pour into serving dishes or a 4-cup mold; chill about 4 hours, or until firm.

To unmold, run knife around edge and shake gently. Unmold onto serving dish. Garnish with orange sections.

Chocolate Chip Mint Dessert

Makes about 6 servings

- 2 envelopes Knox® Unflavored Gelatine
- ½ cup cold milk
- 1 cup very hot milk
- 1 cup heavy cream
- 1 package (6 ounces) semisweet chocolate pieces
- 2 eggs
- ¼ cup sugar
- 1 teaspoon peppermint extract
- 6 ice cubes (about 1 cup)

In a 5-cup blender container, sprinkle Knox Unflavored Gelatine over cold milk. Let stand 3 to 4 minutes. Add hot milk and process at low speed 2 minutes. Add cream, chocolate pieces, eggs, sugar, and peppermint extract; process at high speed until well blended, about 2 minutes. Add ice cubes, 1 at a time, and process at high speed until ice is melted. Pour immediately into dessert dishes. Chill until set.

Cocoa Mousse Dessert

Makes 8 to 10 servings

- 2 envelopes unflavored gelatin
- 1½ cups milk
- 1¼ cups sugar
- ¾ cup Hershey's® Cocoa
- 1 tablespoon light corn syrup
- 3 tablespoons butter
- 1¾ cups milk
- 1½ teaspoons vanilla extract
- 18 split ladyfingers
- 1 cup heavy cream

Mix gelatin and 1½ cups milk in saucepan; allow to soften. Combine sugar and cocoa; add to saucepan. Add corn syrup. Cook and stir until mixture boils. Remove from heat; stir in butter until melted. Blend in 1¾ cups milk and vanilla; pour into large mixer bowl. Cool; chill until almost set. Line 1½-quart mold with ladyfingers. Whip cream until stiff peaks form. Whip chocolate gelatin until smooth. Add whipped cream to chocolate on low speed just until blended. Pour into mold; chill until set. Unmold.

Chocolate Coconut Easter Egg (page 74). Photo courtesy of Knox Gelatine, Inc.

Chocolate Sponge Mold

Makes 8 servings

⅓ **cup sugar**
1 **envelope unflavored gelatin**
¼ **teaspoon salt**
1½ **cups milk**
2 **squares Baker's Unsweetened Chocolate**
3 **egg yolks, lightly beaten**
3 **egg whites**
⅓ **cup sugar**
1 **teaspoon vanilla extract**
1 **cup thawed Birds Eye Cool Whip Non-Dairy Whipped Topping**
 Flaked coconut (optional)

Combine ⅓ cup sugar, the gelatin, and salt in saucepan. Stir in milk; add chocolate. Cook and stir over low heat until chocolate is melted and gelatin is thoroughly dissolved; then blend with rotary beater. Add small amount of hot mixture to egg yolks, mixing well. Return to remaining hot mixture and cook 3 minutes longer, stirring constantly. Chill until slightly thickened.

Beat egg whites until foamy throughout. Gradually beat in ⅓ cup sugar and continue beating until mixture forms stiff, shiny peaks. Gradually fold in chocolate mixture, blending well. Add vanilla. Spoon into 4-cup mold or individual molds. Chill until firm, about 3 hours. Unmold. Garnish with whipped topping, if desired, or spread whipped topping over mold and sprinkle with flaked coconut, if desired.

Chocolate Refrigerator Cake

Makes 6 servings

3 **squares (1 ounce each) unsweetened chocolate**
6 **tablespoons granulated sugar**
3 **tablespoons milk**
3 **eggs, separated**
1 **teaspoon vanilla extract**
⅛ **teaspoon salt**
¾ **cup unsalted butter**
¾ **cup confectioners sugar**
1½ **dozen ladyfingers**
¼ **cup brandy and ¼ cup water, mixed**
½ **cup whipped cream**
 Pistachio nuts and/or cherries

Melt the chocolate with sugar and milk in top of double boiler. Add the beaten egg yolks; cook, stirring, until smooth and thick. Cool; add the vanilla and salt. Cream the butter and ½ cup of confectioners sugar and fold into the chocolate mixture. Fold in the egg whites beaten with the remaining confectioners

sugar. Line a small loaf pan with foil, or make a 6-inch springform pan. Sprinkle ladyfingers with brandy mixture and arrange them in the bottom and around the sides of the pan. You will have to break off small pieces of ladyfingers in order to make them the right size. Spoon in a layer of the chocolate mixture, add the broken ladyfingers, and cover with remaining chocolate mixture. Top with more ladyfingers. Cover with foil and chill in the refrigerator overnight. To serve, if molded in loaf pan, grasp foil liner and loosen the dessert, then invert on a serving plate. Remove foil. If molded in springform pan, remove sides, invert, and remove foil base. Garnish with whipped cream, pistachio nuts, and/or cherries.

Good to know: When preparing molded desserts, think ahead to serving them. A beautiful round dessert should have a round dish, a loaf-shaped dessert an oval or rectangular dish.

Chocolate Containers

An elegant way to serve the best berries of the season, a special dessert, or a cream confection.

Crinkle Cups. Melt 6 squares Baker's Semi-Sweet Chocolate or 1 package (4 ounces) Baker's German's Sweet Chocolate with 2 tablespoons butter or margarine in saucepan over very low heat, stirring constantly. Spread chocolate over inside of 10 aluminum foil baking cups, using a spoon to completely push chocolate over all surfaces in a thin layer. Set cups in muffin pans. Chill until firm, about 1 hour. Fill with chiffon, pudding, ice cream, or berries. Remove foil cups. Makes 6 using sweet chocolate or 10 using semi-sweet chocolate.

For Bonbon Chocolate Crinkle Cups, spread chocolate in 30 paper or aluminum foil bonbon cups. Fill with candy mixtures, liqueurs, or small berries.

Chocolate Cones. Cut waxed paper into six 5-inch squares; cut each square in half to make triangles. Roll each triangle into a cone, making sure that the tip of the cone is tightly closed, so that the chocolate will not leak; tape the cone to secure it. In the top of a small double boiler, over simmering water, melt 6 squares of semisweet chocolate; remove the chocolate from the heat before it is completely melted, and stir it smooth. Using a small, pointed paring knife, spread the inside of each cone with the chocolate, making certain to cover the cone completely. Place the cones on a plate in the freezer until the chocolate is set and firm—only a few minutes. Then—be gentle-handed—peel away the waxed paper. Freeze or refrigerate the cones until you are ready to use them.

Chocolate-Almond Trifle

Makes 8 to 10 servings

⅔ cup sugar
2 tablespoons cornstarch
⅛ teaspoon salt
2 eggs, lightly beaten
3 cups milk, scalded
3 squares Baker's Unsweetened Chocolate
½ teaspoon almond extract or 3 tablespoons almond liqueur
12 ladyfingers, split
1 pint fresh strawberries, hulled and halved
1 can (16 ounces) apricot halves, drained
   Whipped topping, Chocolate Triangles (see index), and strawberries (optional)

Combine sugar, cornstarch, and salt in bowl; add eggs and mix well. Gradually pour in hot milk, stirring constantly. Return to saucepan; cook and stir over very low heat until mixture is smooth and thickened. Remove from heat. Blend in chocolate and extract; stir until chocolate is melted. Cool slightly. Arrange ladyfingers, fruits, and chocolate custard in layers in a serving dish. Chill. Garnish with whipped topping, Chocolate Triangles, and additional strawberries, if desired.

Splendid Bavarian

The majestic Bavarian—the most sky-high, cloud-light of desserts—was first created, it is said, in the 17th century—and probably by a French chef. Garnished lavishly with whipped cream and Chocolate Curls, it is a breathtaking presentation. Bavarians made in plain, unfluted molds can be frosted, like cakes, with whipped cream, then decorated. Other chocolatey garnishes: blender-grated chocolate (toss some chilled Nestlé chocolate morsels into the blender, process for just a few seconds) and chocolate shavings.

Chocolate-Raspberry Trifle

Makes 6 to 8 servings

1 package (3 ounces) ladyfingers
¼ cup rum (optional)
½ cup raspberry preserves
1 6-ounce package (1 cup) Nestlé Toll House Semi-Sweet Chocolate Morsels
1 cup milk
1 cup sour cream
1 package (3¾ ounces) vanilla instant pudding and pie filling
1 cup heavy cream
1 tablespoon confectioners sugar

Arrange ladyfingers on bottom and up sides of a 2½-quart glass bowl. Pour rum evenly over ladyfingers. Spread preserves over ladyfingers. Cover dish with foil and chill in refrigerator about 2 hours.

Melt Nestlé Toll House Semi-Sweet Chocolate Morsels over hot (not boiling) water. Remove from heat and cool 5 minutes. In a small bowl, combine milk, sour cream, and instant pudding powder; beat until thick and creamy. Fold in melted chocolate; spoon carefully into ladyfinger-lined bowl. Chill in refrigerator at least 30 minutes.

In a small bowl, combine heavy cream and confectioners sugar; beat until stiff. Decorate top of trifle with dollops of whipped cream or pipe through a pastry tube. Refrigerate until ready to serve.

Chocolate Bavarian

Makes 12 servings

2 envelopes (2 tablespoons) unflavored gelatin
1 cup sugar, divided
¼ teaspoon salt
4 eggs, separated
2 cups milk
1 12-ounce package (2 cups) Nestlé Toll House Semi-Sweet Chocolate Morsels
2 teaspoons vanilla extract
2 cups heavy cream, whipped
   Whipped cream (optional)
   Chocolate Curls (see index) (optional)

In a large saucepan, combine gelatin, ½ cup sugar, and the salt. In a small bowl, beat egg yolks and milk; stir into gelatin mixture. Add Nestlé Toll House Semi-Sweet Chocolate Morsels and cook over medium heat, stirring constantly, until morsels are melted and gelatin is dissolved (about 8 minutes). Remove from heat and stir in vanilla extract. Chill, stirring occasionally, until mixture mounds when dropped from a spoon. In a small bowl, beat egg whites until stiff but not dry. Gradually add remaining ½ cup sugar, beating until very stiff. Fold in chilled chocolate mixture alternately with whipped cream. Turn into 8-cup decorative mold. Chill in refrigerator until firm. Unmold onto a serving platter. Garnish with whipped cream and/or Chocolate Curls, if desired.

Perky Peppermint Parfaits. Photo courtesy of Knox Gelatine, Inc.

Q. *What do I do to achieve the tempered, melted chocolate some recipes call for in the dipping process?*
A. Melt chocolate and vegetable shortening together in a small bowl in a pan of very warm (120°F.) water (2 to 3 inches below the rim of the bowl). Heat chocolate evenly and uniformly, stirring constantly, to 108°F. Remove bowl from water. Cool, stirring frequently, to 85°F. Continue stirring and scraping down the sides of the bowl until chocolate cools to 80°F. Keep at this temperature 10 minutes, stirring constantly (if necessary, briefly set bowl in warm water to maintain temperature). Place pan in warm water and heat chocolate to 86°F., holding temperature for 5 minutes. This is the correct temperature for dipping and must be maintained throughout the dipping process.

Perky Peppermint Parfaits
Makes 6 servings
    2 envelopes Knox® Unflavored Gelatine
  ½ cup cold milk
    1 cup milk, heated to boiling
    1 cup heavy cream
  ⅓ cup sugar
    2 teaspoons vanilla extract
    3 drops red food coloring
  ¼ cup peppermint candies
    1 cup ice cubes (6 to 8)
1½ cups chocolate wafer crumbs

In a 5-cup blender container, sprinkle Knox Unflavored Gelatine over cold milk; let stand 3 to 4 minutes. Add hot milk; process at low speed 2 minutes. Add heavy cream, sugar, vanilla, food coloring, and peppermint candies. Add ice cubes, 1 at a time, and process at high speed until ice is melted. Let stand until mixture is slightly thickened, about 10 minutes.

In parfait glasses or dessert dishes, alternately layer chocolate crumbs with peppermint mixture. Chill until set, about 40 minutes.

Chocolate Coconut Easter Egg
Makes about 10 servings
    1 envelope Knox® Unflavored Gelatine
    3 tablespoons sugar
    2 eggs, separated
    1 cup milk
    2 tablespoons Irish cream liqueur or ½ teaspoon
        almond extract
    4 squares (1 ounce each) semisweet chocolate
    1 cup whipping or heavy cream
  ½ cup flaked coconut
      Chocolate Curls (see index)

In medium saucepan, mix Knox Unflavored Gelatine with 2 tablespoons sugar; blend in egg yolks beaten with milk. Let stand 1 minute. Stir over low heat until gelatine is completely dissolved, about 5 minutes. Add chocolate and continue cooking over low heat, stirring constantly, until chocolate is melted. With wire whip or rotary beater, beat mixture until chocolate is blended. Stir in liqueur. Pour into large bowl and chill, stirring occasionally, until mixture mounds slightly when dropped from spoon.

In medium bowl, beat egg whites until soft peaks form; gradually add remaining sugar and beat until stiff. Fold egg whites, then ½ cup whipped heavy cream, and coconut into chocolate mixture. Turn into 5-cup mold or bowl; chill until firm. Garnish with remaining whipped cream and, if desired, Chocolate Curls.

Chocolate-Raspberry Trifle (page 73). Courtesy of Nestlé Foods Corporation

Chocolate Lover's Cheesecake Dessert
Makes about 10 servings

1½ cups Hershey's® Mini Chips® Semi-Sweet
    Chocolate
2 packages (8 ounces and 3 ounces) cream cheese
⅓ cup sugar
¼ cup butter, softened
1½ teaspoons vanilla extract
¾ cup chopped pecans
1 cup heavy cream
    Chocolate Glaze (recipe follows)
    Whipped Cream Frosting (recipe follows)
    Chocolate Curls (see index) or chopped nuts
    (optional)

Melt Mini Chips semi-sweet chocolate in top of double boiler over hot water or place in glass mixing bowl and microwave on full power for 1½ minutes; stir until melted. Combine cream cheese, sugar, and butter in large mixer bowl; beat until smooth and creamy. Add vanilla. Beat in melted chocolate and pecans until well blended. Whip heavy cream until stiff peaks form; fold into chocolate cheese mixture. Line a 5-cup heart-shaped mold or 10 individual ½-cup heart-shaped molds with aluminum foil. Spoon mixture into mold(s). Chill completely. Prepare Chocolate Glaze, Whipped Cream Frosting, and Chocolate Curls, if desired. Invert chilled dessert onto serving tray; peel off foil. Glaze top; frost sides and pipe with remaining whipped cream. Decorate with Chocolate Curls or chopped nuts, if desired.
Note: Double Whipped Cream Frosting and Chocolate Glaze recipes for individual molds; eliminate Chocolate Curls.

Chocolate Glaze
1 4-ounce Hershey's® Milk Chocolate Bar
2 tablespoons water

Combine chocolate bar and water in top of double boiler. Place over hot water to melt, stirring occasionally. Cool slightly.

Whipped Cream Frosting
½ cup heavy cream
2 tablespoons confectioners sugar
½ teaspoon vanilla extract

Combine cream, confectioners sugar, and vanilla in small mixer bowl; beat until stiff peaks form.

Frozen Chocolate Pots
Makes 8 servings

1 chocolate bar with almonds (8 ounces)
½ cup Coffee Rich
1 cup small marshmallows
1 package (8 ounces) Richwhip, whipped, or 1
    tub (9 ounces) Rich's Whipped Topping—
    Spoon and Serve
8 whole almonds (optional)
8 Chocolate Curls (see index) (optional)

Melt chocolate bar and marshmallows with Coffee Rich in top of double boiler over simmering water. Mix until blended. Cool in refrigerator or freezer. Fold whipped topping into the cooled chocolate mixture. Pour into eight pot de crème cups, demitasse cups, or juice or wine glasses. Freeze.

Remove from freezer and serve as you would ice cream. Garnish with whipped topping and one almond, or Chocolate Curls, or as desired.

Spiced Rum Chocolate Parfaits
Makes 4 servings

1 cup chocolate cookie crumbs
2 tablespoons Captain Morgan Spiced Rum
1 pint coffee ice cream, softened
    Whipped cream
4 ounces semisweet chocolate pieces
3 tablespoons Captain Morgan Spiced Rum

Combine cookie crumbs and Spiced Rum; place a spoonful in bottoms of parfait glasses. Alternate layers of ice cream and cookies; top with whipped cream. Melt chocolate pieces in heavy saucepan or double boiler; stir in Spiced Rum. Spoon sauce over parfaits.

Super Sundaes

Why stop with just hot fudge and whipped cream? Add some of these chocolate toppings for a really special treat:

    shaved chocolate
    chocolate covered raisins or cherries
    crumbled chocolate or chocolate chip cookies
    chunks of chocolate bars
    pieces of chocolate-mint candies
    crumbled chocolate-peanut butter candies
    chocolate liqueur
    chocolate sprinkles
    brownies, chopped into small cubes
    sweetened cocoa powder

Easy Homemade Chocolate Ice Cream

Makes about 1½ quarts ice cream
   **1 can (14 ounces) Eagle® Brand Sweetened
      Condensed Milk (not evaporated milk)**
   ⅔ cup chocolate-flavored syrup
   2 cups whipping cream, whipped

In large bowl, stir together Eagle Brand and syrup. Fold in whipped cream. Pour into aluminum foil-lined 9 × 5 × 3-inch loaf pan; cover. Freeze 6 hours, or until firm. Scoop ice cream from pan or remove from pan, peel off foil, and slice. Return leftovers to freezer.

French Vanilla

In large bowl, combine Eagle Brand, 2 tablespoons water, 3 beaten egg yolks, and 4 teaspoons vanilla extract. Fold in whipped cream.

Mint Chocolate Chip

In large bowl, combine Eagle Brand, 2 teaspoons peppermint extract, 3 to 4 drops green food color, and 2 tablespoons water. Fold in whipped cream and ½ cup small dark chocolate-flavored baking chips.

Coffee

In large bowl, combine Eagle Brand, 1 tablespoon instant coffee dissolved in 2 tablespoons water, 2 beaten egg yolks, and 4 teaspoons vanilla extract. Fold in whipped cream.

Strawberry

Thaw 1 package (10 ounces) frozen strawberries in syrup. With blender, blend strawberries until smooth. In large bowl, combine strawberries and Eagle Brand. Fold in whipped cream.

Peppermint Candy

In large bowl, combine 3 beaten egg yolks, 2 tablespoons water, Eagle Brand, and 4 teaspoons vanilla extract. Fold in whipped cream and ¼ to ½ cup crushed hard peppermint candy.

Chocolate-Flecked Granita

Makes 4 servings
   ½ cup sugar
   1 to 2 tablespoons Maxwell House Instant Coffee
   2 cups hot water
   2 teaspoons vanilla extract
   **½ square Baker's Unsweetened Chocolate, grated
      Whipped topping (optional)**

Dissolve sugar and instant coffee in hot water. Add vanilla and pour into 8-inch square pan. Freeze until almost firm, about 1 hour. Break up with fork and stir in grated chocolate. Return to freezer and freeze until firm. Break up again with fork and spoon into small brandy glasses or sherbet glasses. Top with prepared whipped topping, if desired.

Blender Chocolate Ice Cream

Makes 1 quart ice cream
   ½ cup sugar
   ½ cup water
   **1 6-ounce package (1 cup) Nestlé Toll House
      Semi-Sweet Chocolate Morsels**
   2 eggs
   2 teaspoons vanilla extract
   ½ teaspoon salt
   1½ cups heavy cream, whipped

In a small saucepan, combine sugar and water. Bring to a boil over moderate heat; boil 3 minutes, then remove from heat. In blender container, combine Nestlé Toll House Semi-Sweet Chocolate Morsels and hot sugar syrup; process at high speed about 6 seconds. Add eggs, vanilla, and salt; blend for about 1 minute. Pour over whipped cream and mix well. Pour into 9 × 5 × 3-inch loaf pan. Freeze until firm.

Cups of Chocolate Cheer

Long before anyone thought of using solid chocolate, chocolate was considered a drink fit for kings. It was not until the eighteenth century that use of solid chocolate surpassed liquid. Even today, there's nothing like a glass of cold chocolate milk to cheer you up on a hot day. Or try one of these chocolate coolers:

Egg Cream

Makes 1 serving
   3 tablespoons chocolate syrup
   ¾ cup very cold milk
   ¼ cup very cold seltzer

Mix syrup with milk; stir well. Add seltzer and stir once.

Chocolate Ice Cream Soda

Makes 1 serving
   2 tablespoons chocolate syrup
   1 cup soda (seltzer or cola)
   1 scoop chocolate (or favorite) ice cream

Mix syrup and soda. Add scoop of ice cream.

Cinnamon-Chocolate Drink

Makes 1 serving
   1 cup milk
   2 tablespoons cocoa powder
   2 tablespoons sugar
   1 teaspoon cinnamon
   1 teaspoon nutmeg

Mix all ingredients in a small saucepan. Heat, stirring constantly, until sugar is dissolved. Chill well before serving.

Super Scoops

Makes 1 quart flavored ice cream

Place 1 quart ice cream in mixing bowl to soften ice cream. Let stand about 5 minutes or until slightly soft. Beat with wooden spoon until thick and of spoonable consistency. Add ingredients as per flavor desired below; mix until well blended. Return to original ice cream container; freeze overnight or until firm. Serve in cones or dessert dishes.

Vibrant Vanilla

Add 1/2 to 3/4 cup chopped, frozen "M&M's" Plain Chocolate Candies and 1/2 teaspoon grated lemon or orange rind (or substitute 1/4 teaspoon orange or lemon extract for grated rind) to softened vanilla ice cream; mix well. Freeze as directed.

Perky Pistachio

Add 1/2 to 3/4 cup chopped, frozen "M&M's" Plain Chocolate Candies, 1/4 teaspoon almond extract, and 8 to 10 drops green food color to softened vanilla ice cream; mix well. Freeze as directed.

Peanut Butter Chip

Add 2 tablespoons creamy peanut butter to softened vanilla ice cream; mix until well blended. Fold in 1/2 to 3/4 cup chopped, frozen "M&M's" Plain Chocolate Candies. Freeze as directed.

Heavenly Hash

Add 3/4 cup marshmallow creme to softened chocolate ice cream; mix until marbled. Fold in 1 cup chopped, toasted almonds and 3/4 to 1 cup chopped, frozen "M&M's" Plain Chocolate Candies. Freeze as directed.

Note: All recipe ingredients double easily to make 1/2 gallon flavored ice cream.

Carnival Ice Cream

Makes 8 or 16 servings

  ½ **gallon vanilla ice cream, softened**
1½ **teaspoons almond extract, rum extract, or peppermint extract**
1½ **cups "M&M's" Plain Chocolate Candies, coarsely chopped and frozen**

Beat together ice cream and extract in large mixing bowl until thick and of spoonable consistency. (Return to freezer if mixture becomes too soft or slightly melted.) Fold in candies. Spoon about ¾ cup mixture into dessert dishes or ½ cup mixture into medium-size muffin pans lined with foil baking cups. Freeze 6 to 8 hours or overnight.

Variations

Spoon ice cream mixture into 9-inch prepared graham cracker crust; freeze. Cut into wedges to serve.

Brownie Bombe

Spoon ice cream mixture into 9×5×3-inch loaf pan; freeze. Scoop into dessert dishes or ice cream cones and serve.

Brownie Bombe

Makes 8 servings

  1 **small package brownie mix**
  1 **quart pistachio ice cream**
  1 **quart strawberry ice cream**
  3 **egg whites, room temperature**
  ½ **teaspoon cream of tartar**
  ½ **cup sugar**
  ½ **teaspoon vanilla extract**

Prepare brownie mix according to package directions; bake in a 9-inch round pie pan. Cool brownie and place on large serving platter.

Allow pistachio ice cream to soften partially; place it on the center of the brownie, and shape it into a mound. Place platter with brownie and pistachio ice cream in freezer until it gets completely hard. Meanwhile, soften strawberry ice cream. With a spatula, spread strawberry ice cream around pistachio ice cream, retaining the mound shape. Work quickly, so that pistachio ice cream does not melt. Return platter to freezer so that both ice creams freeze solidly.

Preheat oven to 450°F. Beat egg whites until foamy. Then add cream of tartar and beat until soft peaks form. Add sugar gradually; continue beating at high speed until stiff peaks form. Fold in vanilla.

Spread meringue over ice cream and brownie base, making sure that all edges are sealed. Place in oven until meringue begins to brown, about 5 minutes. Serve immediately.

Colorful Ice Creamwiches

Makes 14 ice cream sandwiches

- ¾ **cup margarine**
- ¾ **cup creamy peanut butter**
- 1¼ **cups firmly packed light brown sugar**
- 1 **egg**
- 1 **teaspoon vanilla extract**
- 1¼ **cups all-purpose flour**
- 1 **teaspoon baking soda**
- ¼ **teaspoon salt**
- 1 **cup chopped "M&M's" Plain Chocolate Candies**
- 3 **pints chocolate or vanilla ice cream, slightly softened**

Beat together margarine, peanut butter, and sugar until light and fluffy; blend in egg and vanilla. Add combined flour, baking soda, and salt; mix well. Stir in candies. Shape dough to form 1¼-inch balls; place on lightly greased cookie sheet about 3 inches apart. Flatten dough to ¼-inch thickness. Sprinkle with additional chopped candies; press in lightly. Bake at 350°F. for 10 to 12 minutes, or until edges are lightly browned. Cool on cookie sheet about 3 minutes; remove to wire rack to cool thoroughly. For each ice cream sandwich, spread about ½ cup ice cream onto bottom of cooled cookie. Top with second cookie; press together lightly. Wrap in foil; freeze.

Q. *I don't have an ice-cream freezer. Is there any way I can make ice cream without one?*

A. Try the ice-tray freezing method. Follow the recipe for any ice cream up to the point where you pour it into the freezer. Pour the ice-cream mixture into an ice-cube tray or trays, minus the divider. Cover with foil, stick the tray back where it came from, and go about your business. When the top and sides are frozen but the center is still soft, remove the tray from the freezer, turn the ice cream into a bowl, and beat it. Return ice cream to the tray and the tray to the freezer, and let it freeze firm. Beating breaks up frozen lumps, as well as ice crystals, making for a smoother product.

The result is not as good as hand- or electric-churned ice cream, but it is quite acceptable.

Carnival Ice Cream (page 78); Crispy Creamy Freeze (page 81); Colorful Ice Creamwiches. "M&M's" Chocolate Candies

Old-Fashioned Chocolate Ice Cream

Makes 1½ quarts ice cream
- 1 **envelope unflavored gelatin**
- ¾ **cup milk**
- ¾ **cup sugar**
- ¾ **cup Hershey's® Syrup**
- 1 **cup light cream**
- 1 **cup heavy cream**
- 1 **tablespoon vanilla extract**

Soften gelatin in milk for 5 minutes in small saucepan. Add sugar; cook over medium heat, stirring constantly, until gelatin and sugar are dissolved. Remove from heat; pour into large mixer bowl. Add chocolate syrup, light cream, heavy cream, and vanilla. Place in refrigerator freezer, stirring occasionally, until partially frozen. Remove from freezer; beat until slushy. Return to freezer, stirring occasionally during the first hour. Freeze until firm.

Note: May also be frozen in crank-type freezer following freezer manufacturer's directions.

Easy Chocolate Ice Cream

Makes 1½ quarts
- 1⅓ **cups (14-ounce can) sweetened condensed milk**
- ⅔ **cup Hershey's® Syrup**
- 2 **cups heavy cream**

Stir together sweetened condensed milk and chocolate syrup in large bowl. Whip heavy cream until stiff; fold in. Cover; freeze until firm, stirring occasionally during the first hour.

Myers's Mocha Cream Crunch

Makes 1 serving
- 1½ **ounces Myers's Original Rum Cream**
  Coffee ice cream
- 1 **cup crushed chocolate wafers**
  Whipped cream

Combine cookie crumbs with Myers's Original Rum Cream. Place a spoonful of mixture in bottom of parfait glass. Alternate with layers of coffee ice cream. Top with whipped cream.

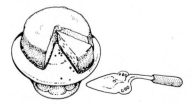

Homemade Is Heavenly

Making ice cream at home as a family project or an everybody-pitch-in party can be fun. And it's no longer the hard work it once was. The ingredients for the mix are easy to come by, and so is the small amount of personpower required. But you do need a freezer of one sort or another.

Churn freezers: These are the old-fashioned jobs—a canister to hold the mixture (the dasher to stir it goes inside), plus an outer tub to hold ice and salt jacketed around the canister, plus power—electric or elbow-grease variety. If the latter, the buddy system is best; a lone cranker is inclined to get cranky over the long haul.

First, fill the freezer canister two-thirds full (ice cream expands as it freezes). Fit the canister into the freezer. Set the dasher in place, and put on the cover securely. Pack crushed ice and rock salt around the canister to the top of the freezer, 6 parts ice to 1 part salt. Turn the handle, adding more ice and salt as necessary, until it becomes very difficult to turn. Then stop—all the cranking in the world won't improve things past this point. Take out ice to below the canister cover; uncover and take out the dasher. Cover the canister with several thicknesses of foil or waxed paper and replace the cover, corking or otherwise plugging the hole in it. Again pack the freezer with ice and salt, 4 parts to 1 this time, and let the whole business stand, covered with a heavy cloth or newspapers, for about 4 hours to ripen. Or, if there's room, place the covered canister in your home freezer for the ripening period. And, of course, if your machine is electric, all that cranking isn't necessary—just follow the maker's instructions. Churn freezers usually produce 6 to 8 quarts of ice cream, making the game well worth the candle.

Little electric freezers: There are two kinds of these, one that goes inside your home freezer, substituting the freezer's cold air for salt and ice; and a tabletop model that uses ice cubes and regular table salt. Both may be battery operated or be plugged into a receptacle (the in-freezer kind has a flat cord that does not interfere with closing the freezer door). Both these freezers make 1 quart, a few models up to 2 quarts of ice cream at a time.

These little jobs are not particularly expensive, but they have a rich relation, product of a San Francisco gourmet food/utensil specialty store, that would knock your eye out in more ways than one. This is a white countertop dingus with a removable stainless steel tub in its center. Fill the tub with whatever ice cream, ice, or sherbet mixture you wish, plug the thing in, turn it on—and that's it. No salt. No ice. The freezer has its own self-contained, sealed refrigeration unit. It makes only a quart at a time, but can turn out a quart every 15 minutes.

Myers's After-Dinner Mint

Makes 1 serving

- 1 ounce Myers's Original Rum Cream
  Mint chocolate chip ice cream
  Whipped cream

Layer Myers's Original Rum Cream and ice cream in parfait glass. Top with whipped cream.

Crispy Creamy Freeze

Makes 9 servings

- ¼ cup vegetable oil
- 1¾ cups "M&M's" Plain Chocolate Candies
- 1½ cups crisp rice cereal
- 1 quart favorite-flavor ice cream, slightly softened

Heat oil in 2-quart heavy saucepan over medium heat about 2 minutes; add 1½ cups candies, reserving ¼ cup for topping. Cook mixture over very low heat, stirring constantly with metal spoon and pressing candies with back of spoon to break up. (Chocolate mixture will be almost melted and pieces of color coating will remain.) Remove from heat; add cereal, mixing lightly until thoroughly coated. Press mixture evenly onto bottom of lightly oiled, prepared★ 9-inch square baking pan. Freeze crust about 30 minutes. Spoon softened ice cream over frozen crust; sprinkle with reserved ¼ cup candies, chopped. Cover with plastic wrap or foil; freeze overnight. Remove from freezer about 5 minutes before serving. Gently remove dessert from pan, using foil liner to lift out. Cut into squares to serve.

★ To prepare pan, line bottom with aluminum foil extending up over 2 sides of pan; lightly oil with 1 to 2 teaspoons vegetable oil.

Easy Spumoni Mold

Makes 8 to 10 servings

- 1 quart chocolate or vanilla ice cream, softened
- 1 cup cold milk
- 1 tablespoon Maxwell House Instant Coffee
- 2 envelopes Dream Whip Whipped Topping Mix
- ½ cup maraschino cherries, quartered, or ½ cup chopped mixed candied fruits
- ½ cup toasted slivered almonds

Press ice cream firmly on bottom and sides of aluminum foil- or plastic wrap-lined 9 × 5 × 3-inch loaf pan, leaving depression in center. Freeze until firm.

Meanwhile, combine milk, instant coffee, and whipped topping mix in deep narrow-bottom mixer bowl. Beat at high speed of electric mixer until topping peaks, about 2 minutes. Continue beating 2 minutes longer. Fold in cherries and almonds. Spoon into center of ice cream shell. Cover with aluminum foil or plastic wrap and freeze at least 4 hours. Unmold and remove foil. Garnish with prepared whipped topping and additional cherries and almonds, if desired.

Toll House Treatwiches

Makes 21 ice cream sandwiches

- 2¼ cups all-purpose flour
- 1 teaspoon baking soda
- 1 teaspoon salt
- 1 cup butter, softened
- ¾ cup sugar
- ¾ cup firmly packed brown sugar
- 1 teaspoon vanilla extract
- 2 eggs
- 1 12-ounce package (2 cups) Nestlé Toll House Semi-Sweet Chocolate Morsels
- 1 cup chopped nuts
- 1 quart ice cream, softened

Preheat oven to 375°F In a small bowl, combine flour, baking soda, and salt; set aside. In a large bowl, combine butter, sugar, brown sugar, and vanilla; beat until creamy. Beat in eggs. Gradually add flour mixture; mix well. Stir in Nestlé Toll House Semi-Sweet Chocolate Morsels and nuts. Drop by rounded tablespoons onto ungreased cookie sheets. Press dough into 2-inch circles. Bake 10 to 12 minutes. Cool 1 minute; remove from cookie sheets. Cool completely. Spread 2 to 3 tablespoons ice cream onto bottom of one cookie. Top with another cookie. Repeat with remaining cookies. Wrap each ice cream sandwich in aluminum foil or plastic wrap. Freeze until ready to serve.

Brownie Ice-Cream Loaf

Makes 10 to 12 servings

1½ cups sugar
 1 cup Bisquick baking mix
 ¾ cup chopped nuts
 ¾ cup margarine or butter, melted
1½ teaspoons vanilla extract
 3 eggs
 3 ounces melted unsweetened chocolate, cooled
 1 quart ice cream, slightly softened
 Confectioners sugar
 Whipped cream
 Fudge sauce

Heat oven to 350°F. Line 15½ × 10½ × 1-inch jelly roll pan with aluminum foil; grease foil. Mix all ingredients except ice cream and confectioners sugar; beat vigorously 30 strokes. Spread in pan. Bake until set, about 25 minutes. Cool brownie in pan on wire rack. Invert on rack or cookie sheet; remove foil. Cut brownie crosswise into 3 equal parts. Place one part brownie on plate; spread with half of the ice cream. Top with another part brownie, the remaining ice cream, and the remaining part brownie. Sprinkle with confectioners sugar. Wrap and freeze until firm, at least 8 hours.

Remove from freezer 10 minutes before serving. Cut into slices; serve with whipped cream or fudge sauce, if desired. Freeze any remaining loaf.

Chocolate Mousse Pie au Rhum

Makes 1 pie

1½ tablespoons sugar
 1 package (8 squares) Baker's Semi-Sweet Chocolate
 ¼ cup water
 8 eggs, separated
 ⅔ cup sugar
1½ teaspoons vanilla extract
 1 teaspoon rum extract★
 Dash of salt
 1 cup sweetened whipped cream or thawed Birds Eye Cool Whip Non-Dairy Whipped Topping
 Chocolate-Dipped Fruit Morsels (recipe follows)

Sprinkle 1½ tablespoons sugar evenly on bottom and sides of well-buttered 9-inch pie pan. Melt chocolate in water in saucepan over very low heat, stirring constantly until smooth. Remove from heat. Beat egg yolks; gradually add ⅔ cup sugar and continue beating until yolks are thick and light in color. Blend

Chocolate Bavarian (page 73). Courtesy of Nestlé Foods Corporation

Brownie Ice-Cream Loaf. Courtesy of Bisquick®

in chocolate, vanilla, and rum extract. Beat egg whites and salt until mixture forms stiff peaks. Fold carefully into chocolate mixture blending well. Measure 4 cups into prepared pie pan. Bake at 350°F. 25 to 30 minutes, or until puffed and firm. Cool 15 minutes; then chill 1 hour. (Center will fall, forming a shell.) Meanwhile, chill remaining chocolate mixture about 1½ hours; spoon into chilled shell. Chill at least 3 hours. Before serving, garnish with sweetened whipped cream and Chocolate-Dipped Fruit Morsels.

★ Or use ¼ cup dark rum; or use 2 tablespoons orange liqueur and omit vanilla.

Chocolate-Dipped Fruit Morsels

Makes 1 to 1½ dozen morsels

 4 squares (1 ounce each) Baker's Semi-Sweet Chocolate
 Assorted fruits: firm strawberries, ½-inch banana slices, fresh pineapple wedges or drained canned pineapple chunks, peeled orange slices, orange wedges, well-drained stemmed maraschino cherries, dried figs, dried dates, or dried apricots

Melt chocolate in saucepan over very low heat, stirring constantly until smooth. Insert wooden picks or skewers into fruit. Dip quickly, 1 at a time, into chocolate. Let stand or chill on rack or waxed paper until chocolate is firm. For best eating quality, chill dipped fresh or canned fruits and serve the same day.

Mud Pie

Makes one 9-inch pie

- 1 can (14 ounces) Eagle® Brand Sweetened Condensed Milk (not evaporated milk)
- 3 egg yolks★
- 4 teaspoons vanilla extract
- 1 cup coarsely crushed cream-filled chocolate sandwich cookies (12 cookies)
- 2 cups whipping cream, whipped (do not use non-dairy whipped topping)
- 1 9-inch chocolate crumb crust
  Chocolate fudge ice cream topping or chocolate-flavored syrup
  Chopped nuts

In large mixer bowl, beat sweetened condensed milk, egg yolks, and vanilla until well blended. Fold in cookies and whipped cream. Pour into 9 × 5 × 3-inch loaf pan or other 2-quart container; cover. Freeze 6 hours, or until firm. Scoop ice cream into prepared crust. Drizzle with topping. Garnish with nuts. Serve. Return leftovers to freezer.
★ Use only Grade A clean, uncracked eggs.

Chocolate Almond Layer Pie

Makes one 9-inch pie

- 1 can (12½ ounces) Solo Almond Filling
- 3 tablespoons crème de cacao, brandy, or desired liqueur
- 1 baked 9-inch pie shell
- 1 pint chocolate ice cream, softened
- ¼ cup chopped toasted almonds
- 3 egg whites
- 6 tablespoons sugar
- ½ teaspoon vanilla extract

Combine almond filling and liqueur and blend well. Spread half of the filling in bottom of baked pie shell. Spread softened ice cream over filling. Top with remaining almond filling. Sprinkle chopped almonds over top. Freeze at least 6 to 8 hours or overnight. Preheat oven to 500°F. Beat egg whites just until stiff. Beat in sugar, 1 tablespoon at a time, and continue beating until mixture is stiff and glossy. Beat in vanilla. Spread meringue over top of pie, making sure that the meringue covers the crust of the pie and seals in the ice cream completely. Bake 3 to 5 minutes, or until meringue is lightly browned. Serve immediately, or return to freezer until serving time.

Chocolate Cappuccino Mousse Pie

Makes one 10-inch pie

- 1 package (8½ ounces) chocolate wafers
- 4 tablespoons butter, melted
- ½ teaspoon ground cinnamon
- ¼ teaspoon ground nutmeg
- 1 12-ounce package (2 cups) Nestlé Toll House Semi-Sweet Chocolate Morsels
- 2 tablespoons butter
- 4 eggs, separated
- 3 tablespoons orange liqueur
- 2 cups heavy cream
- 1½ tablespoons powdered instant coffee
- ⅓ cup sifted confectioners sugar
  Ground cinnamon (optional)
  Ground nutmeg (optional)
  Maraschino cherry slices (optional)

Preheat oven to 325°F. In blender container, grind chocolate wafers until crumbs are very fine. Transfer to a small bowl. Add butter, cinnamon, and nutmeg; mix well. Pat into bottom and up sides of a 10-inch pie plate. Bake 10 minutes. Remove from oven and cool completely.

In a medium heavy-duty saucepan, combine Nestlé Toll House Semi-Sweet Chocolate Morsels, butter, and egg yolks. Cook over very low heat, stirring occasionally, until mixture is melted and smooth. Remove from heat; transfer to a large bowl. In a small bowl, beat egg whites until stiff peaks form. Mix about ¼ cup beaten egg whites into chocolate mixture. Fold in remaining egg whites and orange liqueur. In a small bowl, combine heavy cream, instant coffee, and confectioners sugar. Beat until stiff. Reserve 1 cup whipped cream for garnish. Fold remaining whipped cream into chocolate mixture. Pour into prepared chocolate crumb crust. Chill in refrigerator for 15 minutes until filling is slightly set. Garnish with reserved whipped cream. Lightly sprinkle whipped cream with cinnamon and nutmeg. Top with maraschino cherry slices, if desired. Freeze at least 8 hours, or overnight. Remove from freezer to refrigerator 30 minutes before serving. Cut into small wedges.

Chocolate Icebox Cake

Makes 4 or 5 servings

- 12 ladyfingers, split
- 1 package (4 ounces) Baker's German's Sweet Chocolate
- 1½ tablespoons water
- 1 egg yolk
- 1 tablespoon confectioners sugar
- 1 cup Birds Eye Cool Whip Non-Dairy Whipped Topping
- 1 egg white, stiffly beaten
  Whipped topping (optional)

Line an 8 × 4-inch loaf pan with waxed paper. Place 6 ladyfingers on bottom of pan; set aside 6 for top. Cut remaining ladyfingers in half and place cut side up around sides of pan. Melt chocolate over very low heat, stirring constantly; blend in water. Remove from heat and add egg yolk, beating vigorously until smooth. Blend in sugar; cool. Fold in whipped topping and beaten egg white. Spoon into pan and top with reserved ladyfingers. Chill overnight. Unmold and remove paper. Garnish with additional whipped topping, if desired.

Frozen Mocha Cheesecake
Makes 12 to 15 servings
- 1¼ cups chocolate wafer cookie crumbs (about 24 cookies)
- ¼ cup sugar
- ¼ cup margarine or butter, melted
- 1 package (8 ounces) cream cheese, softened
- 1 can (14 ounces) Eagle® Brand Sweetened Condensed Milk (not evaporated milk)
- ⅔ cup chocolate-flavored syrup
- 2 tablespoons instant coffee
- 1 teaspoon hot water
- 1 cup whipping cream, whipped
  Additional chocolate crumbs (optional)

In small bowl, combine crumbs, sugar, and margarine. In buttered 9-inch springform pan or 13 × 9 × 2-inch baking dish, pat crumbs firmly on bottom and up sides of pan. Chill. In large mixer bowl, beat cheese until fluffy; add Eagle Brand and chocolate syrup. In small bowl, dissolve coffee in water; add to Eagle Brand mixture. Mix well. Fold in whipped cream. Pour into prepared pan. Cover. Freeze 6 hours, or until firm. Garnish with additional chocolate crumbs, if desired. Return leftovers to freezer.

German Chocolate Cheesecake
Makes about 9 servings
- 1 bar (4 ounces) sweet cooking chocolate
- 2 cups milk, divided
- ¼ cup butter or margarine
- 1 cup flaked coconut
- 1 cup finely chopped pecans
- 2 envelopes Knox® Unflavored Gelatine
- ¾ cup sugar, divided
- 3 eggs, separated
- 2 teaspoons vanilla extract
- 2 packages (8 ounces each) cream cheese, softened
  Pecan halves (optional)

In a small saucepan, over low heat, melt chocolate with ¼ cup milk; reserve ⅓ cup of mixture. To remaining chocolate mixture add butter, stirring until it melts. Stir in coconut and pecans. Press mixture onto bottom of a 9-inch-square baking pan and chill.

In a medium saucepan, mix Knox Unflavored Gelatine with ½ cup sugar. Beat egg yolks with remaining 1¾ cups milk; blend into gelatine mixture. Stir over low heat until gelatine is completely dissolved, about 5 minutes. Remove from heat; add vanilla.

In a large bowl, beat cream cheese until smooth; gradually beat in gelatine mixture. Chill, stirring occasionally, until mixture mounds slightly when dropped from a spoon.

In a small bowl, beat egg whites until soft peaks form; gradually add remaining ¼ cup sugar and beat until stiff. Fold in cheese mixture. Into 2 cups cheese mixture, blend reserved chocolate; alternate spoonfuls of chocolate and plain mixtures in prepared pan. Gently swirl with a knife to marble; chill until firm. To serve, cut into squares. Garnish with pecan halves, if desired.

If You're in a Hurry
There are ways to speed up the chilling time of gelatin mixtures—by choosing the right containers or using one of these specially developed speed sets:

The container you use can help hasten the setting. Use metal bowls or molds, rather than glass or china. Metal chills more quickly and the gelatin will be firm in less time than in glass bowls. Individual servings in small molds or serving dishes will also chill more quickly than large servings.

Speed-set method: Completely dissolve gelatin in ¾ cup boiling water (1½ cups for 6-ounce package). Combine ½ cup cold water (1 cup for 6-ounce package) and ice cubes to make 1¼ cups ice and water (2½ cups for 6-ounce package). Add to gelatin, stirring until slightly thickened. If necessary, remove unmelted ice. Chill. Soft-set and ready to eat in about 30 minutes. Do not use this method if mixture is to be molded.

The blender method: Put gelatin (3-ounce package) and ¾ cup boiling water in blender and blend at low speed until dissolved, about 1 minute. Add 1½ cups crushed ice and blend at high speed until ice is melted, about 30 seconds. Pour into individual dishes or serving bowl and chill at least 30 minutes. Mixture is self-layering, with frothy layer on top, clear layer below.

The ice bath: Another way to hasten thickening of gelatin is to place the bowl of gelatin mixture in another bowl of ice and water; stir occasionally as mixture chills to ensure even thickening.

Chocolate Dreams

A confectioner's collection of velvety truffles, spirited balls and nutty clusters, creamy fudges, and crunchy chocolate snacks.

Mocha-Rum Truffles

Makes 5 dozen candies

- 1 12-ounce package (2 cups) Nestlé Toll House Semi-Sweet Chocolate Morsels
- ½ cup butter, softened
- 4 egg yolks
- 2 tablespoons rum
- 2 teaspoons instant coffee
  Confectioners sugar
  Candied fruit and/or Nestlé Milk Chocolate Morsels and/or Nestlé Butterscotch Flavored Morsels (all optional)

Melt Nestlé Toll House Semi-Sweet Chocolate Morsels over hot (not boiling) water; remove from heat but keep chocolate over hot water. Add butter and egg yolks; beat with wire whisk or fork until smooth. In a small bowl, combine rum and coffee. Add chocolate mixture; stir until smooth. Set bowl over an ice bath; chill mixture 20 to 25 minutes, stirring occasionally, until fudgelike in consistency (yet smooth and creamy). Mixture will be quite thick. Fill a pastry bag fitted with rosette tip with a third of the chocolate mixture. Pipe 1-inch rosettes onto cookie sheets.★ Sift confectioners sugar over candies. Decorate with candied fruit and/or Nestlé Milk Chocolate Morsels and/or Nestlé Butterscotch Flavored Morsels, if desired. Repeat with remaining chocolate mixture. Let candies stand at room temperature several hours to season.

★ Chocolate mixture may be shaped into 1-inch balls, then rolled in confectioners sugar.

Chocolate Truffles

Makes 3 dozen candies

- ½ cup heavy cream
- ⅓ cup sugar
- 6 tablespoons sweet or regular butter
- 1 cup (6 ounces) Hershey's® Mini Chips® Semi-Sweet Chocolate
- 1 teaspoon vanilla extract
  Finely chopped nuts, shaved chocolate, or confectioners sugar

Combine heavy cream, sugar, and butter in saucepan; bring just to boil. Remove from heat; immediately add 1 cup Mini Chips semi-sweet chocolate. Stir until chips are melted; add vanilla. Pour into bowl; cool, stirring occasionally. Cover; chill in refrigerator several hours, preferably overnight, to allow mixture to ripen and harden. Form mixture into ½-inch balls, working quickly to prevent melting. Roll in chopped nuts, shaved chocolate, or confectioners sugar. Store in refrigerator; serve cold.

Gift-Giving Truffles

Prepare as above. After shaping into ½-inch balls, place on tray; cover loosely. Chill several hours. Melt 1 cup Mini Chips semi-sweet chocolate with 1 tablespoon shortening in top of double boiler over hot water (avoid getting water in chocolate). Place about ½ teaspoon chocolate in palm of hand, quickly roll truffle in this small amount chocolate, and drop into nuts or finely shaved chocolate, rolling to lightly coat the truffle. Chill completely.

Two-Tone Fudge (page 100); Mocha Rum Truffles; Snow Caps (page 97); Chocolate-Mint Fancies (page 97). Courtesy of Nestlé Foods Corporation

87

Valentine Cranberry Truffles

Makes 6 dozen candies

    1 bag (12 ounces) Ocean Spray Fresh or Frozen
       Cranberries
    1 cup water
    1 cup granulated sugar
    ½ cup firmly packed brown sugar
    1 orange, juice and grated rind
    ⅔ cup brandy
    2 cups toasted walnuts
    2 pounds unsweetened chocolate
    ½ pound butter, cubed
    ⅓ cup honey
    1½ cups powdered cocoa
    ½ cup confectioners sugar
    2 tablespoons honey

In a heavy saucepan, combine cranberries, granulated and brown sugars, the orange juice with its
rind, and water. Bring to a boil, stirring frequently.
Simmer for 15 minutes, until berries are popped and
mixture becomes jellylike. Add the brandy and cook
for 5 more minutes. Let cool. Purée mixture until
smooth, stirring frequently. Pour into a 13×9×2-
inch cake pan and freeze until firm enough to form
balls with a melon scoop. Meanwhile, toast walnuts
for 10 minutes in a 300°F oven. Cool. Chop finely.

Put chopped walnut mixture in a flat pan. Form
"cranberry balls" with melon scooper, dropping them
into the chopped walnuts, rolling them to coat completely, and returning them to the freezer to become
firm once again, approximately 45 minutes.

Chop chocolate into coarse pieces. Place half in top
of a double boiler with ½ pound cubed butter and ⅓
cup honey. Stir over hot, not boiling, water until
ingredients are smooth. Remove from heat and cool
slightly.

Check chocolate-butter mixture. If it has gotten
too thick, put over hot water to remelt. (This mixture
should be thin enough to coat cranberry balls as they
are dipped.) Dip walnut-coated cranberry balls, 1 by
1, into chocolate mixture, coating them rapidly and
completely. Remove balls with 2 forks, thereby allowing the excess chocolate to drain off before plac-
ing them on a lightly oiled or wax-papered plate.
Return balls to freezer and let harden approximately
10 minutes.

Stir together cocoa and confectioners sugar. Set
aside.

Combine remaining chopped chocolate and 2 tablespoons honey in heavy saucepan. Melt over low
heat, stirring constantly. Recoat truffles, 1 at a time,
and roll in cocoa-sugar mixture. Place on waxed
paper to harden. Finished truffles do not need to be
refrigerated but should be kept in cool place.

Chocolate Hearts

In heavy saucepan, over low heat, melt 4 ounces (4
squares) semisweet chocolate with 3 tablespoons butter. Set aside to cool slightly. Pinch paper cupcake
liners into heart shape. Loosely form an 8-inch square
of foil under and around each cupcake holder to help
maintain shape. (Foil need not be in heart shape; just
use as a support for the paper liners.) Slowly spoon
chocolate mixture down sides of paper liners. (If
chocolate runs off sides, cool chocolate further before
proceeding.) Spread chocolate evenly in bottom of
heart. Reshape foil around chocolate hearts as needed
to maintain heart shape. Place each heart in freezer
immediately. Keep frozen until ready to use. Carefully peel paper liners from each heart and fill with
truffles just before serving. *Makes about 6 to 7 Chocolate Hearts.*

Chocolate-Covered Cherries

Makes 4 dozen cherries

    3 cups confectioners sugar
    ⅓ cup butter or margarine
    2 tablespoons milk
    2 jars (10 ounces each) maraschino cherries with
       stems
    8 squares (1 ounce each) semisweet chocolate
       1-inch square paraffin wax, chopped

Cream together sugar, butter, and milk until
smooth. Divide fondant in half; roll each into a 6-
inch log and wrap in Reynolds Plastic Wrap. Chill
until firm. Drain cherries on paper towels. Cut logs
into ¼-inch pieces. Gently pat until large enough to
cover a cherry. Place cherry in center of fondant;
mold to completely cover cherry. Place on foil-lined
cookie sheet. Repeat with remaining cherries. Chill
until firm. Melt chocolate and wax over hot (not
boiling) water, stirring until smooth. Remove from
heat. Hold cherry by stem; dip in chocolate to cover.
If chocolate starts to set, return to heat until melted.
Place dipped cherries on foil sheet. Chill until firm.

Candy Making at Home

Homemade or commercial candy is based on sugar crystals or the lack of them, dividing the confection into two general classifications, sugar-crystal candy and dense-syrup candy. The ingredients used, the proportion of each to the others, the care taken in measuring and combining them, plus cooking temperature and cooking time, determine the kind of candy—and whether or not it's successful.

The Ingredients. The chief component of most candy is granulated sugar. Sugar-and-water syrup, concentrated by boiling down, then turned out and cooled, results in a hard, grainy, crystallized candy hardly worthy of the name. But when other ingredients are added, both to flavor the finished product and to influence the texture of it by controlling or preventing the crystallization, candy as we know it today results.

One of the control ingredients is corn syrup. Combined in proper proportion to sugar, corn syrup makes candy creamy or soft and chewy. Acids—vinegar, cream of tartar, lemon juice—used judiciously, will slow down crystallization, but an excess makes a too-thin, never-congeals candy. Fat—butter, as well as the fat content of milk and/or chocolate—also slows down crystallization, in addition to adding flavor and mellowness.

Those ingredients, and water, are the chief components of most candy, other than flavoring extracts, nuts, and fruit such as raisins that are added after the cooking process is complete.

The Equipment. Candy is boiled and, because it is a sugar mixture, rises high and boils over readily if the pan is too small. So you need a large pan—one with a cover—for candy making. It should be heavy-duty; candy has a nasty habit of sticking and scorching that a heavy pan helps to prevent.

You will also need spoons for stirring and beating. Wooden spoons are the best choice; they never get too hot to handle, and they cut down the clatter when you're beating candy in a metal pan. A large pastry brush is useful for washing down sugar crystals that cling to the sides of the pan.

Most useful of all is a candy thermometer. This gadget, with an easy-read dial and a clip to fasten it to the side of the pan, eliminates all the guesswork of cold-water testing. Removing candy from the heat at the moment it reaches the proper temperature is critical to good results, so such a thermometer is a good investment for the home candy maker—and it can also be used to test the sugar syrup for seafoam and allied frostings, and is useful in jelly making.

The Techniques. Sugar must be completely dissolved for proper texture, so the sugar mixture should be stirred until it comes to a boil. Thereafter, most candies are not stirred—follow the recipe directions. As the candy cooks, crystals of sugar, sometimes in clusters, tend to form on the sides of the pan. Covering the pan during the early part of the boiling period allows steam to accumulate, which washes these crystals back into the candy mixture. Some recipes will tell you to wash these crystals away with a brush; others suggest buttering the sides of the pan to prevent crystal formation. Trust the recipe to guide you to the right technique for the kind of candy you're making.

Candies in which the liquid is water can be cooked over a medium-high heat (always keep a sharp eye out, to make certain that the mixture doesn't stick to the pan and scorch). When milk is the liquid, cook over moderate heat, as milk compounds the tendency to scorching.

Testing, Testing. Cook the mixture to the correct temperature, remove it immediately from the heat once that temperature is reached—those two points are all-important to success. Before the candy thermometer was available, cooks tested the hot syrup by dropping a small amount from a spoon into cold water to determine whether or not it had reached the proper consistency, and a great many cooks still rely on this method. It is, however, not nearly as accurate as a thermometer. Most candy recipes specify a thermometer reading, followed by the alternative cold-water test, such as soft ball or hard ball. If you use a thermometer, keep a sharp eye on it during the last few minutes of cooking. That's when the temperature rises rapidly. If you water-test, be sure that the water is very cold, but don't use ice water. Take a clean cup and spoon, and fresh water, for each test.

To make the cold-water test, remove the pan from the heat and drop a little of the mixture into the water. Use your fingers to gather the drops into a ball and feel it for firmness. If the candy isn't yet ready, return it at once to the heat.

Cautionary Notes. Humidity is the candy cook's enemy. On damp or rainy days, cook candy to a degree or so higher on the thermometer than the recipe calls for. Or, if there's no howling mob clamoring for the product, put off the candy-making session until the weather clears up. Be aware that altitude also affects candy. Temperatures given in recipes are for sea level.

If you are not of a placid disposition, leave candy making to others. It's a phase of cookery that requires a large helping of unflappable patience. Leaving aside the beating, pulling, kneading, or whatever is required, the cooking alone sometimes seems to take just short of forever. And there's no way to hurry it without disaster.

Dipped Fruit Balls

Makes about 3 dozen candies

    2 packages (8 ounces each) pitted dates
    2 cups dried apricots
    1 11½-ounce package (2 cups) Nestlé Milk
         Chocolate Morsels
    2 tablespoons vegetable shortening
       Paper candy liners

Finely chop dates and apricots; mix well. Over hot (not boiling) water, melt Nestlé Milk Chocolate Morsels and vegetable shortening; remove from heat, but keep over hot water. With greased hands, shape date-apricot mixture into 1-inch balls. Dip the balls into melted chocolate mixture. Place on foil-lined cookie sheets. Refrigerate until ready to serve (about 15 to 20 minutes).

Banana Pops (page 104); Halloween Squares (page 45); Chocolate-Covered Pretzels (page 104); Chocolate Caramel Crowns (page 93). Courtesy of Nestlé Foods Corporation

Father's Day Chocolate Golf Balls

Makes 12 golf balls

    5 cups fine fresh chocolate cake crumbs★
    1 cup finely chopped walnuts
    1 tablespoon rum or brandy
    ½ cup Ocean Spray Whole Berry Cranberry Sauce
    2 cans (8 ounces each) or 2 packages (7 ounces
         each) almond paste
    ½ cup confectioners sugar, sifted 10 times

In a large bowl, combine cake crumbs, walnuts, rum, and cranberry sauce; blend thoroughly. Allowing about ¼ cup of mixture for each ball, shape into 12 balls, using palms of hands. Set on baking sheet to firm slightly.

Cut almond paste into 12 equal pieces. Place each piece between 2 sheets of wax paper and roll into a circle 5 inches in diameter. Wrap round of almond paste around each chocolate cake crumb ball. Tuck in ends and round ball; place on baking sheet. Chill in refrigerator one hour to firm almond paste. Remove and roll in sifted sugar. Serve at room temperature.
★ To make crumbs, use your favorite chocolate cake recipe or a frozen chocolate pound cake.

Chocolate Lover's Cheesecake Dessert (page 76); Krunchy Kiss Cookies (page 33); Chocolate Truffles (page 87). Courtesy HERSHEY Food Corporation

Orange-Chocolate Sugar Plums
Makes about 6 dozen candies
 2 cups coarsely chopped pecans
 2 cups coarsely chopped unblanched almonds
 1 cup orange peel preserves, chopped
 ½ cup flaked coconut
 ¼ cup Florida orange juice
 1 package (8 ounces) semisweet chocolate
 1 large egg
   Confectioners sugar

In a large bowl, mix pecans, almonds, orange peel preserves, coconut, and orange juice. In a small saucepan, melt chocolate over moderately low heat; remove from heat and cool 15 minutes. Beat in egg until mixture is smooth. Stir chocolate into nut mixture. When thoroughly mixed, chill 30 to 45 minutes until firm enough to handle. Shape into walnut-size balls. Roll in confectioners sugar. Chill until ready to serve.

Bourbon Balls
Makes 4½ dozen candies
 1 6-ounce package (1 cup) Nestlé Toll House Semi-Sweet Chocolate Morsels
 3 tablespoons corn syrup
 ½ cup bourbon
 2½ cups vanilla wafer crumbs
 ½ cup sifted confectioners sugar
 1 cup finely chopped nuts
   Granulated sugar

Over hot (not boiling) water, melt Nestlé Toll House Semi-Sweet Chocolate Morsels; remove from heat. Blend in corn syrup and bourbon. In a large bowl, combine vanilla wafer crumbs, confectioners sugar, and nuts. Add chocolate mixture; mix well. Let stand about 30 minutes. Form into 1-inch balls. Roll in granulated sugar. Let season in a covered container for several days.

Rocky Road Candy
Makes about 40 squares
 1 package (12 ounces) semisweet chocolate morsels
 1 can (14 ounces) Eagle® Brand Sweetened Condensed Milk (not evaporated milk)
 2 tablespoons margarine or butter
 2 cups dry roasted peanuts
 1 package (10½ ounces) Campfire® Miniature Marshmallows

In heavy saucepan, over low heat, melt morsels with Eagle Brand and margarine; remove from heat. In large bowl, combine nuts and marshmallows; stir in chocolate mixture. Spread in waxed paper-lined 13×9×2-inch pan. Chill 2 hours, or until firm. Remove from pan, peel off waxed paper, and cut into squares. Store loosely covered at room temperature.

Blueberry Clusters
Makes about 2½ dozen clusters
 1 11½-ounce package (2 cups) Nestlé Milk Chocolate Morsels
 ¼ cup vegetable shortening
 36 1¼-inch candy liners
 2 cups fresh blueberries, washed and dried

Over hot (not boiling) water, combine Nestlé Milk Chocolate Morsels and shortening; stir until morsels melt and mixture is smooth. Remove from heat. Place 1 teaspoonful of melted chocolate in candy liner; add 6 to 8 blueberries. Top with additional 2 teaspoonfuls of chocolate, making sure blueberries are well coated. Chill in refrigerator until chocolate is set (20 to 30 minutes). Store in refrigerator until ready to serve.
Note: Blueberry Clusters may be kept at room temperature up to 1 hour. If chocolate becomes sticky, return to refrigerator.

Confections, But Not Really Candy

Many kinds of sweets that don't meet the "candy" definition are nevertheless eaten and enjoyed for the same purpose. There are glacéed fruits and peels, fondant-dipped strawberries, and other berries, crystallized flowers or flower petals, stuffed dried fruits such as dates and prunes, fruit pastes often called leather—peach leather, apricot leather, and so on—and a number of popcorn-based confections. There are also some quick/easy candies for the undermotivated or too-timid candy maker to try—melted chocolate drops with nuts or dry cereal or coconut or, even, chow mein noodles, stirred in, or melted commercial caramels or marshmallows given the same treatment, for example. They are simple to make. Some commercial boxed frosting mixes can be made into acceptable candy, too. Follow instructions on the label.

Chocolate Caramel Crowns

Makes about 4 dozen candies
  1 pound (56) vanilla caramels
  2 tablespoons butter
  1 tablespoon water
  1 11½-ounce package (2 cups) Nestlé Milk
      Chocolate Morsels★
  ½ cup light corn syrup
  2 tablespoons water
      Pecan halves (about 2 cups)

Over boiling water, combine caramels, butter, and water; heat until caramels melt and mixture is smooth. Keep warm over boiling water. Over hot (not boiling) water, combine Nestlé Milk Chocolate Morsels, corn syrup, and water; heat until morsels melt and mixture is smooth. Keep warm over hot water. Place 3 pecan halves, ends touching in center, on greased cookie sheets. Drop caramel mixture by ½ teaspoonfuls onto center of pecans where 3 touch. Drop chocolate mixture over caramel-nut piece by slightly rounded teaspoonfuls. Chill in refrigerator until set (about 30 minutes). Refrigerate until ready to serve.

★ Or substitute 1 12-ounce package (2 cups) Nestlé Toll House Semi-Sweet Chocolate Morsels.

Peanut Butter Stars

Makes 2 dozen tarts
  1 package (3 ounces) cream cheese, softened
  ⅓ cup butter or margarine
  3 tablespoons peanut butter
  1 cup all-purpose flour
  1 egg
  ½ cup dark corn syrup
  ¼ cup sugar
  2 tablespoons butter or margarine, melted
  ½ teaspoon vanilla extract
  ⅓ cup salted peanuts, finely chopped
  24 solid milk chocolate kisses

Preheat oven to 325°F. Combine cream cheese, ⅓ cup butter, peanut butter, and flour in medium mixing bowl. Shape dough into 24 one-inch balls. Cut 24 three-inch circles from multiple thicknesses of Heavy Duty Reynolds Wrap aluminum foil. Carefully separate. Press dough balls onto each circle. Turn up edges of both foil and dough, ¾ inch at 5 points, forming a star. Place on foil-lined cookie sheet.

Beat egg until foamy. Add corn syrup, sugar, butter, and vanilla; beat until smooth. Spoon 2 teaspoons of filling into each star. Sprinkle each filled star with nuts. Bake 20 to 25 minutes, or until lightly browned. Remove from oven. Top each tart with a solid milk chocolate kiss. Cool on wire rack.

Chocolate Cherry Logs

Makes two 12-inch logs
  3 packages (6 ounces each) semisweet chocolate
      chips
  1 can (14 ounces) Eagle® Brand Sweetened
      Condensed Milk (not evaporated milk)
  1 container (6 ounces) candied cherries, chopped
      (about 1 cup)
  1 teaspoon almond extract
  1½ cups slivered almonds, toasted and chopped

In heavy saucepan, over low heat, melt chips with sweetened condensed milk. Remove from heat. Stir in cherries and extract. Chill 30 minutes. Divide in half; place each portion on a 20-inch piece of wax paper. Shape each into 12-inch log. Roll in nuts. Wrap tightly; chill 2 hours or until firm. Remove paper; cut into 1¼-inch slices to serve. Stored covered in refrigerator.

Coconut Creams

Makes about 30 balls
  3 tablespoons butter, softened
  3 tablespoons corn syrup
  1 teaspoon vanilla extract
  ¼ teaspoon salt
  2½ cups sifted confectioners sugar
  1 can (3½ ounces) shredded coconut, chopped
  1 11½-ounce package (2 cups) Nestlé Milk
      Chocolate Morsels
  1 tablespoon vegetable shortening

In a small bowl, combine butter, corn syrup, vanilla, and salt. Gradually add confectioners sugar; beat well. Mixture will be crumbly. Add coconut; knead mixture until smooth and pliable. Roll into 1-inch balls; freeze 10 minutes. Over hot (not boiling) water, combine Nestlé Milk Chocolate Morsels and vegetable shortening; heat until morsels melt and mixture is smooth. Remove from heat, but keep over hot water. Dip coconut balls into melted chocolate; shake off excess chocolate. Place on waxed paper-lined cookie sheets. Chill until firm (about 20 to 30 minutes). Store in refrigerator until ready to serve.

Peppermint Creams

Omit coconut. Add 1 to 2 tablespoons crushed peppermint candy when kneading mixture. Dip as above. Place on waxed paper-lined cookie sheets. Sprinkle tops with crushed peppermint candy. Chill until firm (about 20 to 30 minutes). Serve immediately or store in refrigerator until ready to serve.

Chocolate-Fluted Kiss Cups

Makes 24 cups

2½ **cups Hershey's® Mini Chips® Semi-Sweet Chocolate or 8-ounce Hershey's® Milk Chocolate Bar**

24 **paper petits fours or mini biscuit cases Peanut Butter Filling (recipe follows)**

24 **Hershey's® Kisses® Chocolates**

Melt Mini Chips semi-sweet chocolate or chocolate bar in top of double boiler over hot water; stir until completely melted. Place pleated paper cases in 1¾-inch gem or mini biscuit pans. Coat inside of liners with chocolate using a dry pastry brush. (If chocolate is too thick for coating, add 1 tablespoon shortening, not butter.) Chill 20 minutes; coat any thin spots. Chill completely, preferably overnight. Gently peel paper from cups. Fill, cover, and refrigerate. Before serving, top with a Kisses chocolate.

Peanut Butter Filling

1 **cup creamy peanut butter**

1 **cup confectioners sugar**

1 **tablespoon butter, softened**

Combine peanut butter, confectioners sugar, and butter in a small mixer bowl until smooth.

Chocolate Triangles

4 **squares Baker's Semi-Sweet Chocolate**

1 **tablespoon butter or margarine**

Melt chocolate with butter in saucepan over very low heat, stirring constantly. Pour onto waxed paper-lined baking sheet; spread to about ⅛-inch thickness. Chill until firm, about 15 minutes. Cut into squares, then into triangles, and at once lift gently from paper with a knife. Store on waxed paper in refrigerator or freezer. Use to garnish desserts.

Chocolate-Covered Cherries (page 88). The Reynolds Wrap Kitchen

Milk Chocolate Pralines

Makes 4 dozen candies

   3 cups sugar
  ¾ cup water
  ¼ cup light corn syrup
   1 teaspoon vinegar
  ½ teaspoon salt
   1 11½-ounce package (2 cups) Nestlé Milk
       Chocolate Morsels
   1 cup coarsely chopped pecans
       Pecan halves (optional)

In a large saucepan, combine sugar, water, corn syrup, vinegar, and salt. Bring to full boil, stirring constantly. Boil 3 minutes without stirring. Remove from heat; cool 5 minutes. Add Nestlé Milk Chocolate Morsels; stir quickly until melted. Stir in pecans. Quickly drop by level tablespoonfuls onto foil-lined cookie sheets.★ Garnish with pecan halves, if desired. Refrigerate until set (about 20 minutes). Peel candies off foil to serve. Store in refrigerator.

★ Work as rapidly as possible as mixture tends to set up quickly.

Scotch Toffee

Makes 3 dozen squares

   2 cups Quaker Oats (quick or old fashioned,
       uncooked)
  ⅓ cup butter or margarine, melted
  ½ cup firmly packed brown sugar
  ¼ cup dark corn syrup
  1½ teaspoons vanilla extract
  ½ teaspoon salt
   1 package (6 ounces) semisweet chocolate pieces,
       melted
  ¼ cup chopped nuts

Heat oven to 450°F. Generously grease 11 × 7-inch baking pan. In large bowl, combine oats and butter, mixing well. Add sugar, syrup, vanilla, and salt; blend well. Firmly pack into prepared pan. Bake about 12 minutes. (Mixture will be brown and bubbly.) Cool thoroughly.

Loosen edges; invert pan and tap firmly against cutting board to remove. Spread with chocolate. Sprinkle with nuts. Chill; cut into 36 bars. Store in refrigerator.

No-Cook Candy Roll

Makes 40 pieces

  ¼ cup butter or margarine
  ¼ cup evaporated milk
   1 teaspoon vanilla extract
  ¼ teaspoon salt
   4 cups C & H Powdered Sugar
   2 tablespoons glacéed cherries, chopped
   1 ounce unsweetened chocolate, melted
       Minced nuts

Melt butter in saucepan. Stir in milk, vanilla, and salt. Remove from heat and gradually stir in sugar. Mix well. Measure ½ cup mixture into small bowl. Add cherries and mix well. Work melted chocolate into remaining mixture. Knead with hands until smooth and blended. If chocolate mixture is dry, add evaporated milk by ½ teaspoonfuls until desired consistency is reached.

Divide in half. Roll each piece between waxed paper. Cut into 5 × 10-inch rectangles. Divide cherry candy in half and form into 2 rolls, each 10 inches long. Lay each on chocolate and roll up, then roll in minced nuts. Seal in foil. Refrigerate 1 hour, or until ready to slice. Slice ½ inch thick. With leftover chocolate, make 1-inch balls and roll in nuts.

Chocolate-Almond Divinity

Makes about 3 dozen candies

  ½ cup light corn syrup
   2 cups sugar
  ¼ teaspoon salt
   2 egg whites
  1½ teaspoons vanilla extract
   1 package (6 ounces) semisweet chocolate bits
   1 cup coarsely chopped almonds
       Whole blanched almonds

Combine syrup, sugar, salt, and ½ cup water in saucepan; bring to boil; cook to 248°F (firm-ball stage). Meanwhile, beat egg whites stiff. Gradually beat ½ cup syrup mixture into whites. Return remaining syrup to heat; cook to 272°F; gradually beat it into whites. Beat in vanilla, chocolate, and almonds, beating until chocolate melts. Drop by spoonfuls into paper candy cups (or spread in 9-inch pan). While still soft, top each with a whole almond.

Snow Caps

Makes 3½ dozen candies

- 1 12-ounce package (2 cups) Nestlé Toll House Semi-Sweet Chocolate Morsels
- ¼ cup dark corn syrup
- 1 tablespoon water
- 1 cup chopped nuts
  Granulated sugar
- 1 package (8 ounces) cream cheese, softened
- ⅔ cup sifted confectioners sugar
- 2 teaspoons vanilla extract
  Walnut pieces (optional)

Over hot (not boiling) water, combine Nestlé Toll House Semi-Sweet Chocolate Morsels, corn syrup, and water; heat until morsels melt and mixture is smooth. Stir in chopped nuts. Drop by slightly rounded teaspoonfuls onto waxed paper-lined cookie sheets; press flat with bottom of glass dipped in granulated sugar. Chill in refrigerator for 5 minutes. In a small bowl, combine cream cheese, confectioners sugar, and vanilla; beat until creamy. Top each chocolate mound with 1 teaspoon of cream cheese frosting. Garnish with walnut pieces, if desired. Return to refrigerator and chill until firm. Store in airtight container in refrigerator.

Chocolate-Mint Fancies

Makes 2 dozen candies

- 1 12-ounce package (2 cups) Nestlé Toll House Semi-Sweet Chocolate Morsels, divided
- 4 tablespoons vegetable shortening, divided
- 5 tablespoons butter
- ½ cup light corn syrup
- 4½ cups sifted confectioners sugar, divided
- 1 teaspoon peppermint extract
  Red or green food color

Over hot (not boiling) water, combine 1 cup Nestlé Toll House Semi-Sweet Chocolate Morsels and 2 tablespoons shortening; heat until morsels melt and mixture is smooth. Spread evenly with back of spoon in foil-lined 15 × 10 × 1-inch pan. Chill in refrigerator until firm (about 20 minutes). Carefully invert onto waxed paper-lined cookie sheet. Gently peel off foil. Return to refrigerator.

In a large saucepan, combine butter, corn syrup, and half the confectioners sugar; bring to a full boil, stirring constantly, over medium-low heat. Add remaining confectioners sugar, the peppermint extract, and desired amount of food color; stir vigorously until well blended (about 3 minutes). Remove from heat. Pour mixture (fondant) onto greased cookie sheet. Cool long enough to handle (about 5 minutes).

Knead until soft (about 2 to 3 minutes). Roll out fondant ⅛ inch thick between two pieces of plastic wrap to form a 15 × 10-inch rectangle. Remove top sheet of plastic wrap. Carefully invert fondant onto chocolate bottom layer. Remove second sheet of plastic wrap. Chill 15 minutes.

Over hot (not boiling) water, combine remaining 1 cup Nestlé Toll House Semi-Sweet Chocolate Morsels and 2 tablespoons vegetable shortening; heat until morsels melt and mixture is smooth. Spread evenly over fondant filling. Chill 15 to 20 minutes.

Cut out 24 shapes with a 2-inch cookie cutter. Chill in refrigerator until ready to serve.

Triple Treats

Makes about 2½ dozen candies

- 1 11½-ounce package (2 cups) Nestlé Milk Chocolate Morsels
- 2 tablespoons vegetable shortening
- 30 vanilla caramels
- 3 tablespoons butter
- 2 tablespoons water
- 1 cup coarsely chopped peanuts

Over hot (not boiling) water, combine Nestlé Milk Chocolate Morsels and vegetable shortening; stir until morsels melt and mixture is smooth. Remove from heat. Pour half of melted chocolate into a foil-lined 8-inch square pan; spread evenly. Refrigerate until firm (about 15 minutes). Return remaining chocolate mixture to low heat. Over boiling water, combine caramels, butter, and water. Stir until caramels melt and mixture is smooth. Stir in nuts until well blended. Pour into the chocolate-lined pan; spread evenly. Refrigerate until tacky (about 15 minutes). Top with remaining melted chocolate; spread evenly to cover caramel filling. Return to refrigerator and chill until firm (about 1 hour). Cut into 1 × 2-inch rectangles. Refrigerate until ready to serve.

The Great Swiss Idea

Two centuries after the beginning of the chocolate house fad in England, an inventive Swiss gentleman asked himself a question (probably while sipping a cup of his favorite beverage). Could chocolate be somehow congealed and dried, turned into a solid instead of a liquid, so that it could be eaten rather than drunk? From that cogitation arose the method of producing milk chocolate. When it appeared on the market, the revolution began, until today chocolate for eating outstrips chocolate for drinking by many millions of pounds.

Chocolate Cherry Logs (page 93). Eagle® Brand Sweetened Condensed Milk

Grasshopper Grabs (page 105); Blox of Fudge (page 103). Photo courtesy of Knox Gelatine, Inc.

Peanut Butter Stars (page 93). The Reynolds Wrap Kitchen

Candy Making at Home (page 84). C&H Sugar Company

Creamy Chocolate Penuche

Makes 1¼ pounds candy

  2 cups C & H Granulated Sugar
  1 cup half and half
  2 ounces unsweetened chocolate
  2 tablespoons light corn syrup
  ½ teaspoon salt
  2 tablespoons butter, cut into 6 pieces
  1 teaspoon vanilla extract
  ½ cup coarsely chopped walnuts

Grease 8-inch square pan. Combine sugar, half and half, chocolate, corn syrup, and salt in heavy saucepan. Stir over medium heat until mixture begins to boil. Cook until it reaches 236°F on candy thermometer (soft-ball stage). Wash down any crystals on sides of pan with brush dipped in cold water. Stir frequently to prevent scorching. Pour into clean bowl to prevent graininess. Stir in butter and vanilla; cool to lukewarm (110°F) without stirring. Beat 10 to 15 minutes, until fudge thickens and begins to loose its gloss. Quickly stir in walnuts and spread in pan. Cool and cut into squares.

Peanutty Pillows

Makes about 6½ dozen squares

  1 cup light corn syrup
  ½ cup firmly packed light brown sugar
  1½ cups chunk-style peanut butter
  1 teaspoon vanilla extract
  1 envelope (1 cup) nonfat dry milk powder
  1 cup Hershey's® Mini Chips® Semi-Sweet
     Chocolate

Line 9-inch square pan with aluminum foil; grease foil and set aside. In heavy saucepan, combine corn syrup and sugar, stirring constantly; bring to a full rolling boil. Remove from heat; partially blend in peanut butter, vanilla, and dry milk powder; blend completely. Turn into prepared pan; refrigerate until firm. Cut into 1-inch squares. Wrap individually in plastic wrap or waxed paper, or coat with chocolate. To coat candies: Melt Mini Chips semi-sweet chocolate in top of double boiler over simmering water, stirring constantly to ensure even melting. Cool, stirring occasionally, until chocolate is lukewarm. Dip opposite corners into chocolate or cover entire square, if desired. Place onto waxed paper-covered tray to set. Store in refrigerator or cool place.

Foolproof Chocolate Fudge

Makes about 1¾ pounds candy

  3 packages (6 ounces each) semisweet chocolate
     morsels
  1 can (14 ounces) Eagle® Brand Sweetened
     Condensed Milk (not evaporated milk)
     Dash salt
  1½ teaspoons vanilla extract
  ½ cup chopped nuts, optional

In heavy saucepan, over low heat, melt morsels with Eagle Brand. Remove from heat; stir in remaining ingredients. Spread evenly into waxed paper-lined 8-inch square pan. Chill 2 to 3 hours, or until firm. Turn fudge onto cutting board; peel off paper and cut into squares. Store loosely covered at room temperature.

Butterscotch Fudge

In heavy saucepan, melt 4 (6 ounces each) packages butterscotch-flavored morsels with Eagle Brand; remove from heat. Stir in 2 tablespoons white vinegar, ⅛ teaspoon salt, ½ teaspoon maple flavoring, and 1 cup chopped nuts. Proceed as directed. *Makes about 2¼ pounds.*

White Confetti Fudge

In heavy saucepan, melt 1½ pounds white chocolate with Eagle Brand; remove from heat. Stir in ⅛ teaspoon salt, 1 teaspoon vanilla, and 1 cup chopped mixed candied fruit. Proceed as directed. *Makes about 2½ pounds.*

Marshmallow Cream Fudge

Makes 2¼ pounds candy

  1 jar (7½ to 13 ounces) marshmallow cream
  1½ cups sugar
  ⅔ cup evaporated milk
  ¼ cup butter
  ¼ teaspoon salt
  1 12-ounce package (2 cups) Nestlé Toll House
     Semi-Sweet Chocolate Morsels
  ½ cup chopped nuts
  1 teaspoon vanilla extract

In a medium saucepan, combine marshmallow cream, sugar, evaporated milk, butter, and salt and bring to full boil, stirring constantly over moderate heat. Boil 5 minutes, stirring constantly, over moderate heat. Remove from heat. Add Nestlé Toll House Semi-Sweet Chocolate Morsels; stir until morsels melt and mixture is smooth. Stir in nuts and vanilla. Pour into foil-lined 8-inch square pan. Chill in refrigerator until firm (about 2 hours).

Uncooked Chocolate Fudge

Makes about 1 pound candy
- 3 ounces unsweetened chocolate
- ¼ cup butter or margarine
- 3½ cups C & H Powdered Sugar
- 1 egg
- 2 teaspoons vanilla extract
- 1 cup chopped nuts

Line 8-inch square pan with waxed paper. In heavy saucepan, melt chocolate and butter over low heat. Stir half the sugar into chocolate mixture, then beat in egg and vanilla. Gradually work in remaining sugar. Add nuts. Press into pan. Let set until firm, then turn out and cut into squares.

Carnation Fudge

Makes 2 pounds fudge
- 2 tablespoons butter
- ⅔ cup undiluted Carnation Evaporated Milk
- 1⅔ cups sugar
- ½ teaspoon salt
- 2 cups (4 ounces) miniature marshmallows
- 1½ cups (1½ 6-ounce packages) semisweet chocolate chips
- 1 teaspoon vanilla extract
- ½ cup chopped nuts

Combine butter, evaporated milk, sugar, and salt in saucepan over medium heat, stirring occasionally. Bring to full boil. Cook 4 to 5 minutes, stirring constantly. Remove from heat. Add remaining ingredients. Stir vigorously until marshmallows melt and blend. Pour into 8-inch square buttered pan. Cool. Cut in squares.

Peppermint Fudge

Prepare Carnation Fudge; reduce vanilla to ½ teaspoon and add ¼ teaspoon mint extract. Omit nuts. Sprinkle crushed, hard peppermint candy over top.

Peanut Butter Fudge

Prepare Carnation Fudge; substitute peanut butter chips for chocolate chips. Spread 6 ounces melted chocolate chips over cooled fudge.

Never-Fail Fudge

Makes about 1 pound candy
- 2 cups C & H Powdered Sugar
- 3 ounces cream cheese
- ⅛ teaspoon salt
- ½ teaspoon vanilla extract
- 2 ounces unsweetened chocolate
- ½ cup chopped nuts
- 1 teaspoon whipping cream (optional)

Gradually stir sugar into cream cheese. Add salt and vanilla. Melt chocolate in top of double boiler, cool slightly, and stir into cheese mixture. Add nuts. For softer fudge, add cream. Press into well-greased shallow pan or roll into log. Chill until firm; cut when set.

Two-Tone Fudge

Makes about 2½ pounds candy
- 2½ cups sugar
- ¾ cup evaporated milk
- ⅓ cup butter
- ½ teaspoon salt
- 3 cups miniature marshmallows
- 1 6-ounce package (1 cup) Nestlé Butterscotch Flavored Morsels
- ½ cup chopped walnuts
- ½ teaspoon maple extract
- 1 11½-ounce package (2 cups) Nestlé Milk Chocolate Morsels
- 1 teaspoon vanilla extract

In a large heavy-gauge saucepan, combine sugar, evaporated milk, butter, and salt. Cook, stirring constantly, until mixture comes to full boil. Boil 7 minutes, stirring constantly. Remove from heat; add marshmallows. Mix until marshmallows melt and mixture is smooth. Place half the hot mixture in a bowl. Add Nestlé Butterscotch Flavored Morsels, walnuts, and maple extract. Stir until morsels melt and mixture is smooth; set aside. To remaining mixture, add Nestlé Milk Chocolate Morsels and vanilla. Spread chocolate mixture into foil-lined 9-inch square pan. Pour butterscotch mixture over chocolate layer. Chill in refrigerator until firm (2 to 3 hours). Cut into 1-inch squares.

Coffee Fudge

Makes about 2½ pounds candy
- 3 cups C & H Granulated or Superfine Sugar
- 2 tablespoons instant coffee
- 1 cup milk
- ¼ cup cream
- 2 tablespoons corn syrup
- ¼ cup butter or margarine
- 1 teaspoon vanilla extract
- 1½ cups coarsely chopped pecans

Combine sugar, coffee, milk, cream, and corn syrup in heavy saucepan. Stir over low heat until mixture begins to boil. Cook until it reaches 236°F. on candy thermometer (soft ball stage). Wash down any sugar crystals on sides of pan with brush dipped in cold water. Stir frequently to prevent scorching. Pour into clean bowl to prevent graininess, stir in butter, and cool to lukewarm (110°F.) without stirring. Stir in vanilla, then beat 10 to 15 minutes until fudge loses its gloss. Stir in pecans; beat until candy holds its shape. Drop from teaspoon onto greased cookie sheet or waxed paper to set.

Mocha Fudge

Makes about 1½ pounds candy

   2 tablespoons Taster's Choice freeze-dried instant coffee
   1 tablespoon boiling water
   2 cups firmly packed brown sugar
   ½ cup sour cream
   ⅛ teaspoon salt
   1 6-ounce package (1 cup) Nestlé Toll House Semi-Sweet Chocolate Morsels
   1 cup chopped nuts

In small measuring cup, dissolve Taster's Choice in boiling water. In large saucepan, combine coffee mixture, brown sugar, sour cream, and salt. Cook over moderate heat, stirring constantly, until mixture comes to a full rolling boil. Boil 2 minutes. Remove from heat. Add Nestlé Toll House Semi-Sweet Chocolate Morsels; stir until morsels melt and mixture is smooth. Stir in chopped nuts. Pour into foil-lined 8-inch square pan. Chill in refrigerator until set (about 2 hours). Cut into 1-inch squares.

Quick Nut Fudge

Makes 2 dozen candies

   1 pound Domino Confectioners 10-X Powdered Sugar
   ½ cup cocoa
   ¼ teaspoon salt
   6 tablespoons butter or margarine
   4 tablespoons milk
   1 tablespoon vanilla extract
   1 cup chopped pecans or walnuts

Combine all ingredients except nuts in top of double boiler. Place over simmering water and stir until smooth. Add nuts and mix. Spread candy quickly in buttered 9 × 5 × 3-inch loaf pan. Cool; cut in squares.

Old-Fashioned Cocoa Fudge

Makes about 5 dozen candies

   2 cups sugar
   ½ cup Hershey's® Cocoa
   1 tablespoon corn syrup
   1 cup milk
   1 teaspoon vanilla extract
   ⅓ cup butter or margarine
   1 cup walnuts, broken

In a saucepan, combine sugar, cocoa, corn syrup, and milk. Bring to a boil, stirring constantly. Cook, without stirring, to 234°F on a candy thermometer, or until a small amount dropped into cold water forms a soft ball. Remove from heat. Add butter, vanilla, and nuts. Do not stir. Cool 30 to 35 minutes. Beat until fudge thickens and loses some of its gloss. Spread in a foil-lined 8-inch square pan. Cool. Using foil, lift fudge out of pan. Cut into bite-size pieces. Store in an airtight container in a cool, dry place.

Easy Peanut Butter Fudge

Makes 3 dozen candies

   1 6-ounce package (1 cup) Nestlé Toll House Semi-Sweet Chocolate Morsels
   1 6-ounce package (1 cup) Nestlé Butterscotch Flavored Morsels
   1 cup chunky peanut butter
   1 can (14 ounces) sweetened condensed milk (not evaporated milk), divided
   2 cups oven-toasted rice cereal
   1 cup miniature marshmallows

Over hot (not boiling) water, melt Nestlé Toll House Semi-Sweet Chocolate Morsels and Nestlé Butterscotch Flavored Morsels; set aside. In a large bowl, blend together peanut butter and ¼ cup of the sweetened condensed milk. Stir in cereal. Reserve ½ cup peanut butter mixture and spread remainder into greased 9-inch square pan. Sprinkle miniature marshmallows on top. Combine remaining sweetened condensed milk with chocolate-butterscotch mixture. Spread evenly over marshmallows. Sprinkle reserved peanut butter mixture on top and press in lightly. Chill in refrigerator until firm (at least 2 hours). Cut into 2¼ × 1-inch bars.

Fudge

In the past, fudge was something of a nuisance, had a way of sugaring just when you weren't looking, needed to be beaten within an inch of its life (and yours), and took an unconscionable time to set—if indeed, it didn't balk and refuse to set at all.

But some years back a genius thought up a new way to make fudge. You boil together sugar, evaporated milk, and marshmallow creme (never mind how it sounds—concentrate on how it tastes) for a matter of 5 minutes or so, stirring industriously. You take it off the stove, stir in semisweet chocolate bits, vanilla, and—if you wish—nuts. Turn it into a pan, and wait a very short time until it sets. That's all. It's easy, creamy, and good. Better still, it's failureproof.

If you yearn for a return to the good old days, follow the recipe for the old-fashioned kind of fudge. And for the other fudges: divinity (tricky, this one), penuche, and peanut butter. Make candy for the kids or with the kids. It won't hurt a bit.

Uncooked Chocolate Fudge (page 100); Coffee Fudge (page 100); Never-Fail Fudge (page 100); Creamy Chocolate Penuche (page 99). C&H
Sugar Company

Blox of Fudge

Makes 60 to 80 squares

 4 envelopes Knox₍₎ Unflavored Gelatine
½ cup sugar
1½ cups boiling water
 1 package (12 ounces) semisweet chocolate pieces

In a medium saucepan, mix Knox Unflavored Gelatine with sugar. Add boiling water and stir until gelatine is completely dissolved. Add chocolate pieces; stir with wire whip over low heat until chocolate is melted and thoroughly blended, about 5 minutes. Pour into an 8- or 9-inch square pan; chill until firm. To serve, cut into 1-inch squares.

Variations

For Rocky Road Blox, stir in ½ cup each chopped nuts and marshmallow creme before pouring into pan; for Cherry Fudge Blox, stir in ½ cup chopped maraschino cherries.

Chocolate Crunchies

Makes about 6½ dozen

 1 package (6 ounces) Hershey's₍₎ Semi-Sweet
    Chocolate Chips
 1 tablespoon peanut oil
½ cup smooth peanut butter
 2 tablespoons confectioners sugar
75 to 80 miniature shredded whole wheat biscuits
    Whole peanuts

In a small saucepan over hot water, heat chocolate chips and oil until melted. Stir in peanut butter and sugar until smooth. Dip each miniature biscuit in peanut mixture to coat and place on waxed paper. Top each with a peanut half. Chill.

Ohio Buckeyes

Makes about 5 dozen balls

½ cup margarine
 1 pound peanut butter
 1 pound Domino Confectioners 10-X Powdered
    Sugar
 1 package (6 ounces) chocolate chips, melted

Cream together margarine and peanut butter. Add sugar gradually, beating until blended. Mixture will be crumbly. Shape into 1¼-inch balls. Insert toothpicks and dip balls halfway into melted chocolate. Chill until firm.

Mix 'Ems

Mix together in a plastic bag or container one (or more) of the following combinations:

 1 6-ounce package (1 cup) Nestlé Toll House
    Semi-Sweet Chocolate Morsels or Nestlé
    Butterscotch Flavored Morsels
 1 cup salted peanuts
 1 cup raisins

 1 6-ounce package (1 cup) Nestlé Toll House
    Semi-Sweet Chocolate Morsels or Nestlé
    Butterscotch Flavored Morsels
 1 cup potato sticks
 1 cup coarsely broken pretzel sticks

 1 6-ounce package (1 cup) Nestlé Toll House
    Semi-Sweet Chocolate Morsels or Nestlé
    Butterscotch Flavored Morsels
 1 cup coarsely broken peanut brittle
 1 cup raisins

 1 6-ounce package (1 cup) Nestlé Toll House
    Semi-Sweet Chocolate Morsels
 1 6-ounce package (1 cup) Nestlé Butterscotch
    Flavored Morsels
 1 cup broken corn chips

 1 6-ounce package (1 cup) Nestlé Toll House
    Semi-Sweet Chocolate Morsels or Nestlé
    Butterscotch Flavored Morsels
 1 cup ready-to-eat cereal
 1 cup raisins

 1 6-ounce package (1 cup) Nestlé Toll House
    Semi-Sweet Chocolate Morsels or Nestlé
    Butterscotch Flavored Morsels
 1 package (8 ounces) chopped dates
 1 cup salted cashews

 1 12-ounce package (2 cups) Nestlé Peanut Butter
    Morsels
 2 cups broken graham crackers (about 6 crackers)
 1 cup raisins
 1 cup coconut

 1 12-ounce package (2 cups) Nestlé Peanut Butter
    Morsels
 2 cups bite-size shredded rice biscuits
 1 cup raisins

 1 12-ounce package (2 cups) Nestlé Peanut Butter
    Morsels
 1 12-ounce package (2 cups) Nestlé Milk
    Chocolate Morsels

Ting-a-Lings
Makes about 3½ dozen snacks
  1 package (6 ounces) semisweet chocolate
  1 can (4 ounces) chow mein noodles
  1 package (6 ounces) butterscotch bits
  1 cup roasted peanuts

Melt bits; remove from heat; add remaining ingredients; mix. Drop by spoonfuls on waxed paper.

Toss 'n' Tote Snack Mix
Makes about 10 cups mix
  4 cups popped corn
  2 cups bite-size pretzels
  2 cups bite-size crispy corn cereal squares
  1½ cups "M&M's" Peanut Chocolate Candies
  1 cup raisins

Combine all ingredients. Store in tightly covered container. Serve as a snack.

Chocolate-Covered Pretzels
Makes 25 to 30 pretzels
  1 6-ounce package (1 cup) Nestlé Toll House Semi-Sweet Chocolate Morsels
  2 tablespoons corn syrup
  2 tablespoons vegetable shortening
  1½ teaspoons water
  3 -inch twisted pretzels (25 to 30)

Over hot (not boiling) water, combine Nestlé Toll House Semi-Sweet Chocolate Morsels, corn syrup, shortening and water; stir until morsels melt and mixture is smooth. Remove from heat but keep mixture over hot water. Dip pretzels into chocolate mixture to coat evenly. Place pretzels on wire racks set over waxed paper. Chill in refrigerator and let stand at room temperature until surface dries (about 1 hour).

Banana Pops
Makes 8 pops
  4 ripe bananas, peeled
  8 wooden Popsicle® sticks
  1 6-ounce package (1 cup) Nestlé Toll House Semi-Sweet Chocolate Morsels or Nestlé Milk Chocolate Morsels
  1 tablespoon vegetable shortening
  Chopped nuts (optional)
  Shredded coconut (optional)

Cut bananas in half crosswise. Insert wooden stick in end of each and freeze. Melt Nestlé Toll House Semi-Sweet Chocolate Morsels and shortening over hot (not boiling) water; stir until smooth. Coat each banana half with chocolate mixture; roll immediately in nuts or coconut, if desired. Wrap each pop in aluminum foil or put in freezer bags and store in freezer.

Apple Cartwheels
Makes 32 cartwheels
  8 medium-size apples
  1 6-ounce package (1 cup) Nestlé Toll House Semi-Sweet Chocolate Morsels
  ½ cup peanut butter
  ¼ cup raisins
  1 tablespoon honey

Remove core from each apple, leaving a cavity 1¼ inches in diameter. Set aside. In blender container, process Nestlé Toll House Semi-Sweet Chocolate Morsels 5 seconds, or until morsels are chopped. In a small bowl, mix chopped chocolate, peanut butter, raisins, and honey. Stuff cored apples with chocolate-peanut butter filling. Wrap each apple with plastic wrap. Chill in refrigerator. When ready to serve, slice crosswise in ½-inch slices.

Now That You've Got It Made

Most homemade candies store well, can be kept for several weeks if hidden from marauding snackers. All candies should be stored airtight in a cool dry place. Sticky and chewy kinds—taffies, caramels, and the like—and hard candies should be individually wrapped. The exception to the storage rule is divinity; it stales rapidly and should be eaten within a day or two of making.

Homemade candies—the commercial kind too for that matter—freeze well. Place in a box or other container, individually wrapped or not according to the kind; overwrap with freezer paper or foil.

Cupcake Cones

Makes 24 cones

 1 package (18½ ounces) plain favorite-flavor cake
     mix
 2 packages (1¾ ounces each) small flat bottom ice
     cream cones (about 2 to 3 inches high)
 2 cans (16½ ounces each) prepared canned
     frosting
   "M&M's" Plain or Peanut Chocolate Candies
   Candy sprinkles, cinnamon-flavored candies,
     gumdrops, toasted coconut, or nuts, as
     desired

Prepare cake mix according to package directions. Fill each cone with 3 tablespoons of batter. Place on ungreased cookie sheet about 3 inches apart. Bake at 350°F for 30 to 35 minutes, or until wooden pick inserted in center comes out clean. Cool thoroughly on wire rack. Frost; decorate with candies and toppings, as desired.

S'Mores

Makes 22 snacks

 1 11½-ounce package (2 cups) Nestlé Milk
     Chocolate Morsels
 1 tablespoon vegetable shortening
 22 graham crackers, cut in half crosswise
 22 large marshmallows

Preheat oven to 250°F. Over hot (not boiling) water, combine Nestlé Milk Chocolate Morsels and shortening; heat until morsels melt and mixture is smooth. Remove from heat. Spread 2 teaspoons chocolate mixture onto half the graham cracker halves; set aside. Place remaining graham cracker halves on ungreased 15 × 10 × 1-inch baking pan; place 1 marshmallow on each cracker half. Bake 5 to 7 minutes. Remove from oven. Place chocolate-frosted cracker halves on top, chocolate side down; press.

Grasshopper Grabs

Makes about 100 squares

 6 envelopes Knox® Unflavored Gelatine, divided
 1 package (3 ounces) lime-flavored gelatine
 ¼ cup sugar
 3 cups boiling water, divided
 ⅓ cup green crème de menthe
 3 cups (1½ pints) vanilla ice cream, softened,
     divided
 1 package (4½ ounces) chocolate instant pudding
     mix

In a large bowl, combine 4 envelopes Knox Unflavored Gelatine, the flavored gelatine, and sugar. Add 2 cups boiling water and stir until gelatine is completely dissolved. Stir in crème de menthe and 2 cups ice cream until melted. Pour into a shallow baking pan, 13x9x2 inches; chill until almost set.

In a large bowl, mix 2 envelopes Knox Unflavored Gelatine with the pudding mix. Add 1 cup boiling water and stir until gelatine is completely dissolved. Stir in 1 cup ice cream until melted. Carefully pour onto mint layer; chill until firm. To serve, cut into 1-inch squares.

Chocolate-Dipped Candies

Coating various kinds of candy with chocolate is a most felicitous form of lily-gilding. Nuts and fruits (candied fruits, too), caramels, nougats, and toffees all take kindly to a chocolate bath and, of course, various kinds of flavors of fondant, chocolate-dipped, result in chocolate creams, the home candy maker's crowning achievement.

There is an assortment of equipment available to aid in the making of chocolate-coated candies, such as little wire dippers to hold the candy, special racks, tiny paper bonbon cups, and, indeed, special kinds of chocolate, with a waxy consistency, for the dipping. Some of these are useful, particularly if you are going to make chocolate-dipped candy on a fairly regular basis. But you can get along, at least until you see whether or not you enjoy making such candies, with 2 forks, a candy thermometer, and a double boiler.

Temperature is of first importance—the temperature of the chocolate and of the centers you are dipping in it, and of the room in which you work. Heat and humidity defeat the most skillful chocolate dipper, so choose a cool, dry day and work in a kitchen where the temperature is about 65°F.

Making chocolate-dipped candies requires considerable patience and skill—and a lot of experience and experimenting—before you will be able to produce results like those on display in a good candy store. Consolation: If you use fresh, high-quality ingredients, your candies will taste as good as those from the best candy shops, even though at first they may not equal them in appearance.

Sweet Diversions

*Chocolatey sweet breads, muffins, and coffee cakes —
studded with nuts, filled and creamy—great for
breakfast, brunch or even dessert.*

Streusel Apple-Spice Cake
Makes 12 servings

- ½ cup butter or margarine
- 1 cup sugar
- 2 eggs
- 1 teaspoon vanilla extract
- 2¼ cups all-purpose flour
- ¾ teaspoon baking powder
- ¾ teaspoon ground cinnamon
- ½ teaspoon baking soda
- ¼ teaspoon ground cloves
- ⅛ teaspoon salt
- ¾ cup milk
- 1½ cups chopped, peeled tart apples
- ¾ cup Hershey's® Mini Chips® Semi-Sweet Chocolate
- Streusel Topping (recipe follows)
- 3 tablespoons Hershey's® Mini Chips® Semi-Sweet Chocolate (optional)

Cream butter and sugar in large mixer bowl until
light and fluffy. Add eggs and vanilla; beat well.
Combine flour, baking powder, cinnamon, baking
soda, cloves, and salt; add alternately with milk to
creamed mixture, blending well. Gently fold in
chopped apples and ¾ cup Mini Chips semi-sweet
chocolate. Spoon batter into greased and floured
9 × 5 × 3-inch loaf pan. Prepare Streusel Topping;
sprinkle on top of batter in pan. Bake at 350°F for 70
to 75 minutes, or until tester inserted in center comes
out clean. Cool cake in pan on wire rack 10 minutes.
Remove from pan; turn right side up. Immediately
sprinkle 3 tablespoons Mini Chips semi-sweet chocolate on top, if desired. Cool completely on wire rack.

Streusel Topping
- ½ cup all-purpose flour
- ¼ cup sugar
- ¼ teaspoon baking powder
- 3 tablespoons butter or margarine

Combine flour, sugar, and baking powder in small
bowl; cut in butter to form fine crumbs.

Chocolate Date Nut Loaf
Makes 10 servings

- 3 squares (3 ounces) unsweetened chocolate
- 1¼ cups milk
- ¼ cup vegetable oil
- 1 egg, lightly beaten
- 2 cups all-purpose flour
- ¾ cup sugar
- 1 teaspoon baking powder
- 1 teaspoon baking soda
- 1 teaspoon salt
- 1 cup pitted chopped dates
- ½ cup chopped walnuts

Melt chocolate over hot, not boiling, water. Stir in
milk, oil, and egg. Combine flour, sugar, baking
powder, baking soda, and salt. Add flour mixture,
dates, and walnuts to chocolate mixture and stir until
well mixed. Pour into greased 9 × 5 × 3-inch loaf pan.
Preheat oven to 350°F. Bake 55 to 60 minutes until
toothpick inserted in center comes out clean, rotating
once.

*Crunchy Topped Cocoa Cake (page 27); Streusel Apple-Spice Cake;
Chocolate Quickie Stickies (page 113).* Courtesy HERSHEY Food
Corporation

Chocolate Almond Pumpkin Bread

Makes 1 loaf

1⅔ cups all-purpose flour
1½ cups sugar
2 teaspoons pumpkin pie spice
1 teaspoon baking soda
½ teaspoon salt
¼ teaspoon baking powder
1 cup canned pumpkin
½ cup vegetable oil
⅓ cup water
2 eggs
1 cup chocolate morsels
½ cup chopped natural almonds, toasted

In large bowl, combine flour, sugar, spice, baking soda, salt, and baking powder. Add pumpkin, oil, water, and eggs. Beat to blend thoroughly. Stir in chocolate morsels and almonds. Spoon into greased and floured 9 × 5 × 3-inch loaf pan. Level top. Bake in 350°F oven about 1 hour and 15 minutes, until toothpick inserted in center comes out clean. Cool in pan 15 minutes. Turn out onto rack to cool completely. Wrap and store 24 hours before slicing.

Chocolate-Coconut Bread

Makes 1 loaf

2½ cups all-purpose flour
1½ teaspoons baking soda
1½ teaspoons salt
1 package (3 ounces) cream cheese, softened
¼ cup butter, softened
1 cup sugar
1 egg
3 envelopes (3 ounces) Nestlé Choco-bake Unsweetened Baking Chocolate Flavor
1 teaspoon vanilla extract
1¼ cups sour milk*
¾ cup toasted coconut

Preheat oven to 350°F. In a small bowl, combine flour, baking soda, and salt; set aside. In a large bowl, combine cream cheese, butter, and sugar; beat until creamy. Beat in egg. Add Nestlé Choco-bake Unsweetened Baking Chocolate Flavor and vanilla; mix well. Gradually add flour mixture alternately with sour milk. Stir in coconut. Pour batter into well-greased 9 × 5 × 3-inch loaf pan. Bake 60 to 65 minutes. Cool 10 minutes; remove from pan. Cool completely.

* To make sour milk: Combine 1 tablespoon vinegar or lemon juice and enough sweet milk to equal 1¼ cups. Let stand 5 minutes.

Chocolate Banana Bread

Makes 1 loaf

1½ cups all-purpose flour
½ cup Hershey's₀ Cocoa
⅔ cup sugar
1 teaspoon baking powder
½ teaspoon baking soda
½ teaspoon salt
½ cup shortening
1 cup mashed ripe bananas (about 2 medium)
2 eggs, lightly beaten
Confectioners sugar

Combine flour, cocoa, sugar, baking powder, baking soda, and salt in large mixing bowl. Cut in shortening with pastry blender or 2 knives until mixture resembles coarse crumbs. Add bananas and eggs; stir with fork just until blended. Spread evenly into greased and floured 9 × 5 × 3-inch loaf pan. Bake at 350°F for 50 to 55 minutes, or until cake tester inserted in center comes out clean. Cool in pan 10 minutes; remove from pan. Cool completely; sprinkle with confectioners sugar.

Fruited Chocolate Banana Bread

Stir in 1 cup raisins or finely chopped apricots just before baking.

Cooking with Cocoa

If you want to make a chocolate dessert and have no chocolate on hand, you can substitute cocoa. Use 3 level tablespoons cocoa plus 2 teaspoons shortening for each ounce of baking chocolate the recipe calls for. The shortening is required to make up the fat that chocolate contains but cocoa has in lesser quantity.

In any recipe that calls for cocoa, or in which you're substituting cocoa, mix the cocoa thoroughly with the flour or the sugar called for before adding the eggs or liquids.

Chocolate Surprise Coffee Cake

Makes one 10-inch Bundt® cake

2 packages (¼ ounce each) active dry yeast
¼ cup warm water
½ cup milk
1 cup butter or margarine, softened
1 tablespoon vegetable oil
¼ cup sugar
¼ teaspoon salt
3 cups all-purpose flour, divided
3 eggs, separated
1 6-ounce package (1 cup) Nestlé Toll House Semi-Sweet Chocolate Morsels
1 tablespoon butter, melted
Filling (recipe follows)

In a small bowl, dissolve yeast in warm water; set aside. In medium saucepan, heat milk until scalded. Add butter or margarine and vegetable oil. Cool to lukewarm. Add sugar, salt, and dissolved yeast. In a large bowl, combine 2 cups flour and milk mixture; beat in egg yolks. Beat well until dough is smooth. Stir in remaining cup of flour by hand. Turn out onto floured board. Knead about 10 minutes, until dough is smooth and elastic. Place in greased bowl; turn, cover, and refrigerate overnight.

Preheat oven to 350°F. Divide dough in half and prepare Filling. Roll half of dough into 20 × 12-inch rectangle on a well-floured board. Top with half of filling mixture, leaving 1-inch border on edge. Sprinkle with ½ cup Nestlé Toll House Semi-Sweet Chocolate Morsels. Roll up like jelly roll, starting with 20-inch side. Seal seam. Place in greased Bundt® pan; ends will overlap slightly. Repeat with remaining dough. Place on top of first dough in Bundt® pan, overlapping edges on side of pan opposite first roll. Brush with melted butter. Let rise 30 minutes, or until dough almost reaches top of pan. Bake 60 minutes. Cool 15 minutes. Remove from pan. Serve warm or cold.

Filling
    3 cups chopped walnuts
    1 teaspoon ground cinnamon
    3 tablespoons honey
    ½ cup milk
    ½ cup sugar
    1 teaspoon vanilla extract
    1 cup sugar

In a large saucepan, combine walnuts, cinnamon, honey, milk, and ½ cup sugar. Cook over moderate heat until sugar dissolves and mixture boils. Remove from heat; cool completely. Add vanilla; mix well. In a small bowl, beat egg whites until frothy. Gradually add 1 cup sugar, beating until stiff peaks form. Fold egg whites into walnut mixture. Fills and frosts two 9-inch cake layers.

Cocoa Swirl Coffee Cake
Makes 9 to 12 servings
    1½ cups all-purpose flour
    ¾ cup plus 2 tablespoons sugar
    2½ teaspoons baking powder
    ¾ teaspoon salt
    ¼ cup shortening
    2 eggs, lightly beaten
    ⅔ cup orange juice
    1 teaspoon grated orange peel
    ¾ cup confectioners sugar
    ½ cup chopped nuts
    ¼ cup Hershey's® Cocoa
    3 tablespoons butter, melted
      Orange Glaze (recipe follows)

Combine flour, sugar, baking powder, and salt in mixing bowl. Cut in shortening with pastry blender until mixture resembles coarse crumbs. Add eggs, orange juice, and orange peel; stir just until blended. Set batter aside. Combine confectioners sugar, nuts, and cocoa in a small bowl. Stir in melted butter to form a crumb mixture. Spread ¾ cup reserved batter evenly on bottom of a greased 8-inch square pan. Sprinkle half of crumb mixture over batter. Spread with 1 cup batter and sprinkle with remaining crumb mixture. Cover with remaining batter. Bake at 350°F. for 35 to 40 minutes, or until cake tester inserted in center comes out clean. Cool slightly; spread with Orange Glaze. Serve warm.

Orange Glaze
    1 cup confectioners sugar
    2 tablespoons orange juice
    ¼ teaspoon grated orange peel

Combine confectioners sugar, orange juice, and orange peel in small bowl; blend until smooth. Spread on warm coffee cake.

Toll House Crumb Cake
Makes 24 squares
    1 tablespoon all-purpose flour
    ½ cup firmly packed brown sugar
    2 tablespoons butter, softened
    ½ cup chopped nuts
    1 12-ounce package (2 cups) Nestlé Little Bits
      Semi-Sweet Chocolate, divided
    2 cups all-purpose flour
    1 teaspoon baking powder
    1 teaspoon baking soda
    ½ teaspoon salt
    ½ cup butter, softened
    1 cup sugar
    1 teaspoon vanilla extract
    3 eggs
    1 cup sour cream

In a small bowl, combine flour, brown sugar, and butter; mix well. Stir in nuts and ½ cup Nestlé Little Bits Semi-Sweet Chocolate; set aside.

Preheat oven to 350°F. In a small bowl, combine flour, baking powder, baking soda, and salt; set aside. In a large bowl, combine butter, sugar, and vanilla; mix well. Add eggs, 1 at a time, beating well after each addition. Gradually add flour mixture alternately with sour cream. Fold in remaining 1½ cups Nestlé Little Bits Semi-Sweet Chocolate. Spread into greased 13 × 9 × 2-inch baking pan. Sprinkle topping evenly over batter. Bake 45 to 50 minutes.

Crumble Cake

Makes 12 servings

2½ cups all-purpose flour
  2 teaspoons baking powder
  1 teaspoon salt
  1 cup butter or margarine, divided
1⅓ cups granulated sugar
  3 eggs
  1 cup milk
  1 cup miniature semisweet chocolate pieces, divided
  ½ cup firmly packed brown sugar
  1 cup shredded coconut
  ½ cup chopped walnuts

Combine flour, baking powder, and salt; set aside. Cream ¾ cup butter until smooth. Add sugar and beat until light and fluffy. Beat in eggs, 1 at a time, beating well after each addition. Add flour mixture to egg mixture alternately with milk, beating just until well combined. Stir in ½ cup chocolate pieces. Pour batter into greased 13 × 9 × 2-inch baking dish. Combine brown sugar and remaining ¼ cup butter until crumbly. Add coconut, walnuts, and remaining ½ cup chocolate pieces. Toss to mix; set aside.

Preheat oven to 350°F. Bake 40 to 45 minutes, until toothpick inserted in center comes out clean, rotating once. Sprinkle with coconut-walnut mixture and broil 3 to 4 minutes, until topping melts and is lightly browned. Cool in pan on wire rack. Cut into squares.

Chocolate Coffee Roll

Makes 8 to 10 servings

  1 envelope (¼ ounce) or cake yeast, active dry or compressed
2½ cups sifted all-purpose flour
  ½ cup cocoa
1¼ cups sugar
  ¼ teaspoon salt
  ¼ cup butter
  3 eggs
    Filling (recipe follows)

Oil a cookie sheet. Dissolve the yeast in ¼ cup warm (105 to 115°F) water. Sift the flour, cocoa, sugar, and salt together. Cut in the butter with a pastry blender. Add the eggs, 1 at a time, beating well after each addition. Add the dissolved yeast and beat again. Put into an oiled bowl and turn once to bring oiled side up. Cover and let rise in a warm place, free from draft, until doubled in bulk, about 2 hours. In the meantime, make Filling. When the dough has risen, roll it out into an oblong about ½ inch thick. Spread with the Filling and roll like a jelly roll. Place on cookie sheet. Bake in a preheated 375°F oven for 25 minutes.

Filling

  2 squares (1 ounce each) unsweetened chocolate, melted
  2 tablespoons brandy
  ½ cup honey
  2 cups filberts, ground
  ½ cup dried currants

Mix ingredients thoroughly.

Crumble Cake. Caloric Corporation

Chocolate Date Nut Loaf (page 107). Caloric Corporation

Bird's Nest Coffee Cake

Makes one 9-inch coffee cake
- 1 6-ounce package (1 cup) Nestlé Toll House Semi-Sweet Chocolate Morsels, divided
- ¼ cup blanched slivered almonds, toasted
- 1 teaspoon grated orange rind
- 2¼ to 3¼ cups all-purpose flour
- ¼ cup sugar
- 1 teaspoon salt
- 1 package (¼ ounce) active dry yeast
- ⅔ cup milk
- 2 tablespoons butter
- 2 eggs
  Melted butter
- 5 raw eggs in shells, colored with food color
- 1 tablespoon vegetable shortening

In a small bowl, combine ¾ cup Nestlé Toll House Semi-Sweet Chocolate Morsels, almonds, and orange rind; set aside. In a large bowl, combine 1 cup flour, sugar, salt, and undissolved yeast; set aside. In a small saucepan, combine milk and butter over low heat until liquid is warm (120° to 130°F). Gradually add to flour mixture; beat 2 minutes at medium speed with electric mixer. Add 2 eggs and enough flour to make a thick batter. Beat 2 minutes at high speed; stir in enough additional flour to make a soft dough. Gently stir in morsel-almond mixture. Turn onto a lightly floured board; knead until smooth and elastic (about 8 to 10 minutes). Place in lightly greased bowl, turning dough to grease top. Cover; let rise in a warm place until doubled in bulk (about 1 hour).

Punch down dough; turn onto a lightly floured board and divide in half. Roll each half into a 24-inch rope. Place ropes side by side on a lightly greased cookie sheet and loosely overlap one with the other, starting in the middle. Shape into a ring and seal ends. Brush ring with melted butter. Place colored eggs in spaces in the twist. Cover; let rise in a warm place until doubled in bulk (about 1 hour). About 15 to 20 minutes before ready to bake, preheat oven to 350°F. Bake 30 to 35 minutes. Remove from cookie sheet; cool on rack.

Over hot (not boiling) water, heat remaining ¼ cup Nestlé Toll House Semi-Sweet Chocolate Morsels and the shortening; stir until morsels melt and mixture is smooth. Drizzle chocolate mixture over completely cooled ring to resemble a bird's nest.

Mini Chip Nut Rolls

Makes 4 loaves
- 5 to 5½ cups all-purpose flour
- ½ cup sugar
- 1 teaspoon salt
- 2 packages (¼ ounce each) active dry yeast
- 1 cup sour cream
- ½ cup water
- ¼ cup milk
- ½ cup butter or margarine
- 4 egg yolks, room temperature (reserve whites)
  Walnut Mini Chip Filling (recipe follows)

Mix 2 cups of the flour, the sugar, salt, and undissolved active dry yeast in a large mixer bowl; set aside. Heat sour cream, water, milk, and butter in small saucepan over low heat until very warm (120 to 130°F). Gradually add to dry ingredients; beat 2 minutes on high speed. Add egg yolks and 1 cup of flour; beat 2 minutes on medium speed. Stir in enough additional flour to make a soft dough; turn out onto well-floured board. Knead in enough remaining flour so dough is not sticky and forms smooth ball (about 5 minutes). Cover; let rest 15 minutes. Divide dough into 4 equal pieces.

On lightly floured board, roll each piece of dough to a 12 × 10-inch rectangle. Spread 1¼ cups of Walnut Mini Chip Filling to within ½ inch of edges. Roll dough from long side as for jelly roll; pinch to seal edges. Place on ungreased baking sheet, sealed edges down; cover and let rise in warm place until doubled in bulk (1 to 1½ hours).

Bake at 350°F for 15 minutes; loosely cover with aluminum foil and bake 5 to 10 minutes longer, or until golden brown. Remove from oven and brush lightly with butter; cool completely. Sprinkle with confectioners sugar or glaze with confectioners sugar glaze.

Walnut Mini Chip Filling

Makes 5 cups filling
- 4 egg whites
- ⅔ cup sugar
  Dash salt
- 4 cups ground walnuts
- 1 package (12 ounces) Hershey's® Mini Chips® Semi-Sweet Chocolate

Beat egg whites until foamy in small mixer bowl; gradually add sugar and salt, beating until stiff peaks form. Fold in ground walnuts and Mini Chips semi-sweet chocolate; blend well.

Raisin-Nut Muffins

Makes 2 dozen muffins

2¼ cups all-purpose flour
¾ cup sugar
½ cup Hershey's® Cocoa
1 tablespoon baking powder
1½ teaspoons salt
½ cup shortening
2 eggs, lightly beaten
1¼ cups milk
1 cup raisins
⅓ cup chopped nuts

Combine flour, sugar, cocoa, baking powder, and salt in large mixing bowl. Cut in shortening with pastry blender or 2 knives until mixture resembles coarse crumbs. Combine eggs and milk; add all at once to flour mixture, stirring just until dry ingredients are moistened. Stir raisins and nuts into the mixture. Do not overmix. Fill 24 greased or paper-lined muffin cups (2½ inches in diameter) ⅔ full with batter. Bake at 400°F for 20 minutes, or until cake tester inserted in center comes out clean.
Note: These muffins freeze well. To reheat, place frozen muffins, wrapped in foil, in a 400°F oven for about 20 minutes, or until warm.

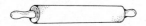

Chocolate Quickie Stickies

Makes 4 dozen rolls

6 tablespoons butter or margarine
3 tablespoons Hershey's® Cocoa
¾ cup firmly packed light brown sugar
5 teaspoons water
1 teaspoon vanilla extract
½ cup coarsely chopped nuts (optional)
2 packages (8 ounces each) refrigerator crescent dinner rolls
2 tablespoons butter or margarine, softened
2 tablespoons sugar
1 tablespoon unsweetened cocoa

Melt 6 tablespoons butter in small saucepan over low heat. Add 3 tablespoons cocoa, the brown sugar, and water. Cook over medium heat, stirring constantly, until mixture comes to a boil. Remove from heat; add vanilla. Spoon about 1 teaspoon chocolate mixture into each of 48 small muffin pans (1¾ inch in diameter). Sprinkle ½ teaspoon nuts, if desired, into each cup; set aside. Separate rolls into 8 rectangles; firmly press diagonal perforations to seal. Spread softened butter evenly over each rectangle. Combine sugar and 1 tablespoon cocoa; sprinkle about 1 tea-spoon mixture over each rectangle. Starting at longer side, roll up. Pinch seams to seal. Cut each roll into 6 equal pieces. Place in prepared pans, cut side down. Bake at 350°F for 11 to 13 minutes, or until light brown. Remove from oven; cool 30 seconds. Invert onto cookie sheet. Let stand 1 minute; remove pan. Serve warm or cool.

Pain au Chocolate

Makes 1 serving

1 croissant
2 tablespoons Nestlé Little Bits Semi-Sweet Chocolate
2 tablespoons confectioners sugar
Hot water
Nestlé Little Bits Semi-Sweet Chocolate (optional)

Slice a prepared croissant horizontally along one side. Do not cut all the way through. Fill with Nestlé Little Bits Semi-Sweet Chocolate. Bake in toaster oven until chocolate melts (about 10 minutes). Meanwhile, add hot water very gradually to confectioners sugar, a few drops at a time. Beat constantly until it forms a glaze thin enough to pour. Drizzle croissant with glaze and sprinkle with additional Little Bits, if desired.

Finer Fillings

The traditional filling for a rolled yeast cake is a mixture of cocoa, sugar, and butter or margarine. It's delicious just like that; but you can make it even better by adding one or more of the following to 1 cup of regular filling:

1 teaspoon cinnamon and ¼ teaspoon nutmeg
1 tablespoon kirsch or other liqueur
¼ cup chopped walnuts, hazelnuts, or pecans
¼ cup raisins, plumped in liqueur or brandy
¼ cup chopped, candied fruit
¼ cup raspberry jam; decrease butter by 2 table-spoons
¼ cup peanut butter; decrease butter by 2 table-spoons
2 tablespoons honey; decrease butter by 1 table-spoon
2 tablespoons chopped chocolate morsels
2 tablespoons chopped butterscotch morsels
2 tablespoons finely chopped cherries or pineapple

Mix well; spread on unbaked yeast dough; roll and bake.

Surprising Sensations

When you want something different, something exotic—
of course, something chocolate—choose from among such
chocolate specialties as bubbly rich fondues, mile-high
cold and hot soufflés, sinfully sauced crêpes, waffles,
cream puffs, and fruit desserts.

Velvet Chocolate Fondue
Makes about 4 servings

  1 package (8 squares) Baker's Semi-Sweet
    Chocolate
  ⅔ cup milk
  ¼ cup sugar
    Dash ground cinnamon
    Fruit: green grapes, apple slices, banana chunks,
      pear wedges, stemmed cherries, or
      tangerines, dried apricots, prunes, or dates

Combine all ingredients except fruit in saucepan. Heat over low heat, stirring constantly, until melted and smooth. Pour into fondue pot or small chafing dish and keep warm while serving. (If heated longer than ½ hour, add additional milk for proper consistency.) Or pour into demitasse cups or small glasses and serve immediately. Accompany fondue with fruit or cake, spearing each with long-handled fork and swirling through chocolate 1 piece at a time.

Double Chocolate Fondue
Prepare Velvet Chocolate Fondue as directed, adding 1 package (4 ounces) Baker's German's Sweet Chocolate and increasing milk to ¾ cup. *Makes 2 cups.*

Honey-Peanut Chocolate Fondue
Prepare Velvet Chocolate Fondue as directed, omitting sugar, reducing milk to ½ cup, and adding ¼ cup creamy peanut butter. *Makes 1¾ cups.*

Brandied Chocolate Fondue
Prepare Velvet Chocolate Fondue as directed, substituting 6 tablespoons light cream or half and half for the milk and omitting the cinnamon. Add 3 tablespoons brandy. *Makes 1⅓ cups.*

Easy Chocolate Fondue
Makes 1 cup

  1 6-ounce package (1 cup) Nestlé Toll House
    Semi-Sweet Chocolate Morsels
  ½ cup corn syrup
  1 teaspoon vanilla extract
    Dash salt
  2 to 3 tablespoons brandy
    Bite-size pieces fruit (apples, bananas, seedless
      grapes, fresh strawberries, maraschino
      cherries, or mandarin orange segments)
    Pound cake, cut into cubes
    Ground nuts or toasted shredded coconut
    (optional)

Combine Nestlé Toll House Semi-Sweet Chocolate Morsels, corn syrup, vanilla, and salt in an electric fondue pot or a large saucepan. Stir over medium heat until morsels melt and mixture is smooth. Add brandy; mix well. Serve with your favorite fruit dippers and/or pound cake cubes. After dipping in chocolate, coat with ground nuts or shredded coconut, if desired.

Velvet Chocolate Fondue. General Foods

Sweet Soufflés

Chocolate or chocolate-fruit soufflés are heavier than savory soufflés; they require some special steps to keep them light and airy.

• Use a bouillie sauce as a base for the soufflé, rather than a cream sauce. Although the bouillie sauce is not as moist as the cream sauce, it will provide a stronger base for the other ingredients. To make a bouillie base, combine 4 tablespoons cornstarch and ⅓ cup milk; whisk until smooth, then add another ⅔ cup milk. Cook, stirring constantly, until the mixture is smooth and very thick. Remove from heat and allow to cool for a few minutes; then fold in 4 egg yolks, 1 at a time; gradually add ½ cup sugar. Stir until well blended, and continue with flavorings.

• If you are using fruit, slice it very thinly; do not use purées, as they tend to be heavy.

• Oversweeten slightly; the rising of the eggs will cause the other parts of the soufflé to be diluted.

• Use a wide-based soufflé dish to give these heavy soufflés a broad base.

• As with all soufflés, it is important that eggs be beaten to their maximum volume. Make sure the bowl you beat your eggs in is perfectly clean; even a trace of grease will cause the eggs to lose volume. Eggs should be at room temperature when you begin.

Black Forest Soufflé

Makes about 8 servings

    1 can (16 ounces) sour pitted cherries, drained
    5 tablespoons kirsch, divided
    4 squares (1 ounce each) semisweet chocolate, divided
    2 envelopes Knox® Unflavored Gelatine
    ¾ cup sugar, divided
    3 eggs, separated
    2 cups milk
 1½ teaspoons vanilla extract
    2 cups heavy cream, divided
      Chocolate Curls (see index)

Chop cherries and marinate in 2 tablespoons kirsch.

Using about ¼ ounce chocolate, make enough Chocolate Curls for garnish.

In a medium saucepan, mix Knox Unflavored Gelatine with ½ cup sugar. Beat egg yolks with milk and add to gelatine mixture with remaining chocolate squares (about 3¾ ounces). Stir over low heat until gelatine is completely dissolved and chocolate melts, 5 to 8 minutes. Remove from heat. Add remaining 3 tablespoons kirsch and vanilla. With wire whip or rotary beater, beat mixture until chocolate is well blended. Chill, stirring occasionally, until mixture mounds slightly when dropped from a spoon.

In a large bowl, beat egg whites until soft peaks form; gradually add remaining ¼ cup sugar and beat until stiff. Fold in gelatine mixture.

In a medium bowl, whip 1¾ cups heavy cream and fold into gelatine mixture with chopped cherries and kirsch. Turn into a 1-quart soufflé dish with a 3-inch collar. Chill until set, about 4 hours. Remove collar. To garnish, top with remaining heavy cream, whipped, and Chocolate Curls.

Chocolate Soufflé with Raspberry Cream

Makes 6 to 8 servings

    1 cup (6 ounces) Hershey's® Mini Chips® Semi-
      Sweet Chocolate
    ¼ cup sugar
    2 tablespoons all-purpose flour
    ¼ teaspoon salt
    1 cup milk
    1 tablespoon butter
    2 teaspoons vanilla extract
    5 egg yolks, lightly beaten
    7 egg whites, at room temperature
    1 tablespoon sugar
      Raspberry Cream (recipe follows)

Butter a 1½-quart soufflé dish or straight-sided casserole; sprinkle with sugar. Measure a length of aluminum foil to go around dish for a collar; fold into thirds lengthwise. Butter and sugar one side of collar and tie with string or tape securely to outside of dish, buttered side in, allowing collar to extend 3 inches above rim. Melt Mini Chips semi-sweet chocolate in top of double boiler over hot (not boiling) water; set aside. Combine ¼ cup sugar, flour, and salt in medium saucepan; gradually add milk. Cook and stir over low heat until mixture boils. Boil and stir 2 minutes. Remove from heat; blend in butter and vanilla. Gradually stir hot mixture into beaten yolks in medium mixing bowl. Add melted chocolate; blend well. Set aside to cool slightly. Beat egg whites in large mixer bowl until foamy; gradually add 1 tablespoon sugar and beat until stiff peaks form. Stir about 1 cup of beaten egg whites into chocolate mixture; gently fold chocolate mixture into remaining egg whites. Pour into prepared soufflé dish. Place on lower oven rack. Bake at 400°F for 35 to 40 minutes, or until set. Carefully remove collar. Serve immediately with Raspberry Cream.

Raspberry Cream

Makes about 2 cups

    1 package (10 ounces) frozen red raspberries,
      thawed
    1 cup heavy cream
    ¼ cup sugar
    1 teaspoon vanilla extract

Drain berries. Mash or purée berry pulp to equal ½ cup. Whip cream, sugar, and vanilla until stiff. Gently fold in raspberry purée.

Spirited Chocolate Soufflé

Makes 16 servings

- 2 envelopes Knox® Unflavored Gelatine
- ½ cup cold water
- ⅔ cup crème de cacao
- 1 package (12 ounces) semisweet chocolate pieces
- 8 eggs, separated
- ⅓ cup firmly packed light brown sugar
- 2 cups heavy cream, whipped
  Sweetened whipped cream (optional)

In a medium saucepan, mix Knox Unflavored Gelatine with water and crème de cacao. Let stand 1 minute. Stir over low heat until gelatine is completely dissolved, about 5 minutes. Add chocolate pieces; stir until melted. Remove from heat; beat in egg yolks 1 at a time. Cool.

In a large bowl, beat egg whites until soft peaks form; gradually add brown sugar and beat until stiff. Fold in chocolate mixture and whipped cream. Turn into a 2-quart soufflé dish with a 2-inch collar. Chill until set, several hours or overnight. Remove collar to serve. Garnish with whipped cream, if desired.

Chocolate-Rum Soufflé

Makes 6 to 8 servings

- Butter
- 2 tablespoons graham cracker crumbs
- 3 tablespoons butter
- 3 tablespoons all-purpose flour
- 1 cup milk
- 1 6-ounce package (1 cup) Nestlé Toll House Semi-Sweet Chocolate Morsels
- 4 eggs, separated
- ¼ cup rum
- 1 teaspoon vanilla extract
  Vanilla ice cream or sweetened whipped cream

Butter bottom and sides of a 6-cup soufflé dish; coat with graham cracker crumbs. In a small saucepan, melt 3 tablespoons butter over medium heat. Blend in flour. Gradually stir in milk. Cook, stirring constantly, until mixture thickens. Stir in Nestlé Toll House Semi-Sweet Chocolate Morsels. Transfer chocolate mixture to a large bowl; cool 10 minutes. Beat in egg yolks, rum, and vanilla; set aside.

Preheat oven to 350°F. In a small bowl, beat egg whites until stiff (not dry) peaks form. Stir ½ cup beaten egg whites into chocolate mixture. Gently fold remaining egg whites into chocolate mixture. Pour into prepared dish. For a top-hat soufflé, run knife through batter in a circle 1 inch from edge of dish, to a depth of 1 inch. Bake 40 minutes. Serve immediately with vanilla ice cream or sweetened whipped cream.

Cocoa Soufflé

Makes 6 to 8 servings

- ¼ cup butter or margarine
- ¼ cup all-purpose flour
- ⅓ cup Hershey's® Cocoa
- ¼ teaspoon salt
- 1 cup milk
- 1 teaspoon vanilla extract
- 4 eggs, separated
- ½ cup sugar
- 2 tablespoons sugar
  Liqueur Whipped Cream (recipe follows)

Grease bottom of 1-quart soufflé dish or straight-sided casserole. Measure a length of aluminum foil to go around dish; fold into thirds lengthwise. Butter one side of foil and tie with string or tape securely to outside of dish (buttered side in); allow foil collar to extend 4 inches above rim. Melt butter in saucepan over low heat; stir in flour, blending well. Remove from heat; add cocoa and salt. Gradually blend in milk. Cook, stirring constantly, over low heat until mixture is thick and smooth and just begins to boil. Remove from heat; add vanilla. Carefully press plastic wrap onto surface; cool 20 minutes.

Beat egg yolks with ½ cup sugar in small mixer bowl until thick and lemon colored. Carefully blend cocoa mixture into egg mixture; set aside. Beat egg whites until foamy in large mixer bowl; gradually add 2 tablespoons sugar and beat until stiff peaks form. Carefully fold cocoa mixture into egg whites just until blended. Pour into dish; place dish in pan containing about 1 inch hot water. Bake at 350°F for 60 to 65 minutes, or until cake tester inserted halfway between edge and center comes out clean. Carefully remove collar; serve immediately with Liqueur Whipped Cream.

Liqueur Whipped Cream

Makes about 1 cup

- ½ cup heavy cream
- 1 tablespoon confectioners sugar
- 1 or 2 teaspoons Grand Marnier or kirsch

Beat heavy cream with confectioners sugar in small mixer bowl until stiff. Fold in liqueur.

Cold Mocha Soufflé

Makes 10 to 12 servings

  1 **envelope unflavored gelatin**
 ¼ **cup cold water**
  1 **package (4 ounces) Baker's German's Sweet Chocolate**
  1 **tablespoon Maxwell House Instant Coffee**
 ¼ **cup water**
  6 **eggs, separated**
 ¼ **cup sugar**
  1 **envelope Dream Whip Whipped Topping Mix**

Soften gelatin in ¼ cup cold water. Heat chocolate in saucepan over low heat with instant coffee and ¼ cup water, stirring until chocolate is melted. Add gelatin; stir to dissolve. Remove from heat.

Combine egg yolks and sugar in top of double boiler. Place over hot water and beat until mixture is thick and light in color, about 4 minutes. Remove from heat. Blend in chocolate mixture, then pour into a bowl. Beat egg whites until stiff, shiny peaks form; fold into chocolate mixture. Cool about 10 minutes. Prepare whipped topping mix as directed on package; fold into chocolate mixture.

Pour into buttered 1½-quart soufflé or serving dish. Chill 3 hours. Garnish with additional whipped topping, if desired.

Note: For a more elegant soufflé, tape 4-inch strip of waxed paper around outside of 1-quart soufflé dish or straight-sided casserole. Brush inside of paper strip with oil. Loosen paper and gently peel away from chilled soufflé.

Individual Chocolate Soufflés

Makes 8 servings

 ½ **cup sugar**
 ⅓ **cup Hershey's® Cocoa**
  3 **tablespoons cornstarch**
 ¾ **cup milk**
 ¼ **cup butter or margarine**
  2 **teaspoons vanilla extract**
  4 **egg yolks**
  4 **egg whites, at room temperature**
 ¼ **teaspoon cream of tartar**
  3 **tablespoons sugar**
    Sweetened whipped cream or whipped topping

Butter eight 6-ounce soufflé dishes; sprinkle with sugar. Measure 8 lengths of aluminum foil to go around dishes for collars. Fold foil lengthwise in quarters. Lightly butter and sugar one side of each collar and tie with string or tape securely to outside of dishes, buttered side in, allowing collar to extend

Party Chocolate Crêpes (page 120). Courtesy of Nestlé Foods Corporation

about 3 inches above rim. Combine ½ cup sugar, cocoa, and cornstarch in a medium saucepan; gradually add milk. Cook and stir over low heat until mixture comes to a boil and is smooth; remove from heat. Stir in butter and vanilla; set aside to cool. Beat egg yolks in small mixer bowl until thick and lemon colored; blend in cocoa mixture. Beat egg whites and cream of tartar in large mixer bowl until foamy. Gradually add 3 tablespoons sugar and beat until stiff peaks form. Stir about 1 cup beaten egg whites into cocoa mixture, then gently fold cocoa mixture into remaining whites just until blended. Pour into prepared dishes. Bake at 325°F for 40 to 45 minutes, or until set but not dry. Carefully remove collars. Immediately serve with sweetened whipped cream or whipped topping.

Cream Puffs (page 119). Caloric Corporation

Quick Napoleons

Makes 24 napoleons
- 2 cups milk
- 1 package (3¾ ounces) vanilla instant pudding and pie filling
- 1 cup heavy cream
- 1 6-ounce package (1 cup) Nestlé Toll House Semi-Sweet Chocolate Morsels
- 24 cinnamon graham crackers
- 1½ cups sifted confectioners sugar
- 2 tablespoons milk
- 1 teaspoon corn syrup

Using 2 cups milk, prepare instant pudding according to package directions. In a small bowl, beat heavy cream until stiff; fold into prepared pudding and chill in refrigerator. Melt Nestlé Toll House Semi-Sweet Chocolate Morsels over hot (not boiling) water. Spread each of 16 crackers with 1 teaspoon melted chocolate. Reserve remaining melted chocolate for frosting. Line a 13x9x2-inch pan with foil and arrange 8 chocolate-covered crackers on bottom. Carefully spread half the chilled pudding mixture evenly over crackers. Repeat with a layer of 8 chocolate-covered crackers and remaining pudding. Set aside; prepare frosting.

In a small bowl, combine confectioners sugar, 2 tablespoons milk, and the corn syrup; blend well. Prepare remaining crackers, 1 at a time; spread crackers with confectioners sugar glaze. Fit a pastry tube with a writing tip and fill with remaining melted chocolate. For a "feathered" look, pipe chocolate over glaze in lengthwise lines about 1 inch apart. Draw a toothpick or knife point through lines, crosswise, in alternating directions, about 1 inch apart. Place frosted graham crackers on top of final pudding layer. Chill overnight. If desired, cut each napoleon in thirds.

> **Q.** *I have a recipe that calls for "canned or fresh pitted cherries." I'd like to use fresh—but how do I get the pits out?*
> **A.** Pitting cherries isn't all that easy a job. For the effete, there are cherry-pitters available—metal gadgets looking rather like a reverse hypodermic with a pair of grabby little tongs on the business end. Or use a thin, pointed knife or the tip of a swivel vegetable peeler. Or press a paper clip into service to hook the stone and pry it out. In any case, don't squeeze— you'll lose juice, flavor, and nutrients. And bear in mind that cherry juice, especially that of dark sweet cherries, stains everything it touches, including clothes, fingers (particularly under fingernails), counters, and utensils. Wash up right away

Black Forest Soufflé (page 116). Photo courtesy of Knox Gelatine, Inc.

Cream Puffs

Makes 8 servings
- ½ cup butter or margarine
- ¼ teaspoon salt
- 1 cup water
- 1 cup all-purpose flour
- 4 eggs
- 2 cups heavy cream
- ¼ cup confectioners sugar
- 3 tablespoons orange-flavored liqueur
- 1 package (6 ounces) semisweet chocolate pieces
- 1 tablespoon milk

Heat butter, salt, and 1 cup water to boiling. Remove from heat and add flour all at once, beating vigorously with wooden spoon until mixture pulls away from side of pan and forms a ball. Let stand 3 to 5 minutes to cool. Beat in eggs, 1 at a time, beating well after each addition, until dough is smooth and glossy. Drop dough onto large ungreased baking sheet in 8 mounds about 3 inches apart. Swirl the top of each mound with back of spoon. Preheat oven to 400°F. Bake cream puffs 45 minutes. Cut a slit in side of each puff and bake 10 minutes, or until crisp and golden. Cool completely on wire rack.

Beat cream until thick. Add sugar and liqueur and beat until stiff; set aside. Melt chocolate with milk, stirring until smooth; set aside. Slice off tops of cream puffs and scoop out uncooked portion. Spoon cream mixture into puffs and replace tops. Drizzle with melted chocolate mixture. Serve immediately or refrigerate.

Party Chocolate Crêpes

Makes 30 filled crêpes

    1 6-ounce package (1 cup) Nestlé Toll House
        Semi-Sweet Chocolate Morsels
    3 tablespoons butter
    1 cup all-purpose flour
    1 cup sifted confectioners sugar
    4 eggs
    ½ cup milk
    ½ cup water
    1 tablespoon vanilla extract
    1 teaspoon salt
      Melted butter
      Confectioners sugar
      Orange Cream Cheese Filling (recipe follows)

Over hot (not boiling) water, combine Nestlé Toll House Semi-Sweet Chocolate Morsels and butter; heat until morsels melt and mixture is smooth. Remove from heat; cool slightly. In blender container, combine cooled chocolate mixture, flour, confectioners sugar, eggs, milk, water, vanilla, and salt; blend at medium speed until smooth (about 2 minutes), scraping sides of container when necessary. Brush a 6- or 8-inch crêpe pan or skillet with melted butter. When butter begins to sizzle, pour about 3 tablespoons batter into pan; turn and tip pan immediately to coat bottom. Cook until top of crêpe begins to dry (about 20 seconds); turn and cook a few seconds. Remove from pan. Repeat with remaining batter. Spread 2 level measuring tablespoonfuls Orange Cream Cheese Filling over each crêpe. Roll up jelly roll fashion; place on a platter. Dust with confectioners sugar.

Orange Cream Cheese Filling

    3 packages (8 ounces each) cream cheese, softened
    ¾ cup sifted confectioners sugar
    ½ cup milk
    2 tablespoons grated orange rind

In a large bowl, combine cream cheese, confectioners sugar, milk, and grated orange rind; beat until smooth and creamy.

Pineapple Chantilly with Almond-Chocolate Sauce

Makes 6 servings

    1 cup whipping cream
    2 tablespoons confectioners sugar
    1 cup fresh or unsweetened canned pineapple
        chunks
    1 cup red grapes, halved and seeded, or sliced
        bananas
    2 tablespoons slivered almonds, toasted
    2 tablespoons rum
      Chocolate-Almond Sauce (recipe follows)

Whip cream until stiff; stir in sugar. At serving time, mix fruit, almonds, and rum into whipped cream. Spoon into sherbert glasses or dessert bowls and top with Chocolate-Almond Sauce.

Chocolate-Almond Sauce

    1 tablespoon toasted slivered almonds
    1 tablespoon rum
    1 cup canned chocolate sundae sauce

Add almonds and rum to chocolate sundae sauce.

Chocolate-Orange Puffs

Makes 16 puffs

    ½ cup water
    ¼ cup butter
    1 tablespoon grated orange rind
      Dash salt
    ½ cup all-purpose flour
    2 eggs
      Confectioners sugar
      Chocolate Filling (recipe follows)

Preheat oven to 450°F. In a small saucepan, combine water, butter, orange rind, and salt; heat until mixture boils. Remove from heat. Add flour; blend until mixture holds together. Add eggs, 1 at a time, beating well after each addition. Drop dough by level tablespoonfuls onto greased cookie sheets. Bake 10 minutes. Reduce heat to 350°F; bake 10 minutes longer. Remove from oven. While still hot, cut a thin slice from top of each puff. Cool completely. Spoon about 1 rounded tablespoonful Chocolate Filling into each puff. Replace top. Dust top with confectioners sugar. Chill in refrigerator for about 1 hour, or until ready to serve.

Chocolate Filling

    1 6-ounce package (1 cup) Nestlé Toll House
        Semi-Sweet Chocolate Morsels
    3 tablespoons orange juice
    ⅔ cup heavy cream
    3 tablespoons confectioners sugar
      Dash salt

Over hot (not boiling) water, combine Nestlé Toll House Semi-Sweet Chocolate Morsels and orange juice; stir until morsels melt and mixture is smooth. Transfer to a large bowl; cool 10 minutes. In a small bowl, combine heavy cream, confectioners sugar, and salt; beat until stiff peaks form. Gently fold into cooled chocolate mixture.

Chocolate Dessert Waffles

Makes 20 waffles

1½ cups milk
  1 cup sugar
  3 envelopes (3 ounces) Nestlé Choco-bake
    Unsweetened Baking Chocolate Flavor
  1 egg
  2 tablespoons vegetable oil
  ¾ teaspoon vanilla extract
  ¾ teaspoon ground cinnamon
  2 cups buttermilk pancake mix
    Ice Cream
    Hot Chocolate Sauce (see index) or Orange-
    Butterscotch Sauce (recipe follows)

In blender container or a large bowl, combine milk, sugar, Nestlé Choco-bake Unsweetened Baking Chocolate Flavor, egg, oil, vanilla, and cinnamon; process at medium speed about 10 seconds or beat well. Add pancake mix; blend until smooth (about 1 minute), scraping sides of container if necessary. To bake waffles, follow manufacturer's instructions for waffle iron. Serve with ice cream and Hot Chocolate Sauce or Orange-Butterscotch Sauce.

Orange-Butterscotch Sauce

Makes ¾ cup sauce

  1 6-ounce package (1 cup) Nestlé Butterscotch
    Flavored Morsels
  ¼ cup evaporated milk
  ¼ teaspoon orange extract

Melt Nestlé Butterscotch Flavored Morsels over hot (not boiling) water. Stir in evaporated milk and orange extract. Blend mixture with a fork or wire whisk until smooth. Serve warm over ice cream or cake.

Ruby Pears with Chocolate Cream

Makes 8 to 10 servings

  2 cans (29 ounces each) pear halves, drained
  2 cups ginger ale
    Juice of 1 orange
    Juice of ½ lime
  2 tablespoons butter or margarine, melted
  1 cinnamon stick
  3 whole cloves
1½ cups red currant jelly
    Chocolate Cream (recipe follows)

Preheat oven to 350°F. Arrange pears, cut side up, in 13×9×2-inch baking pan. In a small bowl, combine ginger ale, orange juice, lime juice, butter, cinnamon stick, and cloves; mix well. Pour over pears. Cover pan with aluminum foil; refrigerate overnight. Remove from refrigerator; allow to sit at room temperature 30 minutes. Cover with aluminum foil. Bake 30 minutes. Remove from oven. Drain pears, reserving 5 tablespoons liquid. Place pears in serving dishes; set aside. In a small saucepan, melt red currant jelly over low heat. Add 3 tablespoons reserved liquid; mix well. Pour equally over pears. Serve with Chocolate Cream.

Chocolate Cream

Makes 3 cups

  1 6-ounce package (1 cup) Nestlé Toll House
    Semi-Sweet Chocolate Morsels
  2 tablespoons honey
1½ tablespoons light rum
1½ cups heavy cream, whipped

Over hot (not boiling) water, combine Nestlé Toll House Semi-Sweet Chocolate Morsels, honey, and 2 tablespoons reserved liquid; stir until morsels melt and mixture is smooth. Remove from heat; transfer to a small bowl. Add rum. Fold in whipped cream.

Chocolate Fruit Soup

Makes 4 servings

  1 6-ounce package (1 cup) Nestlé Toll House
    Semi-Sweet Chocolate Morsels, divided
  1 cup milk
  1 package (10 ounces) frozen raspberries, drained,
    or 1 medium banana
1¼ cups heavy cream
  ½ teaspoon vanilla extract
  ½ teaspoon ground cinnamon
    Whipped cream (optional)
    Grated morsels (optional)

Place ½ cup Nestlé Toll House Semi-Sweet Chocolate Morsels in blender container; process at high speed about 15 seconds, or until reduced to fine particles. Remove from blender and set aside. Over hot (not boiling) water, combine remaining Nestlé Toll House Semi-Sweet Chocolate Morsels and the milk; heat until morsels melt and mixture is combined. (Morsel-milk mixture will contain flecks of chocolate.) In blender container, combine morsel-milk mixture, raspberries or banana, cream, vanilla, and cinnamon. Process at high speed until smooth (about 30 seconds). Pour soup through a fine sieve to remove raspberry seeds. Chill until ready to serve (at least 3 hours). Garnish with whipped cream, if desired, and grated morsels.

Tantalizing Toppers

Sauces and frostings—from old-fashioned hot fudge to new ways with mocha and sour cream—the chocolate final touch for outstanding desserts.

Hot Creamy Fudge Sauce

Makes 1½ cups

½ cup milk
¼ cup butter
¼ teaspoon salt
1 11½-ounce package (2 cups) Nestlé Milk Chocolate Morsels
1 teaspoon vanilla extract

Over hot (not boiling) water, combine milk, butter, and salt; heat until butter melts. Add Nestlé Milk Chocolate Morsels; stir until morsels melt and mixture is smooth. Remove from heat; stir in vanilla. Serve warm over ice cream, cake, waffles, or pancakes.

Hot Fudge Sauce

Makes 1⅓ cups

4 squares (1 ounce each) semisweet chocolate
2 tablespoons margarine or butter
1 can (14 ounces) Eagle® Brand Sweetened Condensed Milk (not evaporated milk)
1 teaspoon vanilla extract
Dash salt

In heavy saucepan, over low heat, melt chocolate and margarine; add remaining ingredients. Cook, stirring constantly, about 5 minutes, or until sauce is slightly thickened. Serve warm over ice cream. Refrigerate leftovers.

To reheat, in small saucepan, combine desired amount of sauce with small amount of water. Over low heat, stir constantly until heated through.

Mocha Fudge

Add 1 teaspoon instant coffee to the margarine and chocolate; proceed as directed.

Choco-Mint

Substitute ½ to 1 teaspoon peppermint extract for vanilla.

Chocolate Almond

Stir in ⅓ cup amaretto liqueur before serving.

Homemade Fudge Sauce

Makes 2 cups

2 squares (1 ounce each) unsweetened chocolate
½ cup water
¼ cup light corn syrup
½ teaspoon salt
2 cups sugar
1 cup smooth peanut butter
½ teaspoon vanilla extract
¾ cup evaporated milk

Combine chocolate, water, corn syrup, salt, and sugar and cook over low heat, stirring until chocolate is melted, to soft-ball stage. Blend in peanut butter and cool to lukewarm. Then stir in vanilla and evaporated milk.

Best Chocolate Sauce

Makes 2 cups

1 package (12 ounces) semisweet chocolate bits
2 squares (2 ounces) unsweetened chocolate
1 cup heavy cream
3 tablespoons brandy

Melt chocolate in top of double boiler over hot water. Stir in cream with a wire whisk to make a smooth mixture. Stir in brandy. Serve hot over ice cream.

Blender Chocolate Ice Cream (page 77); Hot Creamy Fudge Sauce; Hot Chocolate Sauce (page 124); Chocolate Dessert Waffles with Orange-Butterscotch Sauce (page 121). Courtesy of Nestlé Foods Corporation

123

Hot Chocolate Sauce

Makes 1 cup
- ¾ cup sugar
- ¼ cup butter
- 2 envelopes (2 ounces) Nestlé Choco-bake Unsweetened Baking Chocolate Flavor
- 2 tablespoons light corn syrup
  Dash salt
- ¼ cup milk
- 2 teaspoons vanilla extract

In a small saucepan, combine sugar, butter, Nestlé Choco-bake Unsweetened Baking Chocolate Flavor, corn syrup, and salt; mix well. Cook over medium heat, stirring constantly, until sugar dissolves. Add milk; bring to a boil, stirring constantly. Remove from heat; stir in vanilla. Serve warm over ice cream or cake.

Chocolate Drizzle

Makes about ½ cup
- 2 squares Baker's Unsweetened or Semi-Sweet Chocolate
- 2 teaspoons butter or margarine

Melt chocolate and butter in saucepan over low heat, stirring constantly. Cool slightly and drizzle from tip of spoon in thin streams, letting it run down sides of frosted cake. Keep cake in cool place until chocolate is firm.

Hot Mocha Ice Cream Sauce

Makes 1½ cups
- 1 6-ounce package (1 cup) Nestlé Toll House Semi-Sweet Chocolate Morsels
- ¾ cup corn syrup
- ¼ cup milk
- 2 tablespoons butter
- 1 teaspoon instant coffee

In a small saucepan, combine Nestlé Toll House Semi-Sweet Chocolate Morsels and corn syrup; heat over low heat until morsels melt and mixture is smooth. Add milk, butter, and coffee; stir until well blended. Remove from heat; cool 5 minutes. Serve warm over ice cream or cake.

Velvet Fudge Frosting

Makes frosting for two 9-inch round layers
- 3 cups Domino Granulated Sugar
- ½ cup cocoa
- ¼ teaspoon salt
- 1 cup of milk
- 2 tablespoons light corn syrup
- 10 tablespoons butter or margarine
- 1½ teaspoons vanilla extract

Blend sugar, cocoa, and salt in large thick saucepan. Stir milk and corn syrup into mixture. Place over moderate heat, stirring until sugar dissolves. Wipe sugar crystals from side of pan as necessary; cook without stirring until frosting reaches 232°F, or very soft ball stage. Remove from heat. Add butter or margarine without stirring; cool to 110°F, or lukewarm.

Add vanilla. Stir continuously until creamy spreading consistency is reached.

Rich Chocolate Cream Frosting

Makes 3 cups
- 1 12-ounce package (2 cups) Nestlé Toll House Semi-Sweet Chocolate Morsels
- 1 package (8 ounces) cream cheese, softened
- 1 teaspoon vanilla extract
- ½ teaspoon salt
- 3¼ cups sifted confectioners sugar
- 2 tablespoons milk

Melt Nestlé Toll House Semi-Sweet Chocolate Morsels over hot (not boiling) water; remove from heat. In a large bowl, combine melted chocolate, cream cheese, vanilla, and salt; beat well. Beat in confectioners sugar alternately with milk. Fills and frosts two 8- or 9-inch cake layers.

Chocolate Sour Cream Frosting

Makes frosting for two 9-inch round layers
- 1 package (12 ounces) semisweet chocolate chips
- ¾ to 1 cup heavy sour cream
- 1 pound Domino Confectioners 10-X Sugar
- 1 teaspoon vanilla extract

Melt chocolate over hot water. Remove. Add ⅓ of sugar, beating until blended. Alternately add remaining sugar and sour cream, beating until smooth. Add vanilla.

Chocolate Decorations

Special touches such as these make any dessert more delightful. Chocolate curls, trees, butterflies, and doodles are easy to make. Just follow the directions below:

Curls

Place 1 or more squares Baker's Semi-Sweet or Unsweetened Chocolate or several 3-square strips of Baker's German's Sweet Chocolate on a piece of aluminum foil. Let stand in warm place (90° to 100°F.) or in a gas oven with burning pilot light until very slightly softened, 5 to 10 minutes. (Wrapped chocolate may also be warmed by holding between hands.)

Shave chocolate from bottom into curls, using long strokes of vegetable peeler or small sharp knife. Quick strokes make tight curls; slow strokes make looser curls.

If you prefer, melt 4-squares Baker's Semi-Sweet or Unsweetened Chocolate or 1 package (4 ounces) Baker's German's Sweet Chocolate in saucepan over very low heat, stirring constantly. Spread chocolate with spatula or flat pastry brush in a very thin layer on underside of baking sheet. Chill until firm but still pliable, about 10 minutes.

To make curls, slip tip of straight-side metal spatula under chocolate. Push spatula firmly along baking sheet, under chocolate, until a curl forms. Width of curls will vary depending on the width of spatula. If chocolate is too firm to curl, let stand a few minutes at room temperature; chill again if it becomes too soft.

Carefully pick up each chocolate curl by inserting a wooden toothpick in center. Lift onto waxed paper-lined baking sheet. Chill until firm, about 15 minutes. Arrange on pies, desserts, and cakes.

Trees and Butterflies

Melt 2 squares Baker's Semi-Sweet Chocolate or ½ package Baker's German's Sweet Chocolate in saucepan over very low heat, stirring constantly. Remove from heat and stir occasionally until cool to the touch (about 83°F.).

Meanwhile, cut 6x4-inch aluminum foil or parchment rectangles. You will need 2 rectangles for each tree (total of 12); 1 rectangle for each butterfly (total of 6). Fold each rectangle in half with narrow ends together. Open flat, leaving crease down center. Using the dull tip of a spoon handle or the wooden end of a kitchen match, draw the following marks on the foil:

For trees, make a 3-inch line on each center crease, representing a tree trunk. Draw 4 overlapping and diminishing-size triangles on each trunk to form tree branches. (Triangles should be flush with trunk at both ends.)

Pour chocolate into plastic-lined decorating bag fitted with fine writing tip. Pipe chocolate over each tree outline, overlapping branches and trunk lines where they intersect. (Lines of piped chocolate should be about ¼ inch thick.) Reserve leftover chocolate.

For butterflies, make an oval 1½ inches long and ½ inch wide around center crease, representing a butterfly body. Draw antennae; outline wings so they extend about 1 inch on either side of body. Draw matching lacy lines in wings for design.

Pour chocolate into plastic-lined decorating bag fitted with fine writing tip. Pipe chocolate over outlines, overlapping wing patterns and outlines where they meet and where they join the body. (Lines of piped chocolate should be about ⅛ inch thick.) Fill in oval bodies completely, using all remaining chocolate.

Lift foil rectangles into 13x9- and/or 9x9-inch pans so half of each rectangle rests on the pan bottom and the other half is propped up against pan side. (Tree branches will be at right angles to the trunk; butterfly wings will be at right angles to each other.) Chill until chocolate is firm, at least 30 minutes.

Work quickly, and carefully separate foil from chocolate designs with a spatula.

For trees, drizzle some of the reserved chocolate over 2 trunks; gently press together to join. Repeat with remaining chocolate and tree trunks. Chill until firm, at least 30 minutes.

Use trees and butterflies to decorate frosted cakes, cream pies, pudding, and other desserts. Makes 6.

Doodles

Melt 1 square Baker's Semi-Sweet Chocolate or two 3-square strips Baker's German's Sweet Chocolate with 1½ teaspoons butter or margarine in saucepan over very low heat, stirring constantly. Blend in 1½ tablespoons milk. Pour from tip of teaspoon, making lacy circles and free-form designs directly on surface of set pudding, ice cream, chiffon pie, or frosted cake. Chill until chocolate is firm, about 15 minutes. Makes 6 to 8 doodles, each about 2 inches in diameter.

Magic-Quick Chocolate Frosting

Makes about 1½ cups

   2 squares (1 ounce each) unsweetened chocolate
   1 can (14 ounces) Eagle® Brand Sweetened
       Condensed Milk (not evaporated milk)
   Dash salt
   1 tablespoon water
   ½ teaspoon vanilla extract

In heavy saucepan, combine chocolate and Eagle Brand. Over low heat, cook and stir until chocolate melts and mixture thickens (about 10 minutes). Remove from heat. Stir in water; cool. Stir in vanilla. Use to frost one (8-or 9-inch) two-layer cake.

German Sweet Chocolate Frosting

Makes frosting for two 9-inch round layers

   ⅓ cup butter or margarine
   ⅓ cup milk
   2 packages (4 ounces each) German sweet
       chocolate
   1 pound Domino Confectioners 10-X Sugar
   2 egg yolks
   1 teaspoon vanilla extract

Heat butter, milk, and chocolate over low heat until chocolate melts; stir constantly. Remove from heat. Blend in confectioners sugar gradually, beating until smooth. Add egg yolks, 1 at a time, beating well. Add vanilla.

Mocha Butter Frosting

Makes 2½ cups

   6 tablespoons butter or margarine
   Dash salt
   1 package (16 ounces) confectioners sugar
   ¼ cup cocoa
   ¼ cup cold brewed Maxwell House Coffee
   1½ teaspoons vanilla extract

Cream butter with salt. Gradually beat in part of the sugar and the cocoa. Add remaining sugar alternately with coffee, beating well after each addition until smooth and of spreading consistency. Blend in vanilla.

Cups of Chocolate Cheer (page 77)

Frosting Finesse

A professional-looking frosted cake takes just a few more moments than a slap-dash job. Just follow these easy steps:

● Cool cake completely. Place the cake, bottom side up, on several pieces of overlapping waxed paper strips. Brush off any crumbs.

● Frost the sides of the cake first, with long, even, upward strokes from bottom to top. Build the frosting just a little above the top of the cake.

● Spoon a heaping mound of icing on the cake top, and spread it out, blending it neatly with the built-up edges.

● Gently remove waxed paper strips when cake is completely frosted.

Index